To Joh[illegible]

With Be[illegible] wishes

Ray

An Odyssey:
From Ebbw Vale to Tyneside

by

Raymond Hicks

Contents

Acknowledgements

I would like to acknowledge with thanks the contributions made by various people in the production of this book. My sister, Pat, validated many of the dates and some family facts which I was not clear about or had forgotten. The final draft was taken by Mike Brudenell, my son-in-law, who expertly transformed it into a book and also created the picture for the cover. The laborious task of typing and editing the original text was done by Valerie Foxon, Mike's cousin. Final proof-reading and consistency checking was carried out by my daughter, Susan.

I would also like to thank the numerous people, alive or dead, who helped me on my long pilgrimage through life. I was exceptionally fortunate in those who tutored me when I was studying, in the colleagues I had when I was working and the many friends I have had from my younger days in Ebbw Vale through to my retirement in Newcastle.

Raymond Hicks

Preface

A Psalm of Life

Tell me not, in mournful numbers,
Life is but an empty dream!—
For the soul is dead that slumbers,
And things are not what they seem.

Life is real! Life is earnest!
And the grave is not its goal;
Dust thou art, to dust returnest,
Was not spoken of the soul.

Not enjoyment, and not sorrow,
Is our destined end or way;
But to act, that each tomorrow
Find us farther than today.

Art is long, and Time is fleeting,
And our hearts, though stout & brave,
Still, like muffled drums, are beating
Funeral marches to the grave.

In the world's broad field of battle,
In the bivouac of Life,
Be not like dumb, driven cattle!
Be a hero in the strife!

Trust no Future, howe'er pleasant!
Let the dead Past bury its dead!
Act,—act in the living Present!
Heart within, and God o'erhead!

Lives of great men all remind us
We can make our lives sublime,
And, departing, leave behind us
Footprints in the sands of time;

Footprints, that perhaps another,
Sailing o'er life's solemn main,
A forlorn and shipwrecked brother,
Seeing, shall take heart again.

Let us then be up and doing,
With a heart for any fate,
Still achieving, still pursuing,
Learn to labour and to wait.

Henry Wadsworth Longfellow

Introduction

Throughout my life I have often thought about the meaning and significance of the word "education." It was a word I encountered many times in my schooldays, in my youth and as an adult. The culmination of my interest came when the Prime Minister, Tony Blair, used the slogan "Education, Education, Education" as his clarion call to the country during his campaigning speeches. His objective was to get fifty per cent of school-leavers into university education.

I was born in 1925 in the industrial town of Ebbw Vale, located in one of the mining valleys of South Wales. As a result of the closure of its steelworks about fifty per cent of the male population experienced prolonged periods of unemployment between 1929 and 1936. Since all my male relations were miners or steelworkers, it was generally assumed that I would follow them into one of those industries. However, growing up in such an environment had a profound effect on me and I developed a deep fear of being unemployed, being determined to avoid it at all costs.

The word "education" was often used by my mother. She believed that if I had a good education I would not have to work in a coalmine or steelworks, and her great ambition was to see me getting a clean job behind the counter in the Co-op. This was something I had no intention of pursuing, as the idea horrified me.

Although I won a scholarship to a grammar school, I dropped out prematurely with no qualifications. I then worked for seven years as a steelworker, merchant seaman (1942–46), a builder's labourer and a trainee on an opencast coal-site. By the end of this time the wise words of my mother had finally penetrated my thick skull. I realised I would have to get an education if I wanted to be more than a manual worker. Consequently, as a result of a correspondence course and studying in my spare time, I finally got a school certificate, matriculating as an external student of London University. Additional part-time study at a Technical College enabled me to win a scholarship to Cardiff University, where I graduated with a first-class honours degree in civil engineering. A year later I received a MSc as a result of research work in applied mathematics. This was followed by a research award from the Royal Commission for the Exhibition of 1851, which enabled me to get a PhD in the same subject. I could now claim to have acquired a first-class technical education.

Finally, I spent twenty-seven years working in industry, including nuclear power, steelmaking, coalmining, building construction and general engineering. This supplemented my technical education with real experience of working and dealing with people in the UK and overseas.

The culmination of my industrial career was as Managing Director of a well-known Tyneside engineering company with a workforce of 1,800 people.

Because my life has been long, eventful and rewarding it encourages me to hope that the experiences recorded in this book may help young people pursuing a career in twenty-first century Britain, especially those from a deprived background.

Dad, myself, Pat and Ma.

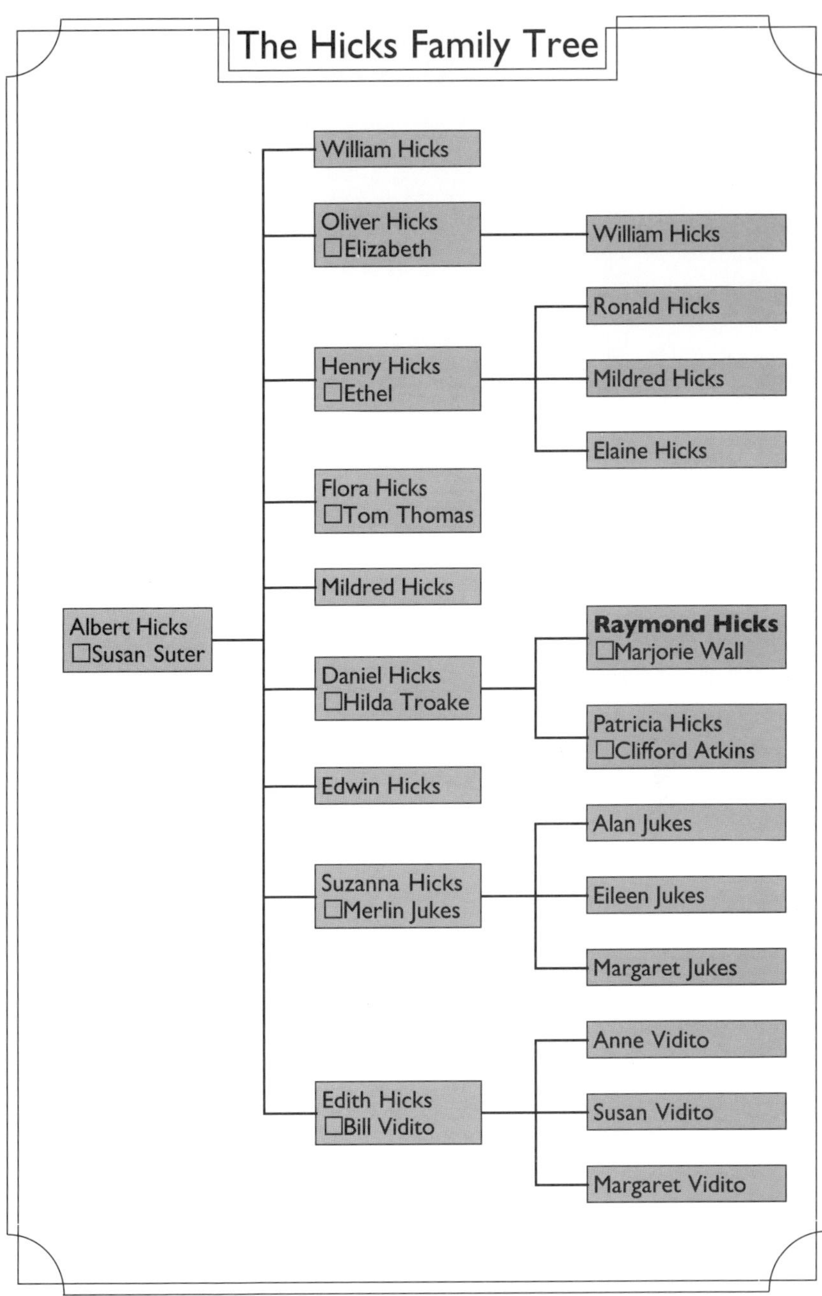
The Hicks Family Tree
Albert Hicks
□Susan Suter
William Hicks
Oliver Hicks
□Elizabeth
William Hicks
Henry Hicks
□Ethel
Ronald Hicks
Mildred Hicks
Elaine Hicks
Flora Hicks
□Tom Thomas
Mildred Hicks
Daniel Hicks
□Hilda Troake
Raymond Hicks
□Marjorie Wall
Patricia Hicks
□Clifford Atkins
Edwin Hicks
Suzanna Hicks
□Merlin Jukes
Alan Jukes
Eileen Jukes
Margaret Jukes
Edith Hicks
□Bill Vidito
Anne Vidito
Susan Vidito
Margaret Vidito

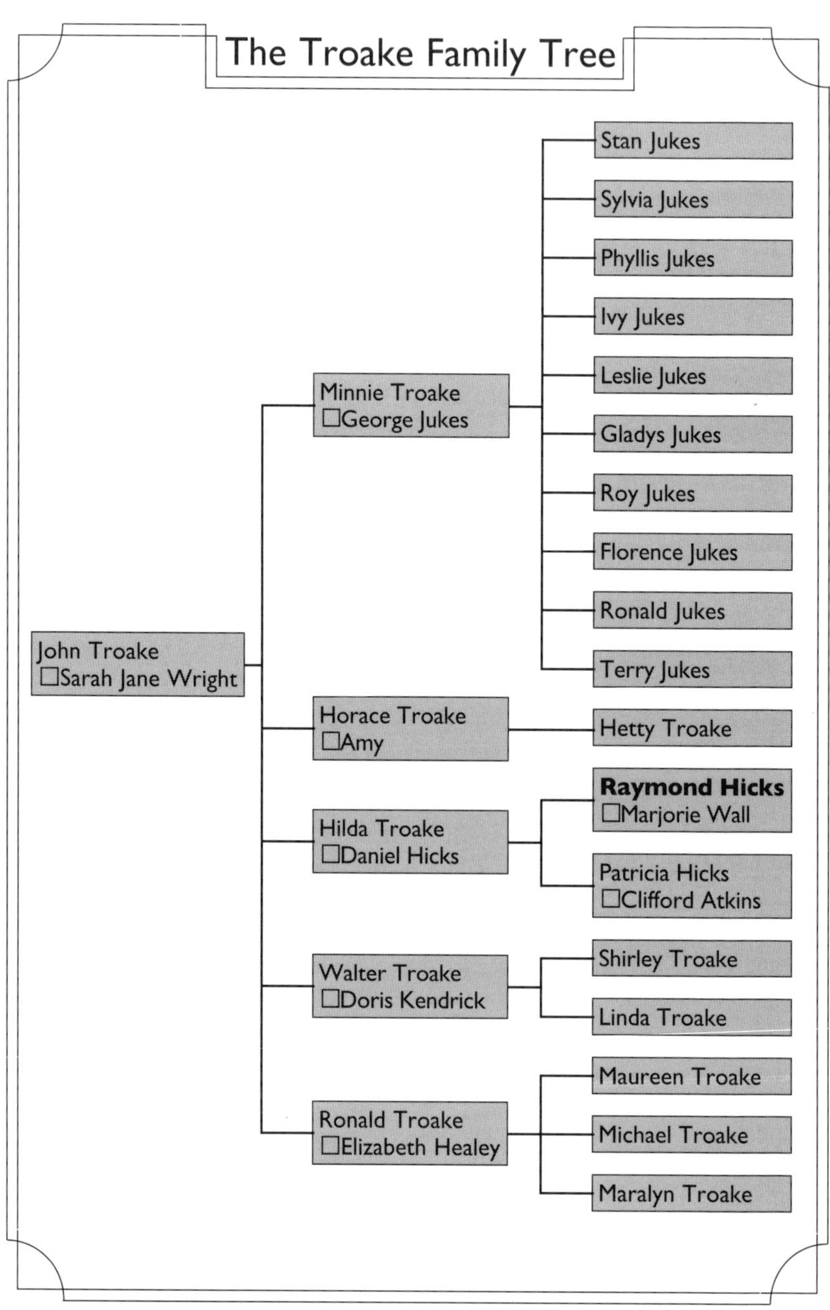
The Troake Family Tree
John Troake
☐Sarah Jane Wright
Minnie Troake
☐George Jukes
Stan Jukes
Sylvia Jukes
Phyllis Jukes
Ivy Jukes
Leslie Jukes
Gladys Jukes
Roy Jukes
Florence Jukes
Ronald Jukes
Terry Jukes
Horace Troake
☐Amy
Hetty Troake
Hilda Troake
☐Daniel Hicks
Raymond Hicks
☐Marjorie Wall
Patricia Hicks
☐Clifford Atkins
Walter Troake
☐Doris Kendrick
Shirley Troake
Linda Troake
Ronald Troake
☐Elizabeth Healey
Maureen Troake
Michael Troake
Maralyn Troake

Chapter 1

Halfway House

My earliest recollection is of lying on my back and looking up to see a dark ring outlined on the ceiling. This came from an old oil-lamp suspended from above. Hanging from the lamp was a long strip of flypaper which had attracted an army of flies that had inevitably come to a sticky end. I was at home in Halfway House, the place where I was born and originally lived with my mother and father, together with my mother's sister Aunty Min, her husband Uncle George and their five children who eventually increased to ten.

I was born on 2nd May 1925 and my cousin Leslie in August of the same year. With two healthy boys born in the same house within three months of each other one would assume that this was a period of satisfaction, if not joy, for the inhabitants of Halfway House. However, the events fell between two tragedies. In the preceding year my father's elder brother was killed while working in the local steelworks, a tragedy amplified by the fact that my father did the same job as his brother, although he worked on a different shift. The other tragedy occurred on St David's Day (1st March) 1927 when an explosion underground at the Marine Colliery killed fifty-two men. The colliery was at Cwm and was the one where my grandfather, his son and Uncle George all worked. Fortunately none of our family was killed but the event cast a shadow over the whole district.

Halfway House was a property that not even the most optimistic and imaginative salesman would be able to describe as desirable. There was no water supply, no sanitation, no electricity and no refuse collection. However, there was a free source of coal at the bottom of the garden which could be foraged from the colliery spoil tip that was slowly approaching the house it would ultimately engulf. The garden was really an area around the house which was part of the hillside. As far as I can remember there were no vegetables or flowers grown there! On one side of the garden, alongside the railway retaining wall, was a line of currant bushes which had clearly given up struggling to live and which produced very few blackcurrants.

The house was located between the small townships of Waunlwyd and Cwm in the District of Ebbw Vale in South Wales. It lay alongside the Great Western Railway which connected Ebbw Vale to Newport about twenty miles away down the steep-sided Ebbw Valley. There was no access to the house except on foot from the main Ebbw Vale to Newport road situated on the side of the mountain about 300 yards uphill from Halfway House.

Running parallel to the Great Western Railway, on the side remote from Halfway House, the River Ebbw emerged from a tunnel which took it under the steelworks site. It could not be seen from the house since the view was blocked by the railway retaining wall. On this side of the valley there were two important industrial tips; one was where molten slag from the iron and steel furnaces was deposited, the other was a second coal tip used by Waunlwyd Colliery. Both of these tips and the one approaching the garden of Halfway House were removed many years later to form the site for the Ebbw Vale Garden Festival in the 1990's. By this time nothing remained of the house where I was born.

The molten slag tipped from the furnaces lit up the sky for several minutes on a dark night. At this time anyone waiting could use the light to run down the hill from the main Newport road to Halfway House.

Except for a small stretch upstream from the first Ebbw Vale colliery and steelworks the River Ebbw was extremely polluted. Since there were collieries sited along the river for twenty miles down the valley to Newport the water became increasingly polluted with coal particles carried in suspension by the current. These were deposited on the river bed as it approached flat country near the sea. Many years later when the collieries were closed, the coal deposits were dredged and the coal sold commercially.

No-one knows the history of the house but it was generally believed to have originally been a pub or a farmhouse. It was double-fronted, with two storeys in the front, and faced the railway retaining wall about ten feet away. It was single-storeyed in the back and had a central door which was the entry commonly used by anyone entering the house. A bunker had been built outside the back entry to the house and this was used to store coal collected from the colliery tip. The location of the house relative to the retaining wall placed it in an ideal position to be flooded during the periods

Half Way House: painted from memory by the author.
The exaggerated perspective enables the proximity of Waunlywd's colliery to be shown.

of heavy rain which were experienced in South Wales. This fact suggests that the house was built before the Great Western Railway.

On the ground floor of Halfway House there were three rooms and a pantry, all of which were covered with flagstones. My aunt and family lived in the front room, and my mother and family in the back. The third room was left bare and used by the children as a playroom. Since this room had no furniture, and the floor was made of flagstones, the children were free to play with no adult interruptions. That is, they could chalk out traditional patterns on the floor to play hopscotch, marbles, etc. The pantry had huge hooks hanging from the ceiling and wide sandstone shelves around the walls. I cannot remember it containing more than bare essentials. It was certainly not well provisioned but the hooks supported the theory that the house was initially part of a farm or pub. On an old map of Ebbw Vale dated 1815 the railway is shown and marked "Monmouthshire Canal and Railroad." My research has shown that this company was formed in 1792 and was responsible for the building of the canal from Crumlin to Newport and for the railway from Crumlin to Ebbw Vale and Beaufort. The original railroad would have been of 3ft 4 inch gauge and consequently of a much lighter construction than the Great Western Railway which was in use when I lived in Halfway House. It was probably a simple tram-road following the contours of the ground, so there would have been no embankment or retaining wall there initially when Halfway House was built. These would have come later when a standard gauge heavy-duty freight service was installed to carry the Great Western Railway traffic.

A spiral stone staircase led to the upstairs rooms in the front of the house and the large loft-room under the roof at the back. Actually, the staircase ended in the first bedroom where we slept. At the back of this room was a door to the room occupied by Aunty Min and Uncle George. Also off the first bedroom was access to the large loft-room occupied by my numerous cousins.

On the outside of the southern gable of the house was a similar staircase, which was fully exposed and which came to an abrupt stop at the top. This suggested that the house was once part of a larger structure. In common with the numerous miners' cottages in the area the house was whitewashed on its outside walls.

The only water supply for the house came from a mountain spring about twenty yards away from the back door. Unfortunately the flow of water, which came from a spout, was very slow so it took a long time to fill a bucket. This has given rise to one of the mysteries surrounding Halfway House. My Uncle George was a collier and my father a steelworker and both needed to bath every day. This was done in the customary galvanised steel bath in front of the fire. The effort needed to get the water from the spring and then heat it on the coal fire must have been a tremendous daily chore and one wonders how they managed to do it.

As there was no road access to Halfway House the inhabitants had no alternative but to tip all their rubbish on their own created rubbish-tip at the side of the house. The sanitary facilities were very primitive, consisting of a wooden privy placed over a stream near the house. This depended on heavy rain periodically to get it flushed. In times of drought one can imagine the difficulties encountered with this arrangement.

Aunty Min had ten children. Unfortunately one of them, named Ronnie, died quite young from rickets. Ultimately she was to raise nine healthy children in Halfway House before she moved to Ebbw Vale about twelve years later. What is amazing is that during this period, when I was growing up, many of the schoolchildren in the area died of diphtheria, TB, rickets and polio yet none of these affected Aunty Min's nine remaining children, that is, my cousins. They all became good, law-abiding adults and prospered in their various fields of endeavour. In fact, seven of them are still alive today.

The first five years of my life seemed to revolve round constant moving from one rented apartment to another. There was a great deal of unemployment in Ebbw Vale at this time; consequently, people living in miners' cottages supplemented their meagre incomes by renting a room to homeless families. This included my family who left Halfway House soon after my birth, although we were to live there again when we ran out of rented rooms in Waunlwyd. The problem was that although people were desperate to take in lodgers to ease their economic plight they found that this arrangement was unworkable when a baby was involved. It appears that by the time I was five and had started school we had lived for two periods in Halfway House with Aunty Min and four or five different houses in the village of Waunlwyd.

One of the houses in Waunlwyd where we lodged for a short time was 22 Garn Terrace, where my father's spinster sister kept house for her two unmarried brothers and two unmarried sisters. 22 Garn Terrace came to play a very important part in my life later on. It is worth noting that it was a typical example of the miners' cottages found in Waunlwyd and elsewhere in the country. There were two small rooms downstairs and a small scullery with a cold-water tap. My mother, father and I must have lived in the small room at the front of the house. Upstairs there were two small bedrooms, each of which could just take a double bed, and also a box-room for a single bed. At the time of our family being accommodated there it housed seven adults and a baby, which was me. How we all managed in such a small house is a mystery, but we were better off than my grandparents and their nine children (there were eleven but two died) when they lived there before I was born. As well as running cold water there was a flush-toilet located at the top of the garden, which was on the hillside.

Although I can remember my first day at school, I'm afraid I cannot conjure up any worthwhile memories of my first five years but my memories did begin to crystallise about this time. My introduction to schooling at Waunlwyd Infant School could only have lasted a few months because we were on the move again. This time our luck had definitely been heaven-sent, since my parents had been allocated a brand-new house on a council estate in Ebbw Vale. By now my memory was beginning to develop and I can vaguely remember riding with my parents on the back of a lorry with a few items of furniture. My parents must have thought they had arrived in heaven. Their one big problem was the employment of my father, who worked as a stoker in the boiler-house at Victoria, a small village in Ebbw Vale. Although the steelworks were closed (1929–1936) a small sheet-mill and the boiler-house remained in operation for some time. However, Dad did have periods when he was unemployed for some considerable time, certainly for one period of nine months and also for other periods of unknown duration.

Chapter 2

Ebbw Vale

Ebbw Vale is essentially a product of the Industrial Revolution since it evolved as a result of the coal, iron ore and limestone found in the area. Prior to 1800 the area was sparsely populated, that is, no more than a few hundred inhabitants. It is situated in a valley formed by moorland giving way to two of a number of mountains which stretch about twenty miles down to Newport and the Bristol Channel. At the height of its industrial development its population grew to more than 30,000.

During the 19th century there was a rapid development of the mineral resources in the area which resulted in iron works, coalmines and quarries being extensively operated in Ebbw Vale and adjacent valley towns, for example Tredegar and Bliana. The housing consisted of rows of whitewashed terraced houses. These had descriptive names like Colliers Row, Furnace Terrace, Pit Row and so on, and were generally described as miners' cottages.

By the 20th century the town had grown considerably. The iron works had given way to large steelworks and although there were fewer pits in the area the ones that were left were much bigger, resulting in a larger production of coal. The housing was still predominantly stone-built terraces but many of them were not whitewashed. They still had only basic facilities: a cold-water tap, an outside toilet and electric light.

As the 20th century progressed there was steady improvement in the quality of the housing. Semi-detached houses were built after the First World War, some of which were privately owned, but these were relatively rarely found. The town also expanded and many improvements were made in the form of entertainment: for example picture-palaces, workmen's halls and Working Men's Institutes. Finally, many new semi-detached houses were built on council estates. These were much sought after by many people who were badly in need of homes, such as our little family.

The town of Ebbw Vale is surrounded by steep mountains and generally highly visible spoil tips resulting from coalmining and the production of iron and steel. Until mining and steel production ended the whole area was usually enveloped in smoke and sulphurous fumes from the steelmaking plant. Many people I have known have stated that their first reaction on seeing Ebbw Vale from a distance was that they were looking at a vision of hell. In sharp contrast to the above, one has only to go two or three miles north-east over the moor (i.e., Llangynidr Moor) to see spread below a panoramic view of Breconshire with a backdrop of the Brecon Beacons and Black Mountains in the distance. A truly beautiful sight.

It is not surprising that my parents were pleased by their good fortune in being offered a council house. It had hot and cold running water, a real bath and an inside toilet. It also boasted a garden, which although completely uncultivated was clearly capable of being so. It was the last house on the estate and backed onto an open field which led to the LMS railway line to Brynmawr, about three miles away. The end of the house led to a cultivated field used for growing hay. I can clearly remember men using scythes to cut the hay at harvest-time. The estate had two streets running parallel to each other with about sixty houses in each street. Our house was 118 Emlyn Avenue. We were located about one mile from the main street in Ebbw Vale, which had quite a good shopping centre with the usual assortment of shops and cafés. The cafés were usually owned by people of Italian origin, who were good citizens and readily accepted by the British citizens. I say British rather than Welsh because the majority of people in Ebbw Vale at this time were from families that moved into the area from Somerset, Yorkshire and so on to work in the mines and steelworks.

Ebbw Vale: shrouded in fumes, circa 1900. An impression painted by the author.

The future looked very bright for our family, but there were ominous dark clouds on our horizon. Although Ebbw Vale had collieries in Waunlwyd and

Aerial view of Ebbw Vale steelworks and town, circa 1960.

Cwm its main source of employment was the steelworks and their future looked very bleak (they were, in fact, completely closed from 1929–1936).

As soon as we settled in our new house I was enrolled in Pont-y-Gof Infant School on the outskirts of Ebbw Vale. This was a small stone building of Victorian vintage and consisted of one big room partitioned off into four small classrooms after assembly in the morning. This little school was to play an important role in my future for two reasons. Firstly, among the group of youngsters was a pretty little fair-haired girl who was to become my wife and, secondly, we had an adored lady teacher who every morning would read to us passages from Longfellow's poem "Hiawatha." I would listen in awe each day to Hiawatha's adventures with his magic mittens and moccasins. It awakened in me a love of poetry which has stayed with me all my life.

The school was about three-quarters of a mile from our home and it was the custom for me to walk there and back each day. I was usually accompanied by the three Hacking children who lived next door but one from us. Joyce, the youngest of the three, was also in my class at the infant school. I have happy memories of this school. All the teachers were ladies who were greatly respected and admired; I cannot recall any bullying or unhappy encounters with other children nor can I remember any disruptive members during lessons.

It was common practice in South Wales at this time that any girls in a family would be sent into service when they were old enough. This happened to my mother and most of my aunts. Usually the girls ended up in London in the homes of professional people, who in many cases were kind to their domestic employees. This happened to my father's sister, Aunty Milly. She worked for a family in Golders Green in London. One day I was surprised when my mother asked me if I would like to go to London for a holiday and stay with Aunty Milly. Without hesitation I said "yes." It would be wonderful to go to London, besides which Aunty Milly was a great favourite of mine and I was sure I would enjoy myself. My enthusiasm waned to some extent when she said I would be travelling alone but I had no need to worry because I would be in the charge of the guards of the train. I had just had my seventh birthday and must have felt quite grown-up to be going to London alone and excitedly looked forward to the great adventure. Arrangements were duly made for me to be away from school for a few weeks. I don't know what reason my mother gave my teacher for my absence but it was clear the teacher fully approved my mother's wish that I should go on a holiday in the middle of a school term. I thought grown-ups acted in a mysterious way on some occasions but I thought no more of the mystery at that time.

I was shepherded to Newport by Aunty Flo, one of Dad's sisters, who lived in Waunlwyd about three miles away. The journey down the valley from Ebbw Vale to Newport was quite exciting. I was particularly thrilled when we left Waunlwyd Station and passed Halfway House on a day when my cousins were probably in school. The colliery tip was still creeping nearer to the house and no doubt some people were foraging for pieces of coal on its flanks. A little later we passed through Cwm and saw Marine Colliery where mum's dad and brothers worked and also Uncle George. At Crumlin we passed under the famous viaduct which much later was featured in a film with Gregory Peck and Sophia Loren. Although it was only twenty miles from Ebbw Vale to Newport the journey took us over an hour. There were about a dozen stops en route and each town we passed seemed to have a colliery. Eventually we reached Newport station and waited excitedly for the arrival of the express train which was to take me to London. When it did arrive Aunty Flo ensured I was safely seated in a suitable compartment and placed under the supervision of the guard, to whom she gave a suitable monetary reward to keep an eye on me during my journey. There were other people in the compartment who knew I was travelling alone and they all went to great lengths to see I was not bored during the long journey.

As we pulled out of Newport station I was told that our journey would take two and a half hours and we would only stop at Swindon and Reading. This information made little impression on me since I was mesmerised by the ruins of a castle which appeared alongside the railway line just outside Newport station. I had never seen a castle before and listened intently as it was explained to me that it was a Norman castle. In answer to my question it was explained that the Normans came from France about 900 years ago and conquered Britain, including Wales. My history lesson was interrupted by the news that we were about to go through a very long tunnel which went under the River Severn. In answer to my next question I was told that it was built by an engineer named Brunel, who built the Great Western

Railway, including such famous stations as Paddington and Temple Meads in Bristol.

By the time we got to Swindon I was convinced that one day I would become an engineer, and my fascination with railways knew no bounds. We passed the famous Swindon locomotive works and standing outside in some sidings were a number of new GWR locomotives. The big ones with tenders were painted an attractive green. I was clearly hooked. From that day to the present I have been a staunch supporter of railways and the GWR in particular.

We continued our journey with a stop at Reading and an interesting run through the outskirts of London until we finally reached Paddington.

I arrived with an improvement in my education as a result of the kindness of my travelling companions. They, I felt, must have arrived exhausted after being subjected to so many questions.

On the platform stood Aunty Milly. She was all smiles and obviously pleased to see I had arrived safely. After she had given me a huge hug and generally made a fuss over me we walked over to the entrance of the Underground station. After examining a very large coloured map of the system we descended an escalator to the platform to board a noisy train which had no visible means of propulsion. I was told it was driven by electricity carried through the rails. After a noisy ride and many stops we arrived at Golders Green and set out on foot to our destination. We finally arrived at the house where Aunty Milly lived and worked and I was presented to the lady of the house and her son, who seemed considerably older than I. I believe his name was Brian. The husband, I was told, was away on business and the whole family were going for a continental holiday in a few days time. This meant that Aunty Milly and I would be alone for the remainder of my stay. With my background of Halfway House and living in miners' cottages and being surrounded by people living on small incomes I felt I had entered a completely new world. The lady of the house, Mrs Evans, and her son were very kind and I liked them at once. The son and I were soon playing together and we rapidly got to the stage where he was showing me his Hornby train set. I was immediately hooked. The whole layout was set out on the floor of one of their rooms and I was very reluctant to leave it even for a meal. I resolved to get one for myself although I had no idea how I was going to get the money for such a desirable purchase.

Sometime later, probably the next day, Aunty Milly told me that Mrs Evans had given her tickets to see Bertram Mills' Circus, which I believe was at Olympia. Although I would have loved to have gone to the circus my heart was with the Hornby trains, which I did not want to leave. However, I was made to realise that it would be ungrateful if I declined to go, so I ended up going to the circus and thoroughly enjoyed the show.

In due course Mr and Mrs Evans and Brian left for their continental holiday and left Aunty Milly in charge of their home. I then embarked on a sightseeing programme arranged by Aunty Milly. This included a whole day at the zoo which, I recall, was in Regent's Park. I found this of great interest and vividly remember being sorry for the lions, who seemed most frustrated in their cages. We also went to the Tower of London and were given a comprehensive history of some of the tragic events which had happened there. One event which sticks in my mind was a visit to the Royal Mint; however, I am not sure if this occurred on this particular visit or at another time when I visited London.

After a week or so my adventures drew to a close and I was put on a train for the return journey to Newport. Again I was put in the care of the guard. When I arrived at Newport I was surprised to find Aunty Flo, and I think Aunty Edith also, waiting for me. They were all smiles when they saw me and I assumed this was because of their great pleasure in seeing me. We got into an empty compartment of the Ebbw Vale train and they immediately told me that my mother had a great surprise waiting for me at home. Could I guess what it was? Now I was never very good at guessing games but on this occasion I was sure I knew what it was. I immediately asked the question, "Is it a Hornby train?" There was clear disappointment on the faces of my two aunts but undaunted they replied, "No, but when you get home you'll find you have a little sister." This disclosure was completely unexpected but I resolved to accept it as one of the trials of life and gradually came to the point where I looked forward to our first meeting. In fact I grew more excited by the prospective meeting with my little sister the nearer we got to Ebbw Vale.

When I finally got home I was surprised to see my mother holding the new addition to our family and binding her around the tummy and chest with a very long and wide bandage. It immediately reminded me of an Egyptian mummy I had seen in a picture-book at school, and my first thought was that she was being prepared for mummification, which really upset me. My mother assured me that this was not the case, and then explained why it was being done. I had no idea what she was talking about but at least I saw it was not being done with any sinister intent. This was the beginning of the wonderful relationship I have with my sister which has lasted more than seventy years and which, I hope, will continue for more years to come.

By now I was old enough to be transferred to Pont-y-Gof Junior School about half a mile from the infant school which I had attended for two years. This was a boys-only school and was the equivalent of a similar girls' school in another location. My daily walk to and from school was now increased but I accepted this with no misgivings. I would be escorted by my two older friends from two doors away, Ralph and Billy Hacking. On rare occasions when the weather was extremely bad we would go on a bus but still walk home.

My new school was built in Victorian times but there was a wooden annexe built after the First World War. Instead of normal foundations the annexe was supported by numerous concrete pillars about two feet high. It was a common arrangement at this time and I remember seeing a whole row of huts of this type, which had been created to house families after the First World War, on the road between Waunlwyd and Cwm above Halfway House. There were two classrooms in the annexe and each was heated by a big pot-bellied iron stove, which burned coal or coke, placed at the front of the class. These stoves generated a great deal of heat which rapidly diminished in intensity inversely as the square of the distance you were seated from them. In the winter it got very cold in Ebbw Vale because of its altitude and it was common practice to operate the stoves at full capacity. The effect of this was quite alarming; the faces of the boys in the front of the class would glow a bright red, while those in the rows behind changed colour by degrees down to an arctic blue for the boys in the back row.

One feature of the annexe which we liked was the fact that it was on pillars, which resulted in a space under the building where we could go during playtime and be away from the watchful eyes of the teachers. We all seemed to collect cigarette cards, play marbles and collect wrappers from toffees that could be used to win a football if you got a complete set, which was extremely unlikely since there was always one team which was missing. We used our time under the annexe to make our swaps of cigarette cards etc.

I cannot remember much about our lessons but I clearly recall using a slate to write on with slate pencils. As a result of my passion for railways I always seemed to be drawing railway layouts on my slate. We moved from the annexe to the main building for some lessons. One lady teacher was very popular because she regularly read stories by Enid Blyton; the characters Hop, Skip and Jump spring easily to my mind. We also had lessons in art and this included getting oddly-shaped jars and painting them in colourful patterns. Old gramophone records were heated and made into flower-bowls. Another favourite was to collect empty matchboxes and glue them into different shapes to make toy furniture. These activities were part of the school learning process. We also had the usual lessons in reading, writing and arithmetic. I recall having a cheap exercise-book which I bought for my own use and I enjoyed making up my own sums in addition, subtraction and multiplication and then working out the answers. My self-imposed homework would then be checked by my mother. We also amused ourselves out of school by making paper boats which we dropped from a bridge into the River Ebbw. This was very exciting when the river was in flood. We also made paper aeroplanes which we launched from a nearby disused colliery tip.

It will be noted that all these activities had one thing in common; they could be pursued without the need for money. I was now getting to the age when I could take note of and comment on my surroundings. It was clear that we boys were all cast in the same mould to a greater or lesser degree. All bore the hallmark of poverty, although the dreaded word was barely used. A word used more often was pride, at least in our house where Ma's pride would not allow her to go to the "parish" for a handout for a pair of boots for me. Boots would be worn with the toecaps so worn that the toes were often visible, trousers would be patched and worn to such an extent that one could see the owner's bottom; underpants were unknown. Jerseys were the standard dress for the body and these usually had holes, particularly in the sleeves. On reflection the wonderful result of all this was that everyone was the same. Consequently, no-one felt superior or inferior to any of his contemporaries.

It was about this time that I began to appreciate what a resourceful person my mother was. Her parents were from Somerset, as were her elder brother and sister, the other six children being born in Ebbw Vale. Three of the children died in infancy and when Ma was seventeen her mother died and she became the housekeeper for her father and substitute mother to her two young brothers, Ron and Walter. Two years later her father remarried and Ma went into service in the next valley. In 1924 she married Dad. They were together for fifty years until Dad died from cancer.

The 1930's were a soul-destroying time for the people of Ebbw Vale, where for seven years about fifty per cent of the male population was unemployed. It took World War II to breathe new life into the town of Ebbw Vale and to give life again to the people who had suffered so much.

Although Ma had received little schooling she seemed to know instinctively how to cope with all the problems she was faced with. She was the driving force in our family. When Dad was unemployed she effectively managed and augmented our meagre family income. She acquired a sewing-machine and began making dresses for our neighbours at two shillings and sixpence a time, that is, twelve and a half pence each at today's price. I can visualise her now, sitting at her sewing-machine at all hours of the day while Dad, my little sister and I were all given domestic chores to be done to her satisfaction. Dad often did the heavy work, such as the weekly laundry which was done in a primitive machine with a handle rotated by hand. He also cultivated the garden and was very proud of the vegetables he grew but he had no interest in growing flowers. He was also responsible for keeping us well stocked with coal which could be obtained from common land in the area. I was the prime dish-washer in the family, a skill which was to prove useful in my adult life. My sister Pat, as soon as she was old enough, was introduced to the art of polishing the furniture. In later years Ma would tell me how difficult it was to live on the seventeen-and-six (87½ pence) dole she received and the extra shilling (5 pence) she got for me as a child. In spite of all this she made it quite clear that if the family wanted something, like new boots, we had it only when she could pay for it. She always warned us of the danger of going into debt. The one source of relief for my family and others who were unemployed was the access they had to a free supply of coal. It may have been illegal but if it was no-one I knew was ever stopped by any authority.

South Wales was famous for the abundance of coal found there. Collieries were located all down the valley almost to Newport on the coast. This was also the case in all the neighbouring valleys. They were mainly deep mines, that is, they were accessed by means of a shaft to get to the coal. These shafts could be more than five hundred feet deep. The coal-seams, however, outcropped on the north-west border of Ebbw Vale, so that the unemployed men could get at the coal by sinking a small shaft of ten feet or so. My father had such a shaft, which he often visited to maintain the stock of coal in our home. As the colliers who were in work were given free coal delivered to their homes the unemployed steelworkers had virtually no outlet for the coal they dug, except for their own use.

One day, when I was about nine, I had an experience worth recording. At this stage of my life I was lucky enough to have my own bedroom. One morning I woke up to receive a heart-stopping shock. In my bed near me was a man fast asleep. I was horrified and stupefied but regaining my composure I went downstairs to see my mother, who was already busy with her daily chores. I looked at her, fearing the shock of my disclosure would make her faint or have a fit, and said, "Ma, there's a man in my bed." To my surprise she took the news quite calmly and looked at me with a smile and said, "O, my love, it's only your Uncle Ron." Uncle Ron was one of Ma's younger brothers. He had decided that he no longer wanted to work in Marine Colliery with grandad and besides he didn't get on too well with his stepmother. This in fact was quite understandable, since Uncle Ron must have been very difficult to control and was a complete tearaway. Ma could testify to this fact as she looked after Uncle Ron when he was a little boy and at the time when she kept house for Grandad when our grandmother died. Notwithstanding this, she was quite happy to see him and look after him again.

Uncle Ron was readily accepted as one of our family and we became friends immediately, in spite of the big difference in our ages. He quickly developed an opinion that I should be better prepared to enter a hard and hostile world; as a result, he took a special interest in toughening me up. I remember that he would lay me on my back on the kitchen table, grasp my two ankles and proceed vigorously to pull me back and push me forward in a sliding motion over the oilcloth that covered the table. I don't think this did me any harm but on the other hand it did me no discernible good. It did, however, raise objections from my mother. He also felt that I should be fully prepared to combat any problems I might have with school bullies. Since no such trouble had occurred this seemed quite unnecessary to me; nevertheless, I was presented with a pair of boxing-gloves for one of my birthdays and was informed that I must begin training at once. My lessons began with me squaring up to Uncle Ron. Since there was a large discrepancy in our respective heights and weights it was clear that I would start with a definite disadvantage; furthermore, in temperament I was inclined to be like my father, who was more of a gentle giant than a battling fighter. My training followed a simple procedure. Uncle Ron would face me kneeling down but this was no great advantage to me since all he had to do to repel any attack was simply to stick out one of his arms to prevent me landing a blow. My mother felt she should take part in the game and consequently put on the gloves. She was short and not very quick and I had no difficulty in landing a hard blow on her nose. She immediately reacted to this and blamed Uncle Ron for teaching me the noble art of boxing. The outcome was that I was forbidden to do any more training with Uncle Ron.

Uncle Ron and I shared a bed, and one of our favourite pastimes was to drape a bed-sheet over the brass corner-posts of the bed and secure the sheet by pressing the brass caps of the bedstead over the corner-posts. In this way we made an extremely well constructed tent. Unfortunately this resulted in the tearing of the corners of the bed-sheet and had the inevitable result of raising my mother's anger, which could be very frightening. We were warned that there would be terrible consequences if we did it again. Knowing that my mother meant what she said, we ensured that we behaved ourselves in the future.

I believe it was always difficult to keep a check on Uncle Ron's activities so my parents were not surprised when one day he admitted he had been to Brecon for a day with his friend Ernie Morgan. It appears they had gone there to join the army, which he had in fact done. They were now new recruits of the South Wales Borderers and were destined subsequently to serve in north-west India for seven years. It came as no surprise to hear of this posting, as it was common practice for young men in the 1930's to join the army or navy to escape from the impoverished areas of South Wales or from the prospect of working in the coalmines for the rest of their lives.

This route to freedom and prosperity was also taken by Cousin Stan at a later date.

I believe Uncle Ron served in Hong Kong for part of his army career, since I recall seeing a photograph which supports this view. What he didn't know was that before his seven years expired Britain would be at war with Germany, so his military service was extended by another six years. I vividly recall my father's words when he was told that Uncle Ron had joined the army. He obviously thought he had taken leave of his senses. Uncle Ron later married Aunty Betty and they produced three more cousins to add to a total of more than two dozen.

Christmas was a time we children all looked forward to with a great deal of anticipation, but the one I remember best gave rise to the great mystery of the mutilated Christmas puddings. It was the custom of my mother to make a large Christmas pudding mix and use it to fill a number of china basins for cooking, each basin covered with a piece of cloth and secured with a length of string. The basins were then placed in a large boiler of water and steamed for a number of hours. The result was about half a dozen fully-cooked Christmas puddings which could be eaten over the festive season as and when required. On one occasion we had all had a satisfying main course at dinner and Ma announced that we were to follow this up with a helping of Christmas pudding. She disappeared to the kitchen to extract the pudding from one of the basins. After cutting the string and removing the covering cloth she tipped the basin upside-down to remove the Christmas pudding and then let out a loud scream. The bottom half of the pudding had been removed—presumably eaten—and the top half replaced in the basin and securely covered again with the cloth and string. She immediately blamed Uncle Ron for this display of vandalism but I noticed that Dad, as well as Uncle Ron, had gone extremely pale.

With the departure of Uncle Ron our daily life settled into a more tranquil phase. A building programme to extend our council estate started in the area between the back of our street and the LMS railway line about a hundred yards away. Lorry loads of bricks appeared and were stacked behind our back garden. This was accepted with some excitement by many of my friends in the area. In the summer, when the evenings remained light, we would play on the site and paid particular attention to the bricks, which we used to construct cabins etc.

Up to this time I had a clear view from our house of the movement of traffic on the railway line, which was only about a hundred yards from the back fence of our garden. This proved an interesting source of adventure for me and others of my age. One activity was to place a halfpenny on the rails and retrieve it after it had been flattened by the passage of a train. This always resulted in the halfpenny coin being transformed into a coin with a larger diameter which we hoped might be accepted as a penny. Unfortunately, this never happened.

The railway was treated as a familiar friend by people in the area. It was a spur line which covered the three miles between Ebbw Vale and Brynmawr. It was a single track and was used by a tank-engine with a single carriage. The engine was permanently attached to the carriage so that it pulled on the outward journey from Ebbw Vale and pushed on its return journey. One of our more adventurous activities was to place our ears to the track and listen for the sound transmitted by the track to let us know a train was coming. Sadly, during the time I lived in Ebbw Vale in the Depression a number of people committed suicide on the railway, doubtless because of the effect of the endless drudgery suffered as a result of unemployment. Also scattered around our area were a number of ponds which had been used for storing water for use in previous steelworks and ironworks. These, too, were used by people to commit suicide, no doubt for the same reason. One of these ponds, called the Blue Lake, is located in an area of moorland where Aneurin Bevan made speeches to the public on his socialist views. A memorial stands on the spot and commemorates his association with Tredegar and Ebbw Vale.

About the time I was nine I joined the cubs. They held their meetings in an old one-storey stone building on the site of the disused Ebbw Vale steelworks about a mile and a half from our house. The area around the stone building was derelict and remote from any kind of human habitation and the whole place was generally scary. I am not sure how I got to our meetings but have no doubt I had to walk there and back every week. I'm sure my parents would have arranged for me to have a companion when I went to a meeting, particularly in winter when the evenings were dark. However I cannot for the life of me remember who this was.

We all looked forward to our cub meetings. The part we liked best, and eagerly anticipated, was the last half-hour or so when our cub-master would get us to sit on the floor in a semicircle around a blazing coal fire. He would then turn off the lights and give us one of his famous ghost stories. Week after week we would sit transfixed while he gave us a new story which would result in my mind imagining all kinds of phantoms arising from the dancing flames of the fire and ensured we wasted no time in our walk home in the dark. Our cub-master was well respected by the boys but one aspect of his character puzzled me. He was reputed to be a Brown-shirt. This description was a complete mystery to me but I later learned that he was a fascist of some kind, apparently a supporter of the Italian dictator Mussolini. This was decidedly frowned on in the 1930's and I'm sure my parents would not have approved of my being a cub if they had known this.

As cubs we were expected to wear the cub uniform. This was chiefly a green jersey on which to sew any badges we earned. The proper cub jersey was beyond the means of most people to buy so we had to make do with the assorted colours of the jerseys we wore to school. The striking cub hat, with its radiating gold ribs, was something most of us managed to acquire and was proudly worn during our cub meetings and outings.

The one thing I must be thankful for was that the cubs gave me an introduction to the meaning of such words as pride, truthfulness, honour, doing things for oneself and helping people at all times. This was the beginning of an education which continued for many years when I became a keen and loyal boy scout until I left Ebbw Vale for war service.

One of the most unpleasant incidents in my life happened about the time I was nine years old. I developed scarlet fever and became desperately ill for six weeks or so. The doctor thought I might have diphtheria and there was great concern about my recovery, which apparently was in some doubt. The illness was very common in our town and many children died from it. My parents were understandably very worried. They had every reason to be since in the next few years many of our neighbours' children died from TB, rickets, polio and diphtheria. These included my friend Melvin Holland, who lived in the house opposite ours, and Billy Jones and Frank Newman who were in school with me and lived two hundred yards from us. There were others on our estate who died young but were not so well known to me as those mentioned above. Billy Hacking, who lived in the house next door and who took me to school, went away to live on a farm for the state of his health. I was not told what his health problem was but it's a safe bet to say it was TB.

Some time after Uncle Ron left us to join the army, his place in our household was taken by his elder brother Walter. I believe he left home for more or less the same reason as Uncle Ron, that is, he could not get on with his stepmother. However Uncle Walter was no tearaway and there was never any prospect of his joining the army. He was and remained a coalminer all his life. When he moved in with us he was seriously courting a young lady who fascinated sister Pat and me because she had wonderful long red hair and was always ready to burst into laughter. We definitely liked her and we were delighted when we heard she and Uncle Walter were to get married. When they did they set up house in Cwm, where Uncle Walter worked in the local Marine Colliery.

Uncle Walter and Aunty Doris, both of whom are now dead, had two daughters so that our list of cousins continued to grow. I should explain that sister Pat has always been, and remains, the focal point for all news relating to our family, particularly our cousins. She is in touch regularly with most of them, including the ones in Canada, and many of them visit her at her home in Barry.

We were still making regular visits to Aunty Min at Halfway House. She and Ma were inseparable. On one such visit I was surprised to find Cousin Stan at home when normally he would be at work in Cwm Colliery where he worked underground with his father. Uncle George was a fully fledged collier and as such would have his own particular stall in the pit where he had sole rights for digging coal, paid according to the actual tonnage he produced each shift, and he paid Cousin Stan as his helper. I believe Uncle George was in a position to earn very good pay; however, the work was extremely arduous and not surprisingly Stan wanted to relinquish his job in the pit. When I saw him on this occasion he proudly proclaimed that he, like Uncle Ron, had joined the army. In his case I believe it was the Royal Artillery and not the South Wales Borderers like Uncle Ron. In any event he was subsequently destined to serve in India. Many years later Stan was to play a very important role in my future.

At home Uncle Walter had left us but he was soon replaced by another lodger who was a workmate of Dad's. His name was Howells and he came from the next valley, from the village of Nant-Y-Glo. I recall that Ma was not very enthusiastic about taking another lodger and reluctantly accepted the fact that the income it brought in really was needed. I believe he was married but separated from his wife.

Ma was still making dresses etc for the neighbours and no doubt saving some of her income for a rainy day. She was very insistent that we should scrape enough money together to enable us to have a holiday occasionally. We usually stayed in furnished rooms for a week in Weston-super-Mare or with distant relatives in Port Talbot.

By this time my little sister was no longer a baby but had in fact started at an infant school in the Rassau, an old part of Ebbw Vale about a mile away. By this time, 1937, there were clear signs that better times were returning to Ebbw Vale and children were better dressed. Pat was particularly lucky because of Ma's ability to make her a new dress from the surplus material she always had. In spite of the fact that I was seven years older than Pat we always got on well together and I loved my little sister. We invented our own games when we were at home. These included lions and tigers, our version of shipwreck (which utilised Ma's large linen-basket as a lifeboat) and our version of the toughening-up procedure invented by Uncle Ron. In this case I took the part of Uncle Ron and Pat was the one being toughened. We also played popular board games with Ma and Dad. I recall that Ludo was very popular.

I don't know if it was the result of being a cub or the influence of other boys in the area but I got to the stage where I was very keen on the idea of camping out all night. As some of my friends felt the same way we finally got to the point where we acquired some old sacks, poles and rope to make a presentable tent. It was located on common ground on the remote side of the LMS railway. Having made the tent we had the difficult task of convincing our parents that we would come to no harm and pleaded with them for permission to stay out all night. With some reluctance my parents gave me the necessary permission. However some of my friends were not so lucky and their parents flatly refused to let them stay out overnight. We fortunate ones gathered at our camping-site with piles of blankets and other essentials, such as food, and settled in for the night. I think we all prayed that it would not rain since our tent was clearly not waterproof. We settled down to sleep packed like sardines in a can as the tent was severely overloaded by the excess number of campers. It suddenly occurred to me and my friends that we were on the side of the railway line where there were no houses and our nearest neighbours were in the local cemetery a quarter of a mile away. We talked a good deal, doubtless to keep up our courage, when suddenly we heard ghostly footsteps approaching, to be followed by a formless head at the entrance to the tent and we were caught in the beam of a torch. We had all bravely immersed ourselves deeper in our blankets when a man's deep voice revealed that our intruder was the father of one of the boys, who wanted to reassure himself that we were all OK. The only other incident which occurred that night was the appearance of one of the boys who had been refused permission to camp out. It appears he was sent to bed at home but had crawled out of the bedroom window to come and join us. I wonder what the reaction of his parents was when next morning he was found not to be at home.

This venture increased my desire to own my own real tent, and an opportunity occurred later that summer when my mother revealed plans for a family holiday in Weston-super-Mare. My master plan was that I should not accompany them on their holiday but should stay at home with Aunty Flo and her brothers in Waunlwyd. The money saved could then be used to buy me a tent. This was agreed and I became the proud owner of a canvas tent approximately six feet long and four and a half feet wide costing eight shillings and sixpence (42½). You got a lot for your money in those days.

I had the tent before I went to Waunlwyd to stay with my aunt for the duration of my parents' holiday. This was ideal because I was able to arrange a safari with Trevor Pernel, who lived next door, and another friend. We decided to go over the mountain and camp in the Silent Valley. This seemed a reasonable idea since cubs and scouts camped there every year. The great drawback was that it lived up to its name; it was silent and spooky. As it grew darker we remembered that the farm in the valley was reputed to be haunted and we got really scared. Suddenly we reacted in unison and hastily packed our belongings and raced over the hill and down the other side to Waunlwyd.

When we arrived back at my aunt's home she was dumbfounded. How could three intrepid explorers be afraid of the dark? And anyway everybody knew that Jones' farm was not haunted. It took Uncles Ted and Will a long time to forget this particular adventure and they reminded me of it on many future occasions. Sadly, not long after our camping trip Trevor died. I had returned home and learned later of his death, which I believe must have been expected although I had no idea of the cause. Trevor was just one of the youngsters who died at this time.

During my tuition at Pont-y-Gof Junior Boys' School I was surprised one day to hear the teacher say that we were to be given a swimming lesson. This was indeed news of earth-shattering importance and amazement. There was definitely no swimming-pool in the area and we were sure there was not enough water flowing in the River Ebbw to make even paddling worthwhile. There were, however, more than a dozen ponds around the area which had been formed to store water for the iron and steelworks which originally existed in Ebbw Vale and surrounding districts. These were often used for swimming by older boys and men, but we were sure we would not be given our swimming lesson in one of these.

Eventually we were marched outside to the playground and stood in rows that were spaced to give us enough room to stretch our arms. An older boy then stood in front of us and went through the motions of doing the breast-stroke. It all seemed futile to us at the time. However it has since occurred to me that there was some logic in the exercise because there were plans afoot to build a swimming-pool in Ebbw Vale. It appears that a group of unemployed men had got together and decided to construct a pool. I presume they were unpaid but got money for the materials from the Council or other worthy body.

Ebbw Vale swimming pool.

The pool was sited in a field adjacent to the River Ebbw. The source of the water supply for the pool was from an old drift-mine about four hundred yards away which constantly disgorged a steady stream of cold, clear spring-water. The water went direct to the swimming-pool, where it was heated and chemically treated before being used. The pool was located about half a mile from my home and, as might be expected, I was a regular patron of the facility along with many of my friends. In the summer it was open until quite late in the evenings and on some occasions we even had midnight bathing.

After the middle of the 1930's war-clouds began to appear all over Europe and people began to be fearful of the effect on our country and on themselves. Italy was already at war with Abyssinia and Mussolini, her boastful dictator, was constantly making warlike threats. But it was the developments in Germany which posed the greatest worry to our peaceful existence. It was for family reasons, oddly enough, that I remember this period. One day we heard the devastating news that Uncle George had been knocked down and killed by a train as he walked from the village of Cwm to his home at Halfway House. It was of course illegal for anyone to trespass on the railway but it was natural for Uncle George as it was the shortest and the easiest route to his job as a miner at Marine Colliery. The effect of his death was instant and catastrophic. Aunty Min had nine children and was pregnant with her tenth. The eldest son, Stan, was a soldier in the army and was stationed in India and her next eldest son, Leslie, was about eleven and far too young to be a breadwinner (Cousin Leslie and I were born in Halfway House in the same year). Therefore Aunty Min was left to look after six children, and one due to be born, in a house where there was no man with a job. In addition there were two older daughters but I believe they were not living at home at the time. Presumably they would have been away as domestic servants.

Because of the appalling living conditions in Halfway House and the lack of income it became a matter of life or death to get the family moved to some acceptable accommodation and my mother finally succeeded in getting them a council house within two hundred yards of where we lived. This heralded a whole new chapter in the lives of our family. It was exciting to have a whole family of cousins living so near.

By about 1936 the dark clouds over Ebbw Vale started to get lighter. There were signs of a new steelworks to be built there and, because of the growing conviction that we would soon be involved in a war with Germany, it was assumed there would be an urgent requirement for steelmaking capacity. With the development of a new steelworks the town would be relieved of the chronic unemployment which had lasted for seven years. It would also help to relieve the unemployment level in the towns in adjacent valleys. The development in the town which excited the children on our council estate was the building of a new school on a greenfield site situated about three hundred yards from our house.

By now I had passed my eleventh birthday and was beginning to spend more time with Dad's sister and two brothers at Waunlwyd. I was also getting to an age when I was spending less time at play with children living nearby. Up to the age of about eleven we played mainly in the streets after school. There was little traffic on the roads of the council estate so we were quite safe playing there.

Boys often played marbles, whip and top, hoop and guider, strong horses and weak donkeys. Girls played hopscotch and skipping. Both sexes enjoyed roller-skating when someone was lucky enough to own skates. Usually the skater would only have one skate so they would propel themselves along with one foot on the ground and one on the skate. This invariably resulted in one shoe being worn out much quicker than the other.

In the winter it got quite cold in Ebbw Vale because of its altitude. On these occasions we would throw buckets of water on the road, which would quickly freeze to make a first-rate slide. When there was snow we would make a toboggan and slide down the numerous hills and inclines in the area. Ma liked this sport and would always enjoy a ride with us. She was twenty-two when I was born so she was still quite young when Pat and I were growing up. If there was no snow about we could always find sheets of cardboard to sit on and slide down grassy banks. The Rolls Royce of transport was a gambo made out of a set of pram-wheels. This was great fun and we could attain quite high speeds on a hill.

One incident in my early years which sticks in my mind is the strange adventure of our dog, Gyp. He was an out-and-out mongrel who appeared in our lives from a mysterious source. His appearance coincided with one of the periods when Dad was unemployed. Gyp had the undesirable habit of barking excessively on the slightest provocation. This proved to be too much for Ma to bear, along with her anxieties about managing the household problems associated with unemployment. One day in desperation she said to my father, "Dan, for pity's sake take that dog out and lose him." Dad, who was always happy to comply when Ma wanted help, called me and Gyp to accompany him as he set out to accomplish his assignment. We walked around the streets and fields surrounding our home for what seemed like hours but every time we looked around Gyp was seen happily wagging his tail and following us. Eventually we turned round to find Gyp was not there. Dad and I with great speed made for home, expecting Ma to be very pleased to see us. With a warning glint in her eyes she turned to Dad and said, "Dan, where is the dog?" Dad naturally said we had lost him. Ma replied in her most belligerent voice, "Well, you both go out again and don't come back till you have found him." Dad and I knew we had no alternative but to leave our house and retrace the route we had just negotiated. So with heavy hearts and tired legs we set off to look for Gyp. After what seemed like hours we reached the conclusion that he had completely disappeared and we had to admit defeat. This left us with the unenviable task of returning home to tell Ma of our failure. In due course we arrived home and timidly opened the door and stepped into our humble living-room. The scene before us was one of total tranquillity and domestic bliss. Ma was sitting at her sewing-machine, happily making yet another dress for one of her neighbours, while little Pat was busy playing with a doll. Lying on a rug in front of the coal-fire was Gyp. He was fast asleep and seemed to have a cheeky smile on his face. On reflection, I think Ma knew Gyp would have no trouble finding his way home and she had enjoyed getting Dad and me out of the house for a while. It was clear I had a lot to learn about women, but my education was progressing.

Chapter 3

Waunlwyd

The small township of Waunlwyd lies about three miles down the valley from the town-centre of Ebbw Vale. It was built by the owners of Waunlwyd Colliery for their workers, people who moved into the area for work in the 19th century and who were mainly from Dorset and Somerset.

The village consisted of about eight rows of terraced houses, most of which followed the contours of the mountain on which they are built and the rest followed inclined lines from one contoured terrace to another. Halfway House was within the village boundary but remote from the contoured streets.

My father's parents moved from Silton in Dorset, bringing their eldest son William, to a district of Ebbw Vale called Briery Hill, where their next son, Oliver, was born. They then moved to Victoria, about two miles away, where Uncle Harry was born. In 1900–01 they moved again to nearby Waunlwyd, where Aunty Flo and all their subsequent children were born, including my father. In all they had eleven children, eight of whom were born in Garn Terrace, Waunlwyd, although two died when young.

My father and three of his brothers were steelworkers, while my grandfather and Uncle Will were colliers. Uncle Oliver was killed in the steelworks in 1924.

From the time we moved to Ebbw Vale my parents made regular visits to Aunty Min at Halfway House and to Aunty Flo and Uncles Will and Ted at 22 Garn Terrace. I loved these visits, which went on for many years. Those to Halfway House meant I played with my cousins, whose number increased regularly until there were nine. We seemed to have limitless freedom as there were no roads or neighbours nearby and when it was fine we could play in the fields at the foot of the mountain. When it was raining, as it often was, we played in the playroom at Halfway House. My visits to Garn Terrace were completely different. Because there were no children in the house my spinster aunt and her bachelor brothers gave me a great deal of attention; in fact they spoiled me by granting me my every wish. As Garn Terrace was on the highest street it meant we had open access to

Looking across to the steelworks from Garn Terrace. Painted from memory by the author.

the mountain through the back-gate of the garden; in contrast, if you stood at the front door of your house you would overlook the roofs of the houses in the terrace below. With a terrace of this sort there were, of course, no houses on the other side of the street. At this time (1930–36) the steelworks were closed and the general appearance of the bottom of the valley was one of industrial dereliction. In later years when the steelworks were in full production I could sit on the doorstep at the front of the house and have a panoramic view of the steelmaking furnaces and the iron-making blast-furnaces, which were no more than half a mile away as the crow flies. When the wind was blowing across the valley in the direction of Waunlwyd it was not possible to see anything as we would be enveloped in smoke. One sight which always fascinated me was the industrial locomotive which pushed two or more railway-mounted ladle-trucks to the spoil-tip near Halfway House and tipped the molten slag over the extreme edge. The result was like a miniature volcano that lit up the sky at night.

In the early days, when my sister Pat was still a baby, we would walk the three miles or so to Garn Terrace with Pat in her pram. Three miles may not seem far but the journey was a succession of hills, both up and down, typical of any walk in South Wales. Halfway House, which was about a mile from Garn Terrace, had to be visited by bus as there was no access by pram.

I had a number of friends in Waunlwyd about my own age. One was the boy next door, Trevor Pernel, another was Ewart Jones. Trevor's dad and uncle were permanently unemployed, as was my Uncle Ted. It always amused me to see Uncle Ted go next door when he wanted a haircut, and the exercise was reversed when Trevor's uncle came to Uncle Ted for the same purpose.

The economic depression lasted for seven years until the new steelworks were built. During this time I effectively had two homes, living at Ebbw Vale during schooldays and at Garn Terrace at the weekends. This arrangement was made at my request as I enjoyed the freedom of the fields and woods around Waunlwyd rather more than living on a council estate in Ebbw Vale. My uncles also had time to take me for walks in the surrounding countryside and my friends and I were free to explore the area, particularly the valley between Ebbw Vale and the Abertillery Mountain.

This was known as the Silent Valley (Cwm Rhydech), uninhabited apart from a single farm.

A large proportion of the men in Waunlwyd were unemployed and it was interesting to study their day-to-day behaviour. In the winter on fine days they would congregate at the end of Garn Terrace and sit on stones with their backs against the gable of the house at the end. This was because the house would have a roaring fire at its gable-end so the men outside could benefit from the warm stonework. It was noticeable that steelworkers would always sit on stones while the colliers would crouch for hours on their haunches, a natural result of working underground in coal-seams which were not high enough to allow them to stand upright. In summer the men would sit in a row on a castellated stone wall backing onto a garden in a terrace of houses lower down the hill. I would sometimes sit with the men and listen to their talk and dreams for the future. It was always the same: what they would do if they had a job or their plans to emigrate if they had the money to buy a passage on a boat. Some of them did manage to get to America or Australia but these were usually the single men. The married men with a family had little hope of getting away.

On a number of occasions when I was in the company of adults I recall the reactions of men present when someone used a swear-word in the presence of a child or a lady. The reaction was always one of strong disapproval and a reminder to the offender to mind his language.

In common with other men in the area Uncle Ted was the provider of coal for the household. Unlike my father, who had a ready supply of coal near the surface of the ground on common land about a mile from home, Uncle Ted had to get coal from an outcrop on the side of Abertillery Mountain. This meant digging a tunnel horizontally into the side of the mountain until the coal was reached. This might be only a few yards initially but would become much further as the tunnel continued to be dug over time. Light was obtained using a candle and the coal was dug using a pick and shovel. It was then shovelled into a sack, loaded onto a home-made sledge and dragged to the entrance of the tunnel. Sometimes I would go into the mine and haul the sledge to the entrance, although Uncle Ted never allowed me actually to dig the coal as this was considered too dangerous. Once the coal was outside the mine ready for transport to Garn Terrace, Uncle Ted would hide the sledge and tools in a suitable place away from prying eyes, thieves and other men using the mine. All this happened when I was in my early teens. As my mother would have been horrified if she knew what I was doing I deemed it prudent not to tell her. The big problem with Uncle Ted's drift-mine was that it was located in a very inconvenient place for Garn Terrace. As the crow flies the mine was only a mile away but in practice one had to go down the mountainside to the bottom of Cwm Rhydech and then climb up the other side to the top of a hill leading down to Garn Terrace. Uncle Ted always dug two sacks of coal of about a hundredweight each. To transport them home he would carry one bag a few hundred yards to a convenient spot, where he would leave it and go back for the second sack, this process being repeated until Garn Terrace was reached. There was an immense amount of work and energy expended in this operation and, if Uncle Ted were lucky, he might sell a bag of coal for a shilling (5 pence today). This was, however, unlikely as coal was a commodity which everyone in Waunlwyd had in abundance. In fact the garden of 22 Garn Terrace had a large tip of coal as a result of Uncle Ted's labour. Ironically, as a Waunlwyd collier Uncle Will was given free coal by the colliery. The concessionary coal was always dumped on the road outside the house. The usual amount was, I think, about a ton. As the coal was kept in the garden at the back of the house it meant the full load would have to be carried through the house, a bucketful at a time, invariably resulting in a trail of coal-dust and footprints that would have to be scrubbed away at the end of the operation. Aunty Flo never looked forward to a delivery of free coal.

One of the attractions of spending my weekends with my aunt and uncles in Garn Terrace was that they would let me stay up late at night, sometimes as late as eleven o'clock, which was very late indeed compared with my home bedtime. The evenings were the times when my uncles were more inclined to talk about serious matters, and one evening they surprised me with a discussion on the merits of keeping pigeons. Pigeons were a popular hobby in South Wales at that time but I had not realised my uncles were interested in the subject. Discussion included probable costs and the best location, it being finally decided that the best spot for a pigeon-loft was on the hillside beyond the back garden, using timber purchased from a local builder's yard. The timber would have to be collected and brought to the site by my uncles with some modest help from myself. They pored over the rough plans they had concocted and decided to go ahead. By now both uncles were in work and therefore in a position to buy the timber. While all the planning and talks were going on I became uneasy because I could not see how I fitted into this grand project. My uncles saw my concern and came up with the imaginative suggestion that I should be made the loft-manager. I was very pleased with this proposal as I felt that very few boys (I was about eleven at the time) would have the chance to start their careers in a managerial capacity. I had no ideas what my responsibilities would be but was assured all would be explained when the loft was completed and we had a reasonable stock of pigeons. This all happened at the start of the summer holidays so I had a lot of extra time to spend at Garn Terrace.

For some weeks frantic efforts were made to get the loft completed as quickly as possible. We first had to buy the timber and carry it, plank by plank, from the timber-merchant to Garn Terrace, no easy job since the journey was all uphill. We then had to cut the wood and construct the numerous nesting-boxes required for the birds. In a surprisingly short time we were ready to buy some pigeons from local fanciers. The time had now come for me to take up my responsibilities as loft-manager. My first assignment was to clean out the loft every day, as pigeons are extremely cavalier about their bodily functions and their droppings were liberally scattered about the loft floor and in the individual perch-boxes. The task entailed the use of a scraper to accumulate the droppings in one spot, where they could be shovelled up and disposed of. The floor then had to be rubbed with powdered lime, presumably to kill off pests and parasites. I also had to see that there was plenty of fresh water available for drinking and bathing. It was fun to see the birds take a bath as they always seemed to leave the floor of the loft covered in feathers.

The pigeons soon began to breed and I found I had the job of training the young birds to return to the loft after they were allowed to fly unfettered in the sky over the village. I would take them in a basket to a suitable spot on the side of the mountain, about a quarter of a mile from the loft, where they were then released. After a short period of flying they would return to the loft. This procedure was repeated regularly and each time the pigeons were taken further afield. Eventually the birds would be put on a train in baskets and released when they reached their destination, which could be as far as Scotland or Belgium on race occasions.

During the race we would not know exactly when they would arrive home so one of my uncles would be on hand outside the loft to receive the bird when it arrived. Then came an important part of my responsibilities; a ring would be retrieved from the leg of the pigeon and I had to run with this ring to a central clocking-in point to record officially the time taken to complete the race. This was done by all participants and a group of officials would announce the winner. There were prizes allocated for various parts of the race and the officials had to make judgements allowing for the fact that the lofts competing could be miles apart.

With hindsight I can see that keeping and racing pigeons was a very worthwhile hobby, and can quite understand how working-men can find it a satisfying relief from the daily monotony of hard labour in the coalmines or elsewhere.

The sequel to the pigeon-keeping was that Uncle Will acquired a whippet and, having convinced himself that Spot had racing potential, was determined to train him for future glory on the dog-tracks of South Wales. Uncle Ted was not so convinced and wanted nothing to do with the scheme. He was of the opinion that Spot was too fat in the body and too short in the legs. I also had great reservations, as I feared I would be given another management job to go with my pigeon responsibilities. What actually happened was this. The first thing we had to do was to test Spot's racing potential. So Uncle Will and I wandered around the brow of a nearby hill until we finally found a relatively flat piece of ground: no mean

Author bathing his dog (1938).
Back garden of 22 Garn Terrace, Waunlywd.
Mountainside in background.

achievement since flat ground was very rare in and around Waunlwyd. The plan was that I would place myself about 100 yards ahead of Uncle Will and Spot then, at a pre-arranged signal, would start running away whilst furiously waving an old rag and shouting loudly to encourage Spot to chase the imaginary rabbit. Needless to say, Spot's performance was abysmal. It was obvious even to Uncle Will that Spot would be hard-pressed to catch a three-legged rabbit and showed no signs whatsoever that he had any enthusiasm for a chase. The episode convinced Uncle Will, a man of acute perception, that any further effort on our part to train Spot would be pointless, and so this traumatic failure was promptly accepted and forgotten. Uncle Will always gave me the impression that he was a great philosopher, and in this instance his grasp of reality struck me profoundly. He suggested instead that we should go fishing, an idea which immediately appealed to me.

I then embarked on a period of serious fishing, mostly with Uncle Will. Our equipment was very primitive since little was available commercially, with the exception of hooks which could be tied to a length of gut, also available to buy. Our lack of worthwhile results was, however, down to the fact that any fish caught in one or other of the numerous ponds in the area could be guaranteed to be no more than three inches long. These were usually perch. Although our fishing trips were not productive they sowed in my mind the seeds of an interest that has remained with me all my life.

One evening, while we were sitting up late, my uncles started talking about my future. They were giving it serious thought but could only come up with two possibilities: I should either be a steelworker or a collier. This was perhaps unsurprising given their respective experiences of available work but what was surprising was the depth of their opinions. Uncle Will, the collier, was quite sure that working in a colliery was far better than the steelworks and outlined the dangers of an environment where you were surrounded by molten iron or steel. Furthermore, he reminded me of Uncle Oliver's fatal accident in the steelworks. Uncle Ted, on the other hand, was firmly of the opinion that I would be better off in the steelworks than working underground. At this time he had just started work again after being unemployed for seven years and I thought his argument was therefore rather less valid. Nonetheless, on balance I did favour the steelworks option at the time. I have remembered my uncles' remarks all my life and have often wondered if well-meaning people, who have never actually done any manual labour, know what they are talking about when they profess to shed tears for the lot of manual workers in industry. Most men I have worked with were happy to have a job with security for them and their families.

Uncle Will eating his lunch whilst working underground at the colliery. An impression painted by the author.

It was when I was staying in Garn Terrace that I met a young man who was to have a profound influence on me. He was a collier called Douglas Griffiths and I would guess he was about twenty years old when I first met him, on being taken to his home by one of my aunts. The great thing about Douglas was that he was passionately fond of drawing and I can vividly remember some of the pictures he produced of clipper ships and cathedrals. I'd watch him for hours and would try to emulate him by copying some of his work. This was largely unsuccessful but I would never miss an opportunity to visit him. He had other interests too and one I found astounding was his ability to play tunes on a carpenter's saw. On one occasion I found him and his elder brother, Cliff, playing with a contraption seemingly made up of numerous wires and which produced indistinct noises. I was told he and Cliff were making a crystal set: an early form of wireless. I shall always remember Douglas Griffiths for awaking in me a desire to draw, although that desire was not truly realised until I was over seventy.

My earliest recollections of Waunlwyd conjure up pictures of terraced streets with roads that were made from stones dry-mixed with earth. It wasn't until some years later that the roads there were covered with tar macadam like that found on the main roads in the area. Generally speaking there were few vehicles on the roads apart from the buses running from Cwm to Ebbw Vale. One day I was fascinated by the arrival of a heavy-duty lorry driven by a coal-fired steam-engine. It was being used to deliver casks of beer from a brewery. The normal means of delivery was by beautiful cart-horses, happily not replaced to any great extent by the lorry. On some days we would have a visit from a lorry which carried a small carousel on its deck and, for a halfpenny, we could get an exciting ride on its roundabout. A rag-and-bone man came round periodically with a horse and cart and for an armful of old clothes we were rewarded with a goldfish, which invariably had a pathetically short life. A source of revenue, usually a reward of a halfpenny, was to collect potato peelings for a man who kept pigs. I do not remember seeing a bicycle in Waunlwyd, although they were fairly common in Ebbw Vale, for the probable reason that the roads involved steep climbs.

Every day as the miners came home from work they could be seen walking up the hills leading to their terraced houses. In my early years they came home completely black from the coal-dust and would be going home to wash in the customary galvanised steel bath in front of a coal-fire. Later pithead baths were installed in most collieries so that the miners went home fully bathed and in clean clothes, although some stubbornly continued to bathe at home.

We did not play in the streets in Waunlwyd, as we did on the council estate in Ebbw Vale, as the terraced design of the housing made ball games highly frustrating. A ball kicked a little too hard could disappear over the roofs of the houses in the terrace below. Most of the play took place on the hillside behind Garn Terrace where there was an assortment of deciduous trees that we enjoyed climbing for a number of reasons. A favourite place for playing was an old disused quarry at the back of Waunlwyd School. A striking feature, which gave me food for thought, was that there seemed to be fewer children around in Waunlwyd than on our council estate in Ebbw Vale. I have now concluded that this was because the estate held a high proportion of young families living in their first home, as indeed were we.

Sadly, as the new steelworks got into full production the effect of the attendant pollution proved to be devastating for Waunlwyd. The blast-furnaces producing iron and the Bessemer converters producing steel were very close to it with the result that it was often enveloped in clouds of smoke and sulphurous fumes. The effect on the woods, where I loved to walk and play, was devastating. Within a few short years the beautiful deciduous trees were dead. It is a mystery to me that there were no mass deaths of people living in the area, who must have been constantly breathing in the pollution.

A tramway was constructed from the furnaces up the hill, alongside Garn Terrace, over the top and into the Silent Valley. It was used to carry the solidified molten slag from the furnaces to a tipping area, which rapidly assumed the form of a huge unsightly pyramid. This completely vandalised the beautiful valley where I had loved to walk and camp with the Boy Scouts. It was the price the people of Ebbw Vale paid to regain employment in their area. In one of my picture-books portraying old Ebbw Vale there is a particular picture of Waunlwyd. The caption reads "Waunlwyd, the most polluted village in the country."

Although my uncles Will and Ted were uneducated insofar as they had very little formal schooling I learned a great deal from them during the years when I spent my weekends with them at Waunlwyd. Through them I acquired an interest in walking in the woods and on the mountains near to Garn Terrace. I loved to go out of the gate at the end of the back-garden and climb up the hill behind the house and then beyond to the top of the mountain. The mountains on both sides of the Ebbw valley were about 1800 feet high. It was a wonderful feeling to lie on one's back in the grass and listen to the singing of the skylarks. I learned that men with little education can have a satisfying life even though others may feel they are to be pitied because they work in a pit or labour in a steelworks. Provided they have a steady job and have other interests they can be quite contented.

They often have a store of wisdom which can be of immense comfort in times of trouble and, although they may not have had much schooling, their knowledge is particularly valuable because it came from their actual experience and was not simply a theory expressed in a book.

Later I was to leave school at sixteen to work in the steelworks. I would then no longer spent my weekends in Waunlwyd; my sister Pat and cousin Alan took my place there instead. My early years in Ebbw Vale during the long depression in the 1930's came back to me many years later when I was reading Goethe's *Faust*. Dr Faust was an academic who spent the best years of his life studying and searching for knowledge. He became depressed and said to himself,

"I drag myself through learned bric-à-brac
And shall I there discover what I lack,
And learn by reading countless volumes through
That mortals mostly live on misery's rack,
That happiness is known to just a few?"

Picking up a human skull, he continues,

"You hollow skull, what has your grin to say,
But that a mortal brain, with trouble tossed,
Sought once, like mine, the sweetness of the day,
And strove for truth, and in the gloam was lost."

Faust had reached a state of complete hopelessness and misery, very much like the people of Waunlwyd in Ebbw Vale who were unemployed for so long when I was a boy.

Chapter 4

Glyncoed School

By 1936 life had taken a turn for the better as far as the youngsters on our council estate were concerned. The new school of Glyncoed had been opened at the end of the summer holidays. Compared with the old Victorian schools I had attended in the past Glyncoed was vastly superior. It was built entirely of bricks, with large windows on outside walls. In plan it was rectangular with a large grass quadrangle in the middle. Around the quadrangle the classrooms were arranged with their doors opening onto a cloistered passageway glazed on the side facing inwards to the quadrangle. Along one of the shorter sides of the building there was a well-equipped gymnasium and on the opposite side was a two-storey section for the headmaster, teachers and administration, which formed the front face of the building. The school was on a six-acre site with a large area devoted to playing-fields for the pupils. The whole school area was surrounded by fields, which in the years to come were used to develop a companion junior school and also more houses. My future wife, Marjorie, was one of my fellow students.

Many of the pupils were known to me from my days at Pont-y-Gof Junior Boys' School; there were also others from the small township of Beaufort, which was included in the catchment area for the school. One of these was my cousin, Billy Hicks: the son of Dad's brother Oliver, who was killed in the steelworks before Billy was born.

There were two features of the school which particularly appealed to me. One was the gymnasium, which I thoroughly enjoyed, and the other was the workshop where we were taught the rudiments of carpentry. I did well at this subject and consequently convinced myself that I would become a carpenter. In fact I became so enthusiastic that I asked for and received as a Christmas present, some tools for my own use. Unfortunately my enthusiasm for carpentry got me into trouble. My parents and sister went out for the day allowing me to stay at home to practise my carpentry skills. I decided that the kitchen was the best place to work and the table made a first-class bench. When my family returned home it was to find me standing in a pool of wood-shavings with a liberal sprinkling of sawdust covering the furniture. Ma went ballistic and started chasing me with a brush. I smartly ducked out of her way and locked myself in the toilet. My life was never in danger but it took Ma a long time to calm down and allow me to come out of the toilet.

Ma's father was a lay preacher and a strict parent. This clearly influenced Ma, who was a great disciplinarian. If we misbehaved we were punished, but never unfairly, and afterwards she always told us she loved us and we knew she meant it. She had a simple but effective way of teaching us right from wrong. At a very early age she taught us the Ten Commandments, which comprehensively covered every possible avenue of misbehaviour. One of the most frequently invoked commandments was "Honour thy father and thy mother." Pat tells a story which illustrates Ma's twin obsessions with discipline and respect for her children. One day she was shopping in the main street of Ebbw Vale and Pat was being particularly difficult and unresponsive to Ma's threats of punishment if she did not behave. Eventually Ma turned to Pat and said, "Pat, I've had enough and I'm going to punish you. However, I don't want to embarrass you in front of these people in the street, so we'll go behind the shops and do it there." Pat, of course, survived and relates this story with love even after more than fifty years. It still makes us laugh today as it was so typical of our mother.

Ma always referred to us as children, never as kids. She sometimes explained that kids were young goats and it was insulting to refer to children as kids. I sympathise with her reasoning.

Dad was a quiet man. He was six feet tall and strong as a result of the manual work he did all his life. In brief, he was a gentle giant. In matters of discipline Ma used Dad as a back-up threat. She would often say, "If you don't behave, I'll tell your father." We took notice of this threat to pacify her, but we knew that Dad could never bring himself to raise a finger to hurt his children.

When he was young Dad contracted TB and became very ill, causing him to leave school at an early age and to be hospitalised at Cefn Marbly and later be sent to live on a farm; consequently he had no worthwhile education. He was, however, very conscious of the need for good behaviour both at home and socially. He did not go to church and as far as I know had no firm religious convictions. Ma, on the other hand, was a lifelong member of St David's Church in Beaufort, where she was a chorister and church worker. She ensured that Pat and I went regularly to Sunday School. I seemed to have been born with an insatiable thirst for knowledge but I could never accept information from any source without convincing myself that I had the truth. Sunday School engendered an interest in biblical issues but without satisfying my search for proof.

Although Ma had little education herself she instinctively realised how important a good education was. About the time I started at Glyncoed School I became aware of her determination to see that Pat and I were adequately educated. It wasn't quite clear to me what this meant but I began to hear more and more about the necessity of winning a scholarship to Ebbw Vale Grammar School.

By now it was evident that the Ebbw Vale steelworks would soon be completed and in operation, so that there would be an army of workers to be recruited. It would be the largest integrated steelworks in Europe and would require more than ten thousand workers, far more than could be supplied by the population of Ebbw Vale. Many of the workers would have to be recruited from Tredegar, Abertillery and other valley towns. With this prospect in mind Dad's view was that I should get a job in the steelworks as soon as possible and contribute to the family income. As was to be expected, Ma's view prevailed and I was reconciled to winning the scholarship to the grammar school. Oddly enough I cannot remember sitting an examination, although I presume I must have done so. In fact I cannot recall any subjects such as Mathematics and English being taught in Pont-y-Gof or at Glyncoed, but I have no doubt they were and that I must have been an inattentive pupil. Some occasions, however, do stand out in my memory. The first occurred during my junior boys' school days when I remember our teacher talking to us about the poverty which existed in the country as a whole. She was fully aware of the unemployment and deprivation in Ebbw Vale, the misery and suffering they brought to our parents and the effect they had on the children. She explained that families in the East End of London were suffering from the same economic depression, but their plight was different from ours. Their children were far worse off than we were since they were trapped in a very large urban environment where areas of green fields and woodland were rare. We, on the other hand, were surrounded by unspoiled hills and woods which we could enjoy simply by leaving our gardens by the back gate. I think there was a lot of truth in what she said. Clearly, the parents in both areas had identical problems but we could at least take advantage of our natural surroundings.

The second incident I remember clearly. In Glyncoed School we had a couple of boys who were generally disruptive and tended to bully other boys. One day they were sent for by the headmaster for being particularly difficult, and we knew they were in for some kind of punishment, possibly six strokes of the cane or worse. It is interesting that the general feeling of the pupils was relief that the headmaster had taken them in hand in this way, and we believed that they deserved the cane and wished it had been applied earlier. There were no complaints from parents, who usually sided with the teachers in such matters.

Another memory is of a particular lesson we had at Glyncoed. The teacher talked about industry in general and the effect it had on Ebbw Vale. He explained why some industries failed and later were born again. I assumed he was thinking of the steelworks and its closure for economic reasons and its revival as a result of the importance of steel in the pending war and the need to get the unemployed back to work. He also spoke of other industries which were based on the recovery of natural resources, and explained that their success was very dependent on the ease with which these could be extracted. He was, I'm sure, thinking of the coal industry. His point was that the more coal we extracted, the greater the distance between the coal-face and the bottom of the shaft. The point would finally be reached when it would no longer be economically sensible to extract the coal. He called this the Law of Diminishing Returns. I did not know it at the time but both of these industries would affect my future.

One Christmas a party was arranged for us at school. This took place in the gymnasium, where arrangements had been made for us to play games and to be entertained. This proved to be a great success as the school was co-educational, a completely new experience for all of us. While the boys were taught woodwork the girls were taught cookery, and for this purpose the school boasted a well-equipped kitchen. It was evident that for our party a great deal of work had to be done to see we had an exciting meal, so the girls had been especially busy in the kitchen making sure we had plenty of nice things to eat such as jellies and cakes.

The games we played were traditional for youngsters of our age—musical chairs and pass-the-parcel. We made some attempts to dance but most of the boys were embarrassed and not very happy with this form of enjoyment. At the appropriate time we were invited by our teachers to pair up with a partner to have our Christmas tea. This was a novel idea as we had little experience of mixing with the opposite sex. Marjorie and I found ourselves drawn to one another and ended up walking hand in hand to the party. We became friends and married partners until she died over fifty years later.

By the time I attended Glyncoed School I was old enough to leave the cubs and join the local scout troop, the Second Beaufort Scout Troop. As a result of this I made a number of very good friends, the most important being Tommy Jones, who lived about two hundred yards from me. Tom was our troop leader and we were to remain close friends until I left Ebbw Vale. Our Scoutmaster was Elwyn Thomas, who became well-known in Ebbw Vale and the whole of South Wales for his scouting activities, ultimately becoming Commissioner for the area. We called our Scoutmaster Skipper and he had had a very interesting life. He was one of the young men who had left Ebbw Vale to live in Australia for a number of years, no doubt to find work during the depression. He would get us to sit around an imaginary campfire (it was actually a pot-bellied stove) and sing some of the well-known scout songs. He would also tell us of his adventures in Australia, which we boys were always pleased to hear.

One particular story he told was of an Australian man on walkabout in the outback who was bitten by a deadly poisonous snake. To save his life he apparently cut off his own hand. I had great difficulty in believing this story.

Our scoutmaster led us in the pursuit of scouting ideals and constantly reminded us "to help other people at all times."

One of the pursuits of serious boy scouts is to earn proficiency badges. There are a multitude of these badges and many boys learned skills they could not have acquired otherwise. We had a garden shed which I used as a modest workshop, and in there I learned to repair shoes and earn a cobbler's badge, gaining other badges for carpentry, cooking, first aid, life-saving, needlework, etc. Winning these badges made me sufficiently skilled, for example, to repair my father's and my own shoes. I also made wooden feeding-troughs for a farmer's pigs, for which I was duly paid. My cooking prowess was the cause of some concern as I was always using the small paraffin stove to cook for myself and friends. My parents thought the use of the stove was dangerous, which I suppose it was. As far as I can remember, the only cooking I did where danger was involved was frying sausages.

Camping was a passion with me and I spent many nights in my tent, which I often pitched on the back lawn. The life-saving badge was of doubtful value so far as I could see. We were told that people drowning invariably panicked and became violent and dangerous to approach. The recommended solution to this problem was to knock the victim out so that he could be safely rescued. I always had serious doubts about the wisdom of this approach, being only eleven years old myself and scarcely able to do this.

The church, or chapel, played an important role in the lives of people from Ebbw Vale and other valley towns. For many it was the only means of respite from life's daily grind. It was common practice for the churches and chapels to arrange an annual outing for its members to the seaside. In our area this meant Barry Island, about forty miles away. This outing was mirrored in other valley towns and usually on the same day. We always

Sunday School children from churches and chapels in Beaufort waiting at the railway station for their trip to Barry.

became very excited as the day for the outing approached. In preparation for the trip all sandwiches, cakes and so on were carefully packed along with such items as bathing costumes, towels, beach-balls, etc as well as the indispensable bucket and spade. On the morning of the great day we would meet at the railway station to wait excitedly for our special train, which would be shared with people from neighbouring churches and chapels in the Beaufort district of Ebbw Vale and from those in the main area of the town of Ebbw Vale. We were constantly told to keep away from the platform edge because of the danger of being pushed over in the throng. The train was always of the type with individual compartments, with no corridor toilet facilities. We were all repeatedly reminded to attend to our toilet needs before we boarded the train. On the train's arrival we would all pile into a compartment, each family ensuring it was all safely on board and together. As our train departed from Beaufort it meant we would go down the Tredegar valley, which was the route taken by the LMS railway. People from Waunlwyd and Cwm would leave from the Ebbw Vale GWR station and follow a route down the Ebbw valley.

The trip down the valley was of great interest to young and old alike. In spite of the fact that we passed numerous collieries with their distinctive winding-gear and pithead slag-tips, each one a replica of the previous, there was no diminution of excitement. Eventually we would arrive at the flat land adjacent to the Bristol Channel and finally get a glimpse of the sea. For many people this would be their first encounter with the sea.

As we approached our destination we passed through Cadoxton and saw the start of the Barry Docks. We saw many ships being loaded with coal for export. Coming into the area leading into Barry Island station we passed through sidings housing a number of stationary trains, all headed by engines with large boards in front of their boilers. These boards had distinctive numbers painted on them to identify the train for a particular church outing.

The morning was invariably spent on the sands, which would be crowded with day-trippers from all over South Wales, in the sea and building sand castles. There were the usual bulletins from the loudspeaker about children being lost (and found) as a result of the dense crowds on the beach. At lunchtime we would eat our sandwiches, which for some strange reason always contained a liberal dusting of sand along with the usual filling of ham. In the afternoon, after another dip in the sea, we would visit one or other of the pleasant parks which were easy to reach from the beach. Alternatively we would walk to Cold Knapp and enjoy ourselves on the boating lake. The greatest treat of all was kept for the evening, when we visited the funfair. For this we were allocated a modest amount of money for rides on the various amusements but were cautioned that there would be no more money once we had spent up.

One of my enduring memories of Barry Island was seeing and hearing a massive wheel-mounted organ in the middle of the fairground. Its frontage was a mass of golden instruments and artefacts flanked by two life-size figures of regal-looking ladies. It was powered by a massive steam-tractor, which presumably generated the electricity required for its moving parts. The songs it played were stored on an array of punched cards joined together on their long sides, thus forming an endless ribbon of cards folded like a concertina. These cards contained a medley of well-known songs that were played continuously and included such songs as Land of my Fathers, God Bless the Prince of Wales and other favourites. These organ-produced songs would blend with the noise of the fairground all day long to evoke an unforgettable memory.

About fifty years later I was attending a fête at the racecourse in York, when suddenly the loud noise of a mighty organ could be heard. I went over to investigate and there in all its glory was White's Mammoth Gavioli Coliseum Organ. It was the very one I was enchanted by when I went to Barry Island as a boy. It carried a huge board outlining its history and recorded that it was then eighty years old and had been rescued and repaired by a preservation society from Chester-le-Street.

After an hour or two at the funfair we caught our special train back to Ebbw Vale. We all arrived home very happy, our later life sustained by memories of a bygone age. Like so many others, the Barry Island day-trips have been replaced by cheap flights to Spain and elsewhere.

The churches and chapels were also involved in other aspects of our lives. For example, every year at Whitsuntide there were massive parades in the town to celebrate Whit Monday. Every church and chapel in the district would be represented and each had its own banner and was led by senior members, who formed a choir with the children following behind. The marching was accompanied by the singing of hymns chosen by the churches, who had their own particular favourites. There was no confusion, since the choirs did not attempt to sing at the same time and were not in competition. The march would pass through the main street of Ebbw Vale or through the corresponding streets of the outlying districts. Our church went through Beaufort to the top of Beaufort Hill and back, a distance of about two miles. After the march we returned to our church, where we would be given a tea-party and, in the case of the younger children especially, play some games. There was also a carnival in the town once a year to raise funds for the local hospital. The participants would be representatives of various local businesses or organisations. I usually got involved because of being a scout.

One of the legacies of my upbringing during the depression was an enduring compulsion to retain any item which might conceivably be of some use in the future. My mother constantly reminded us that "to waste not was to want not." This resulted in collections of buttons cut off worn clothing, numerous short lengths of string salvaged from parcels, odd screws and nails and so on. This habit was adopted by a whole generation of people, who became incapable of throwing anything away: a practice that remains with many of them today, including me. On one occasion about seventy years ago my mother came downstairs proudly waving a corset above her head. "I'll never wear one of these again," she said, and let it languish on the kitchen table before throwing its unwanted parts away. On close inspection I found that the corset was reinforced with a number of steel ribs about ten inches long. I found that when the steel was flexed it sprang back to its original shape. This was a property it needed to fulfil its function in the corset and it persuaded me not to throw it away. I realised that here were items worth retaining, although I had no idea what use I could make of them.

About forty years later, during one of my trout-fishing trips, I had the misfortune to break the retaining strip on my landing-net. The strip allowed the net to be clipped to my belt when not in use. I could not get a replacement part and was very reluctant to buy a new net so I examined the contents of my junk-box to see if I could find a way of repairing the old one. There, languishing in the box, were the steel corset-ribs I had kept so long ago. They were a perfect solution to my problem and my landing-net is still in use today. Even now, as I approach the end of my life, I have difficulty in parting with disposable items. All ice-cream cartons, jam jars and good sheets of cardboard are carefully stowed away. I have an unshakeable belief that one day I may find a use for them. I feel sorry for my children who, one day, will have the unenviable task of throwing away so much of the contents of my home.

One day during the summer holidays of 1937 my mother called me to say that the results of the grammar school scholarship exams were to be published that day. Apparently they were to appear in the window of a well-known solicitor's office in Ebbw Vale. Understandably I was excited and waited anxiously for the published results. When I finally saw the list of successful pupils I was thrilled to find my name on it, along with that of Marjorie Wall. The next few weeks were used to prepare me for entry to the grammar school. This meant a new school cap, which was blue with a distinctive gold band, the only item of dress compulsory for the boys: but I believe the girls had to have a regulation gymslip. I also had to have a satchel to carry my books home, a portfolio for drawing and a woodworker's apron. I was fortunate that Ma was capable of making the last two items.

My mother was thrilled and proud as I was the first member of her family, and my father's family, to win a grammar school place. I was not so sure I would like my new school and looked forward to my first day with some trepidation.

Chapter 5

Grammar School

In the autumn of 1937 I looked forward with mixed feelings to starting in the grammar school. On the one hand I felt proud that I had won a scholarship and resolved to do my best to succeed when I got there, but on the other hand I had heard from older boys that new pupils were treated sadistically by established pupils. It was rumoured that the new boys would have to go through an initiation ceremony that was too gruesome to contemplate. Of course we newcomers were made apprehensive by these stories and dreaded the coming of the first day.

Like most propaganda, the facts had been grossly exaggerated. There was an initiation of sorts, which occurred at playtime on the first day. We new boys were chased by the other pupils, given a few slaps and then released as they moved on to the next victim. On the whole the initiation was but a trivial event, hardly worth mentioning. The older pupils actually treated us well and we soon began to admire them for their superior knowledge and their prowess at sport.

The school itself was of Victorian vintage, being a single-storey stone building with a pleasing elevation from the front main side where school photographs were taken. There was an old galvanised steel annexe within the grounds, which I believe was originally part of a church, that was used in my day as a classroom for teaching woodwork. There was another building in the school grounds, brick-built and relatively new. It housed the gymnasium and was also used for assembly. We also had properly equipped laboratories for chemistry and physics. Just outside the main entrance was a very large field which was used for our sporting activities, rugby for the boys and hockey for the girls.

The teaching staff concentrated on their own particular subjects and in the main were good at their jobs; in fact, it was a school in which I should have been happy and done well. Unfortunately there were some aspects of the school which were to contribute to my failure as a pupil. One feature was that all its staff had to speak Welsh; furthermore the learning of Welsh was compulsory for all students. Our days began with assembly, where we would sing the Welsh national anthem and recite, in Welsh, the Lord's Prayer. Finally, the headmaster was dedicated to ensuring that all his pupils remembered they were Welsh and this became a problem of major proportions for me, as my grandparents had come from Somerset and Dorset and those living spoke with a broad West Country accent, as did some of their children. Although I thought of myself as Welsh, and was particularly supportive of the national rugby team when they played England, I could not see any relevance in learning Welsh to my main objective in ultimately getting a good job.

Although I have difficulty remembering lessons from my earlier schooldays I have no problem with those from my time in the grammar school. My studies covered many subjects which were new to me. As well as Welsh and French they included biology, physics and chemistry. I can vividly recall my first lesson in physics, which was about the composition of matter. The teacher stood in front of the class and stated confidently, "Matter cannot be created or destroyed." This was, of course, before our modern understanding of nuclear physics and the discovery of the atom bomb. On the whole I liked physics, was lukewarm as far as chemistry, biology, English and history were concerned and disliked Welsh and French. Geography was of some interest insofar as it awoke in me a curiosity about other countries. My great interests, however, were in mathematics—particularly geometry—and carpentry. From my earliest days in the grammar school I was favoured by Mr Gratton, who took us for woodwork. This was doubtless because of my enthusiasm and the fact that I had done some work in this area in Glyncoed School previously. When he learned of my interest in Hornby trains it was not long before he allowed me to do work of my own choosing. The first project was an elaborate railway station about three feet long, which I was eventually allowed to take home. This was followed by a galleon.

Mr Gratton was also a great favourite in another field of endeavour: he coached us in rugby, which to us boys was a religion rather than a sport. We had to supply our own kit but the official items were considered to be too expensive at a time when unemployment was still high so we were generally kitted out in old cast-off shirts and boots. The difficulty then was to identify the boys playing on your side, since both teams were dressed in a variety of coloured and patterned shirts. The one problem we had with playing rugby was the possibility of getting injured. Usually injuries were quite minor; I had a number of cuts which needed stitches; the only serious accident I learned of was to a boy in my sister's class who broke his neck during a game and died. This was some time after I left school, as my sister is seven years my junior.

My teachers were generally very good and most, I believe, liked me as I caused no trouble in class. I thought our French teacher, Miss O'Riordan, who was approaching her retirement, was a truly regal lady. If I met her on the street it would give me great pleasure to doff my cap and smile at her, or open a door if she was about to enter or leave a room. Sadly my admiration for her was not matched by my progress in learning French. Each time I was given a list of words to learn as homework I would conveniently forget about them and go out and play with my friends when I got home. The same situation prevailed with Miss Rees, our Welsh teacher. She was young, good-looking and well-liked by all her pupils. She was also the girlfriend of Mr Samuel, another teacher at the school, who was lodging with the Hacking family in the house next door to ours. Ma was a great friend of Mrs Hacking and through her got to know Mr Samuel. From him she learned that I was well-liked by the teaching staff but, however, that they felt I did not apply myself seriously to my studies.

The one subject that I appeared to handle without difficulty was maths, particularly Euclidean geometry. The teacher would hand out stencilled sheets of problems which we were expected to solve during the lesson. Usually I could do these without too much difficulty. But the great thing was that I felt it was a joy to do, rather like doing a puzzle for fun. The feeling that it was all fun stayed with me when we did trigonometry and, later, algebra and higher mathematics: a feeling which remains with me to this day. Even now I often solve problems for fun, enjoying the fact that the whole logical process is sheer poetry.

My schooling seemed to proceed along parallel lines. In subjects I liked I made good progress but in those I didn't like I made no progress at all. My parents had very little education and could not help me with my homework and I made use of this by claiming I had done my homework or had none to do. I realise now that I was only fooling myself, having lost sight of the fact that I had to pass in all relevant subjects if I wanted to matriculate at the end of my schooldays. I did not realise that if I failed to matriculate I would drastically reduce my chances of getting a worthwhile job when I became an adult.

As it was a Welsh school great emphasis was placed on music, especially singing. Mr Harrison, our music teacher, was not impressed by my contribution to singing lessons and pronounced that I was tone-deaf. I loved singing and felt that his assessment of my voice was wrong and discouraging. I think he would have been gratified if he knew that years later I was to become a member of the Ebbw Vale Male-Voice Choir and many years after that a member of the Stockton-on-Tees Male-Voice Choir.

On one memorable occasion the headmaster summoned all pupils to assemble in the gymnasium. This was very mysterious as the whole floor area was filled with chairs. When we were seated he explained that we were to be privileged to hear a complete recording of a famous opera called *Tosca*. This unwelcome rendition was to be given by Mr Brewer, the local radio enthusiast, on his gramophone. I don't think any of us had any idea what *Tosca* was or what there was about it to interest us for up to two hours. Our worst fears were aroused when we were told to listen intently and appreciate Mr Brewer's kindness in visiting us and going to so much trouble on our behalf. We were then solemnly reminded that any bad behaviour would be severely punished at the end of the concert.

Never in the whole history of classical music has so much pain been inflicted on so many by one man; it was unadulterated torture that put me off listening to opera for more than fifteen years. I am now a great lover of opera but I think it was a grave mistake to inflict it on children of the 11–15 age range. I have no doubt it completely destroyed any hope the headmaster had of getting his students to appreciate opera. How many young people have been put off Shakespeare because they were obliged to study whole plays rather than selected passages which have great beauty or deep philosophical wisdom? Hamlet's soliloquy which begins "To be or not to be, that is the question," is a good example—one does not have to read the whole play to appreciate it. The same applies to the books of Charles Dickens. He was a great writer but many students have been put off by too early an introduction to his works.

The school gymnasium had a special fascination for me and I was chosen as a member of the school team that performed in public on one special occasion, possibly Prize-Giving Day at the Ebbw Vale Workmen's Hall.

During the period I was at Glyncoed and the grammar school I continued to spend my weekends with my Aunty Flo and her two brothers in Waunlwyd. By now there was great activity going on in the valley below Garn Terrace, where work was well under way to complete the building of the new steelworks, which would cover a site about two miles long, spreading down the valley from Ebbw Vale to Waunlwyd. During this time I took great pleasure in sitting on the doorstep of my aunt's house and watching the various engineering projects that were unfolding about half a mile away down the mountain in the valley site below. Prominent was the construction of the blast-furnaces to be used for the production of iron. These were massive cylindrical structures connected by conveyors to stockyards holding the raw materials for iron-making. The newly-made iron was then used for the manufacture of steel in the Bessemer converters and open-hearth furnaces, housed in a corrugated steel mill being constructed adjacent to the blast-furnaces.

At this time the mountainside around Waunlwyd had a fair population of deciduous trees which conveniently provided acorns and other boyish delights. I did not know it then but when the furnaces started producing their iron and steel the concomitant pollution would envelop Waunlwyd in clouds of sulphurous fumes and kill those trees. I had a friend in Waunlwyd called Ewart Jones, who also won a scholarship to Ebbw Vale County School. He lived in an adjacent street about a hundred yards from the home of my aunt in Garn Terrace.

After our first two years in the grammar school we were all re-organised into three specialist groups according to academic interests. The groups were science, art and commercial. Ewart and I went into the science stream and shared a double desk until we left school. Marjorie went into the commercial group. My group was composed mainly of boys.

In school we wrote with a simple pen and ink, the common practice in those days. Ewart had a gift for writing which I could never understand. If he was given a clean sheet of paper and asked to write something the page would be completely covered in ink-blots before he had finished. He had a very inventive mind and was always coming up with new ideas. One day he surprised me by showing me his latest acquisition. It was a pen with no nib and was called a "Biro." I asked him what it had which other pens did not. He said its main property was that it could be used to write underwater. This struck me as a feature which would be of little use to Ewart.

In the summer of 1939 I went camping again with the scouts. By this time the Ebbw Vale steelworks was in full production and everyone seemed to be talking about war, which was now inevitable. I was fourteen and all the boys in the camp were about my age. We were naturally aware that if war came we might be involved in it one way or another. We all sat round our campfire on a calm, warm night and had our usual singsong but we were all anxious about the war and its possible effect on us. In reply to our questions Skipper informed us that if war came there would be devastating air-raids and in his view it would be over in six months. This was one time when his views were incorrect. At the time we accepted what he said and continued our camping holiday with no worries about the future.

It was at this camp that we were caught in a violent rainstorm, accompanied by frightening bursts of thunder and lightning. We were all comfortably installed in our sleeping-bags and quite happy to remain in our tent where we were at least dry. Our scoutmaster, however, was concerned since we were surrounded by trees. With little explanation he hastily got us all out of our tents to shelter behind a stone wall with groundsheets over our heads. We had a very unpleasant night but were assured it was the right thing to do under the circumstances.

By this time the steelworks were in full production. Overnight thousands of jobs were created for men in Ebbw Vale and in the adjacent valleys. Uncle Ted was working again after seven years. Dad also had a new job in the mills, where red-hot ingots of steel were rolled into ribbons about 3mm thick and a metre wide. These ribbons of steel were automatically rolled into huge coils weighing several tons while still very hot but no longer glowing. They were then allowed to cool before being pickled in a continuous bath and then re-rolled into a size suitable for the manufacture of car bodies etc, or given a further reduction in thickness and coated with tin for the purposes of canning food.

All this came at a high price. Waunlwyd was on most days covered by sulphurous clouds blown over from the plant, and a small-gauge tramway was built up the mountain adjacent to Garn Terrace that was used to dump blast-furnace slag over the top of the hill into the Silent Valley. This was a devastating development since it spelt the end of a valley of great beauty and peace. It seemed that all of Ebbw Vale was to be surrounded by rubbish-tips of coal-spoil and slag.

In school I continued to be out of my depth in French and Welsh because of my inability to apply myself to their study. My progress in English and biology was modest and by no means satisfactory. Only in maths and physics was I really making progress. I still took a great delight in doing woodwork but this was not of great significance as far as my overall performance was concerned.

I now began to feel that continuing in the grammar school was a pointless endeavour for a number of reasons, the most important being that I would never succeed in passing the matriculation examinations. My ambition was to become a carpenter, an aspiration I was likely achieve even if I dropped out of school. To my surprise I found that Ewart felt the same way, so we planned to ask the headmaster for a transfer to the Ebbw Vale Technical School. There we would get tuition in the various trades open to craftsmen and be relieved of the burden of learning foreign languages.

Another factor contributed to my lack of progress at school. As soon as war broke out various sections of the town formed Air-Raid Precaution Groups (ARPs). These were composed mostly of men who were in no danger of being called up because of their age or occupation, but boys were also being recruited to do minor jobs such as run messages for the Special Police and ARP wardens. Being a Boy Scout I was recruited as a messenger-boy. The task did not impose any great strain on my modest brain but it had one disadvantage for a boy in the grammar school striving to reach certain academic targets: I was duty-bound to report to the ARP headquarters whenever an air-raid alarm sounded. This usually happened at night after I'd gone to bed and consequently I would attend school the next day decidedly the worse for wear owing to lack of sleep. As one would expect, none of this contributed to an improvement in my French and Welsh.

A particular incident sticks in my mind. I was often assigned the duty of accompanying a Special Policeman on his rounds. He had the appropriate uniform and would go round the neighbourhood keeping a sharp look-out for houses with defects in their blackout arrangements. One night he found a house which was not completely blacked out. Clearly appalled by this lapse on the part of the unlucky householder he pulled himself up to his maximum height and gave a very loud knock at the door. A lady opened the door, displaying a full head of curlers and a great deal of displeasure. My policeman colleague said, "Madam, you are showing a light and I must report you to the proper authority." Taking out his notebook and pencil he said, "What is your name?" The woman turned a vivid red and looked set to explode at any second. Looking at the policeman she said, "Mr Davies, are you daft? You know who I am—I live next door to you." There seemed to be no answer to her question.

On one memorable occasion we had the normal end-of-term examinations in all the subjects we were studying and I distinguished myself by scoring a zero in French and in Welsh, an achievement which has never been emulated by any other pupil since. It did, however, lead me to the logical conclusion that I would never succeed in the grammar school. The net result was that I saw the headmaster and suggested that I would probably be better off transferring to the Ebbw Vale Technical School. The headmaster, with palpable relief and pleasure, readily agreed to this idea and Ewart Jones and I were duly transferred. My parents were very disappointed with my transfer, as it indicated complete failure on my part to achieve any worthwhile success in my education. This was a crushing blow to my mother, who expected far more from me.

I left grammar school with no feelings of regret. It had been an experience that would ultimately prove invaluable to me in my future pursuit of a career, but in the autumn of 1940 I was incapable of making a mature assessment of what I had done. At the time my thoughts were very much influenced by the traumatic development of the war in France, as the country had been overrun, and by the Battle of Britain, which was in full swing. I knew instinctively that sooner or later I would be involved in some way.

The Ebbw Vale Technical School was designed to prepare boys for a craft career in industry, such as fitter, carpenter, electrician and the like. It was small in comparison with the grammar school; in fact I would say that there were only about 150 pupils, and its premises consisted of a number of rooms and workshops above the Workmen's Institute. On the ground floor of the building were the Ebbw Vale library and a billiard hall. In the entrance hall was a large model of a tramp-steamer, a subject of great fascination to me. I often stood to look at it when entering the school and would wonder what life would be like on such a ship. Early in the war we would hear or read of merchant ships being torpedoed and sunk more or less every day. This was at a time identified as "The Phoney War" but there was no phoney war for the crews of merchant ships.

Lessons at the technical school proved more to my liking. Great emphasis was placed on mathematics, to my great delight, and it was soon clear that the teachers had faith in my ability to do well. What's more, I enjoyed going to school and felt I had made a good decision in making the transfer to the "Tech." My sessions in the workshops were frequent and very much enjoyed. Metalwork became a new component of my education and I was taught to use a lathe and other pieces of metal-working equipment. I also continued with lessons in carpentry. There was every reason to suppose that, like my friends at school, I would eventually end up being apprenticed to one of the trades found in the steelworks. Now that I was free from the labour of learning foreign languages I began making good progress in non-scientific subjects such as English and geography.

Many of the boys at school were already known to me, such as Tom Jones. He was destined to become a fitter in the steelworks, the lot of many other boys in the school. Others became carpenters, electricians and so on. They all had a security and status which seemed highly desirable to me. Tom Jones was a year ahead of me at school and often talked of the studies in front of me. One day he said something to me which has stayed in my head. He had been extolling the beauty of mathematics and tried to explain to me the wonders of calculus, which I would soon be studying. It was a world where finite quantities could be made infinitely large or infinitely small and yet yield finite tangible results. We had the same teacher for the subject, whom we both highly respected, and apparently he offered Tom and his fellow-pupils the then astonishing hypothesis that God must be a mathematician. I gave this a lot of thought and discussed it with Tom at the time. I still think about it now when in contemplative mood; however I cannot find sufficient reason to believe that it's true. It was about this time that we became aware of Einstein's Theory of Relativity.

One of the great attractions of the technical school was that it was directly above the billiard hall that belonged to the Institute. We boys were not encouraged to play there but we were tolerated provided we behaved ourselves. It was quite common, therefore, for us to play a game of snooker during our lunch-break. Unfortunately I had an affliction which made me unpopular with the other boys: I was incapable of distinguishing between the green and blue balls because of colour-blindness. Nobody wanted to have me as a partner since I was constantly conceding points for foul play.

The war was advancing with a constant stream of defeats in various areas, such as Norway and North Africa. There was now very little news concerning the Battle of the Atlantic and the daily sinking of merchant ships, presumably to shield the public from the dismal news that we were constantly losing encounters with the German U-boats. At school it was anticipated that there might be air-raids in Ebbw Vale because of the strategic value of the steelworks. So a plan was devised to disperse the whole population of schoolchildren between carefully selected private homes in the area. I was one of a group of four boys who were allocated to a home belonging to one of my co-pupils from the grammar school.

The grammar school was having its daily routine drastically changed to cope with wartime requirements. A grammar school from Kent was evacuated to Ebbw Vale and shared the same premises as the local pupils. The problem of overcrowding was solved by the Ebbw Vale pupils attending in the mornings and the Kentish evacuees in the afternoons. Aunty Flo had two boys billeted with her. I still visited and spent my weekends with her at Garn Terrace and became good friends with the boys. At home a number of older boys had been called up or had volunteered for the armed forces. Billy and Ralph Hacking becoming air-gunners in the RAF. They had been great friends of mine for many years and in my junior school days had escorted me the mile or so to Pont-y-Gof School along with their sister, Joyce. In the house on the other side of ours the son of Mr and Mrs O'Donnell was also called up and he, too, became an air-crew member of the RAF. Unfortunately he went missing and was presumed killed.

As far as I was concerned I was fifteen and still a messenger for the ARP, turning out each time the siren sounded, although this was not as often as initially had been the case. In any event it did not have a significant effect on my studies, which were going well. By now I was confident of doing reasonably well in the approaching end-of-year examinations. But the unexpected happened and at a crucial time I developed scarlet fever for the second time. Although it was not serious enough to put me in any danger, it did prevent me from going to school over the critical period of the examinations. This was indeed serious and I had to think about my future, bearing in mind that I would have to choose between leaving school or possibly taking up my studies again in the next academic year. This was the prelude to a protracted period of conflict at home where I was at variance with the views of my parents. My mother was determined that I should continue my education so that I would not end up working as an ordinary labourer in the steelworks or the pits. She was obsessed with the idea that I should have a good job where I would be able to wear a collar and tie and not get dirty as a result of my labours. This to me was a prospect too hideous to contemplate. I knew she meant well but her desired occupation did not seem to me to be a man's job. My father was convinced I should get a job in the steelworks and help with the economy of the family. I thought this was a better idea than working as a shop-assistant behind a counter. With my grandfathers, father, uncles and cousins all being working-class men in the coal and steel industries I felt that industrial work was in my blood. Besides, I had a great respect for all the male members of our extensive family and quite naturally saw nothing wrong with the way they earned a living. Finally I decided I would like to work in the steelworks, with a preference for an apprenticeship of one sort or another. Unfortunately my attempts to be accepted as an apprentice were not successful, so I accepted a post as stores' boy in the works store servicing the blast-furnaces etc.

In retrospect I realise that my dropping out of grammar school was a bitter blow to my mother, who had worked so hard to keep me there. However I console myself with the thought that if I had studied hard, stayed in school and matriculated, my career would have come to an abrupt end since there was no possibility of my going to university. My parents could not have afforded to send me and, at that stage, I would not have succeeded in getting a scholarship as I was too immature and not sufficiently motivated to compete. So if I had stayed in school and by some miracle matriculated I would probably have ended up with a respectable white-collar job and eventually become frustrated and unhappy. Deep down in my soul there must have been a burning ambition and inflexible determination waiting to break out. Before that could happen, though, I would have to experience seven years of living in the real world of men who earn their living by the sweat of their brow rather than with a pen. This was a phase of my education which was to change my life irrevocably. In the end I was to achieve all the objectives my mother had worked for and I believe I was eventually redeemed.

Tosca

I must have been about thirteen—
That's as near as I can tell—
When with a hundred or so
  school friends
I was cruelly sent to hell.

Our headmaster, may he rest in peace,
Decided we were sufficiently mature
To listen to some gramophone records:
Specially chosen to make us pure.

Being Welsh and fond of singing,
This special rendition was to be
Verdi's celebrated opera Tosca;
This portion of culture to be given free.

We all sat in the assembly hall,
When we were given the news that day.
I whispered to Glyn beside me,
"Who is this Tosca anyway?"

He said it was an Italian café,
Located in the valley next to us.
I somehow felt this was not so
And prayed the maestro had
  missed his bus!

Mr Brewer was to be our tormentor:
A respected and well-known Radio Am.
He approached his gramophone
  with gusto;
His ferocity filled us with alarm.

Never in the history of classical music,
Not even since civilisation began,
Has so much pain been inflicted
On so many innocent children
  by one man.

In our seats we shuffled and fidgeted:
The culture lasted
  for two hours or more.
We silently lifted hands and prayed,
"Please God,
  show Mr Brewer the door."

When the agony finally ended,
Most children were too stiff to move.
Some banged their heads in desperation
To get their brains back in the groove.

For me, the result was catastrophic:
It was years before I again tried
To see and listen to an opera—
When I did, I could have cried.

Raymond Hicks

Chapter 6

The Steelworks

Just after my sixteenth birthday in May 1941 I took up my post in the steelworks at a princely wage of seventeen-and-six (87½ pence) a week. My duties were trivial and did nothing to convince me I had done the right thing in leaving school. My time was spent arranging items in storage bins and labelling them for future reference and mundane tasks like sweeping the floor of the stores. There was, however, one side of my duties that was welcome and which enabled me to get to grips with some of the interesting aspects of steel-making. I was often sent on errands that enabled me to wander around the works in the areas immediately surrounding the stores. These were the areas where iron and steel were actually produced: the blast-furnaces and steel furnaces.

Three basic materials are needed to produce iron and steel, together with some special additives needed in small quantities. Those materials are: (1) iron ore, which came from abroad, as all the indigenous supply had been exhausted in the previous century; (2) coal, found in abundance in South Wales; and (3) limestone, which was also plentiful in the areas of moorland north-west of Ebbw Vale, where the coal measures outcrop and give way to large areas of this rock.

The first important step in steel-making is to turn the available coal into coke by firing it in large batteries of coke-ovens. This process was accompanied by copious emissions of fumes and dirty smoke which inevitably engulfed "Garden City," a small village of several streets directly opposite the coke-ovens.

The three basic ingredients were loaded into the top of the blast-furnace and fired from below with a plentiful supply of air blown in to generate a very high temperature. The ingredients were melted and turned into a pool of molten iron. When the process was deemed to be complete a furnace-man would puncture a hole in the bottom region of the furnace to release a spectacular stream of molten pig-iron for collection in massive, rail-mounted ladles. The molten iron was then taken by rail to the nearby steel-making plant, where it was converted into steel either in large open-hearth furnaces or in Bessemer converters. This latter process was extremely spectacular since it produced streams of molten steel reminiscent of a volcano overflowing the lip of its crater.

All the above will be of little interest to most people but it is worth noting, as I have already said, that the process caused appalling pollution.

Now that I was sixteen my service as a messenger-boy with the ARP came to an end and I joined the Home Guard. Actually I was prompted to take this step by some of my friends, who pointed out that for certain duties the Home Guard was paid. For example, a 24-hour guard was kept on the drill hall, which served as HQ for the Home Guard, and if you were on duty all night you would be paid twenty shillings. As that was more than my weekly wage as a stores' boy, it seemed a very good payment for just being on duty all night. I cannot remember the reason for the all-night vigil, unless it was fear that we would be the target of German parachutists interested in the steelworks. I'm not sure what we would have done if such a raid had occurred.

In the Home Guard we were given a uniform and a 303 rifle but no ammunition; however, we did use our rifles when training on a local firing-range. When these occasions came along I was quite pleased as I was considered to be a good shot. We also went on manoeuvres and, in accordance with good army practice, we would have the usual games; that is, one group would be the enemy and the other group the Brits. I disliked the drilling we had to do as I resented being ordered to do things which to me seemed completely unnecessary. Sometime after the war, when television became a household essential, a series called *Dad's Army* became very popular with the public. I'm sure it created in people's minds a picture of the Home Guard that, although very entertaining, was not a good representation of the Home Guard as I found it to be in Ebbw Vale. The men were mainly tough, down-to-earth steelworkers and coalminers exempted from military service by virtue of their occupations. They were all deeply resentful of the war started by Germany and, I'm sure, would have given a good account of themselves if called to do so.

There was also a sizeable proportion of young men in our division who in a year or so would be in the armed forces or the Merchant Navy. My great friend in the Home Guard was Bobby Clubb. Bobby was the son of a miner and lived about a hundred yards from me. He had had no secondary

Ebbw Vale blast furnaces, at the steelworks where the author worked as a boy. Painted from memory by the author.

education but did have a knowledge of opera and poetry and was very intelligent. He worked near me in the rolling-mills and eventually served on the same ship as me in the Merchant Navy. At this time my favourite poet was Kipling, who would also be the first choice of many of my shipmates.

After two or three months working as a stores' boy I became completely disenchanted with the job and started to make enquiries about possible openings for me elsewhere in the steelworks. By now the war had progressed to the stage where many young men of the workforce had been called up for military service. This resulted in boys of my age being employed in jobs normally filled by men. As a result of talking with friends I applied for and got a job in the rolling-mills at a man's wage. This started at about three pounds per week but could increase to five with overtime or by working on a more demanding machine. We worked a four-shift system of days, afternoons, nights and floating. The floating shift occurred every four weeks and entailed working two days on each of the three normal shifts. A few of my friends and my cousin Leslie worked in the same department as I did.

On the whole I liked working in the cutting-lines, which were a part of the cold rolling-mills. But deep down I knew that I wanted to get away from Ebbw Vale and gain experience of the outside world, just as Uncle Ron and Cousin Stan had by joining the army many years before. I knew I would not be happy in the army, navy or RAF because of a deep-rooted dislike of military discipline; furthermore I was only sixteen, so the obvious choice for me was to join the Merchant Navy as a boy rating. In pursuit of this idea I went to Newport, twenty miles away, and visited the dock area where I could gaze on the merchant ships from outside the forbidden area and even see some of them in dry dock. I also went to a number of shipping offices to offer my services as a boy rating, that is, a cabin boy or galley boy. It was all to no avail, the general presumption being that only men over eighteen were required. I reluctantly returned to Ebbw Vale with a firm resolve to try again when I was older.

By now my parents knew of my desire to go to sea and had instantly united in their opposition to the idea, putting forward all sorts of arguments to support their disapproval. Their greatest fear was that I would ruin my life since they believed that I would be consorting with degenerates outside the accepted orbit of good moral behaviour and would be in grave danger of following their sinful ways. They were saying all this without knowing anything about the lives and behaviour of seafaring people and were repeating what they had heard from other people, who themselves were probably talking about something of which they had no experience.

I returned to my job in the steelworks deeply disappointed with my failed attempt to join the Merchant Navy. But I soon recovered my usual cheerful outlook on life and resolved to try again later when I was older and, I hoped, more mature. My situation in the rolling-mills was not disagreeable, although some of us had minor accidents such as cuts on the arms which needed stitches. These happened in spite of the fact that we had to wear gloves and steel-studded gauntlets on our arms below the elbow.

I had a number of friends working with me and we were all maturing in various ways. One of our great topics of conversation and debate was our future in the light of the vicissitudes of the war. Another topic was politics. It seemed to me that everybody in the area was a supporter of the Labour Party, really not surprising bearing in mind the poverty and privation experienced over the last decade. The MP for our area was a local man, Aneurin Bevan, and he was idolised by almost everybody as a great socialist.

Most of the people of Ebbw Vale were of the opinion that everyone would be better off if the wealth of the country was equally shared between them. I had serious doubts about this theory as a result of my experiences of living on a council estate through the depression years. I can recall that most of the people living on our estate were families belonging to miners or steelworkers and that a large proportion of them experienced long-term unemployment while I lived there. These people were all living on the dole and were essentially getting the same state benefits yet they fell into two distinct groups. On the one hand you would find the families who kept their garden tidy and well cared for and the inside of their homes would be neat and clean while their children were well-disciplined and good-mannered; on the other hand there were families who completely ignored their gardens, which were overgrown and filled with rubbish, and the insides of their homes were neglected while the children were allowed to roam freely without any apparent control. All this has left me with a firm conviction that it's not just equality of wealth that's important to our lives but other factors too.

While I was working and serving in the Home Guard I still kept up my interest in the scouts. By now I had exhausted most of the subjects which enabled me to win proficiency badges but there was one area I still had to tackle. This was map-making. I decided to make a map of Ebbw Vale incorporating all the streets in the town and its immediate surroundings. This took up many months of my spare time but in the end the map was completed to my satisfaction. The exercise led me further afield, as much as ten miles away from my home, and it wasn't long before I got involved in exploring the limestone area mentioned earlier. At Trevyl I found the quarry where limestone was mined and supplied to the steelworks for the manufacture of iron. The moorland was extensively covered with large depressions caused by subsidence of the ground above the caves that covered vast underground areas. I spent many enjoyable days exploring these caves which, many years later, were explored by expert cavers and pronounced to be among the most extensive in Europe. On one occasion I succeeded in finding the cave that, it is reputed, was used by Chartist rebels as a hideout during an uprising by workers against their taskmasters.

As my seventeenth birthday came nearer I found myself thinking more and more about trying once again to join the Merchant Navy. Once again I found myself on a train going down the valley to Newport and subsequently presenting myself at the recruitment office, called "The Pool." This time I had the not-so-bright idea of not being quite truthful about my age and, when asked, I said I was eighteen. The examining officer looked at me and seemed satisfied that I was of age and started taking down all the facts he thought relevant. He finally asked where I was employed and I replied that I was a steel-worker. He seemed suitably impressed by this disclosure and was clearly thinking I was a good candidate for a job in the ship's engine-room. To my great relief he suggested that if I was interested he would arrange for me to go on a two-week course at Gravesend and on its completion I would be offered a job on a ship as a coal-trimmer. If I had known what a coal-trimmer was I might not have been so keen to say "yes" to the invitation, but I was so excited at the prospect of going to sea that I readily accepted the offer. I was then instructed to quit my job and report back to the recruiting office where I would be given a posting to the Gravesend Training School.

I returned home to give my news to my parents, who were decidedly unhappy at the turn of events. My mother was tearful and told me several times how dangerous the Merchant Navy was and I might well be killed. My father joined in the condemnation of my actions and concluded that I was a fool to volunteer for such a job and would probably pay for it with my life. I replied that I would rather die on my feet than live on my knees, which was what would happen if Germany won the war. This seemed to convince my parents there was nothing they could say or do to make me change my mind and they eventually came to terms with the idea I was going to leave home, maybe for good.

My next action was to give notice to my employers at the steelworks. This was accepted by the company and I was given my last wage, along with my employment cards to hand to my new employer. This was to be my undoing. In complete ignorance of the significance of the employment card I handed it to the recruitment officer at the Pool. He stared at it for a moment or two before commenting on my deception about my age. Consequently I was not eligible for the job of coal-trimmer or anything else until I could prove I was eighteen and an adult. I returned home from Newport in a state of acute depression. Not only had I failed to get into the Merchant Navy but I had lost my job as well and had no tangible means of support. The obvious thing to do was to apply for another job in the steelworks but I could not bring myself to do that because I believed I would find a way of going to sea eventually.

My parents must have been deeply disappointed with me as their dreams of me getting a good education and a good white-collar job were now in ruins. But if this was so they never showed their true feelings and I was welcomed back to my home with no reminders of my failure nor any recriminations. They probably saw me as following in the footsteps of Uncle Ron and Cousin Stan, who had got out of Ebbw Vale by joining the army before the war. However I was beginning to exhibit a characteristic that would serve me well in years to come: when I cared passionately about an objective I would keep at it until I finally succeeded. The thought occurred to me that after leaving the army Cousin Stan had got a job in Liverpool as a policeman and, as Liverpool was of prime importance as a control base for the Battle of the Atlantic, perhaps he could help me in my quest to go to sea. Cousin Stan wrote back with information of great importance to me. It appeared that he was assigned to the patrol of the docks and he was convinced he could help me to get a ship. He was married and assured me that he and his wife Nora would give me free board and lodgings if I should decide to go to Liverpool. This would really be a big step into the unknown and would necessitate a train journey which I could ill afford. However, assuming it would be a one-way journey, I bought a single ticket and embarked on a train for Liverpool. I had very little in the way of luggage and had no clothing suitable for life at sea, but this did not dampen my enthusiasm and I felt that I was on my way to an important adventure.

On arrival at Lime Street Station I was met by Cousin Stan, who still had the infectious smile and grin I could remember from a time many years ago when we were at Halfway House and he told me he had joined the army. He took me on a tram along Queen's Drive and we got off at the stop for Cherry Avenue. (Funny how I can remember these details after sixty years!). I met Nora, his wife, for the first time. She was beautiful to look at and delightful company. I thought how lucky Stan was.

From the moment I entered Stan's house and met Nora I was made to feel at home. She was a great cook and she looked after me like a younger brother. Stan spent a great deal of time with me and showed me some places worth visiting in Liverpool, notably the Liver Building and the pier-head, where a ferry could be taken to cross the Mersey. I would go there daily and take a ride on the ferry. It was a joy to feel the ship move underfoot in unison with the movement of the river. I couldn't wait to get on an ocean-going steamer and really go to sea. During this time Stan was busily exploring possible openings for me on various foreign ships. He was confident that he would eventually be successful.

Chapter 7

Part I – **Dutch Merchant Navy**

Introductory Note

During the four years I was at sea (1942–46) I served on two Dutch merchant ships and six British; usually we sailed in convoy but not always. There is little merit in covering each voyage in detail since some were without incident but I give the return convoy of my first voyage, *HX229,* some prominence as a number of books have been written about it. I have consulted my Dutch payslips and these confirm I was a crew member of *Ganymedes,* which formed part of the convoy. So I have written in some detail about this voyage, supported by information from the following books which both list *Ganymedes:*

- *Convoy,* written by Martin Middlebrook, a British historian.
- *The Critical Convoy Battles of March 1943,* by Jurgen Röhwer, a German wartime naval officer.

My second voyage was more or less a duplication of the first and once again we ran into U-boat trouble in the North Atlantic, an episode covered in the book *Dönitz and the Wolf-packs,* by Bernard Edwards.

"Oh, where are you going to, all you Big Steamers,
With England's own coal, up and down the salt seas?"
"We are going to fetch you your bread and your butter,
Your beef, pork, and mutton, eggs, apples and cheese."

"For the bread that you eat and the biscuits you nibble,
The sweets that you suck and the joints that you carve,
They are brought to you daily by all us Big Steamers—
And if anyone hinders our coming you'll starve!"

(Rudyard Kipling)

This extract comes from a poem we all had to learn when I was a schoolboy.

Now that we were at war the merchant ships were also responsible for our imports of war materials such as aviation fuel and high explosives, tanks and planes, etc.

My *Ganymedes* papers confirm that I made my second crossing to New York between the end of April 1943 and the middle of May 1943. This implies that we were probably part of *Convoy ONS 5*. The books do not specify the names of the ships in the convoy but the times indicate that *Ganymedes* was probably one of them. Bernard Edwards also describes the attacks by a U-boat pack on *Convoy ONS 154* in late December 1942. This convoy was outward-bound from the UK to Halifax in Canada. It was attacked repeatedly, with the tragic loss of fourteen merchant ships that were torpedoed. My *Ganymedes* records indicate we were in the North Atlantic at the end of December 1942 and in New York and Trinidad in the January of 1943. This clearly puts us in the battle-zone at the crucial time of the convoy battle but I have no means of proving that we formed part of *Convoy ONS 154,* although I remember being under a U-boat attack on that voyage.

The details of the British ships I served on are tabulated in my seaman's logbook, in particular my five voyages to New York on the *Queen Elizabeth* and my three voyages to India, Ceylon and Singapore on the liner *Capetown Castle*.

With the help of Cousin Stan the day finally arrived when I achieved my long-awaited ambition. Our repeated visits to the offices of the Netherland Shipping and Trading Committee Ltd resulted in my being offered a berth on their freighter *SS Ganymedes* as a pantry-boy and I was to join the ship immediately. I was not sure what the duties of a pantry-boy were but was assured they were more or less the same as those of a cabin-boy. I was not told where we were going or when we would sail. This information was never given to the crew for reasons of security, as every effort was made to ensure that the enemy did not gain knowledge of our plans. Thus, duly armed with official authorisation, I presented myself at the security office on the gates of, I think, Gladstone Dock. The dock-gate policeman directed me to the wharf where *Ganymedes* was moored and being loaded for the next trip.

As I walked along the dockside I began wondering what *Ganymedes* would look like. Most of the ships I passed were freighters, loading or unloading their cargo using their own steam-derricks or dockside cranes. Some of these were grand-looking vessels which I hoped *Ganymedes* would resemble, but I wasn't really worried as long as she would take me to sea. Some were troopships, like the French liner *Pasteur* which was in Liverpool at that time, and some were in a sorry state because of enemy action and were being repaired. When Stan had told me there were seven miles of docks in Liverpool I found it difficult to believe. But now, with the ships and activity I saw all around me, I was prepared to believe him. Finally I found myself alongside *Ganymedes*. She was small in comparison with the other ships moored around her. She weighed fewer than 3,000 tons but she was relatively modern. Today ships of 300,000 tons are quite common. *Ganymedes* was flush-decked with a cruiser stern (i.e., rear) and burned oil as her primary source of fuel. One unusual feature was her masts, which were situated between hatches 1 and 2 and hatches 4 and 5. These were double, with a cross-member like the posts on a rugby field. To a rugby enthusiast from the South Wales mining valleys this seemed to be a very good omen.

With a mixture of excitement and trepidation I stepped on to the gangplank and climbed aboard. Because the ship was small her deck was only a few feet above the quayside. The gangplank was therefore aligned almost horizontally with the dock. In fact it would have been a simple jump from ship to shore. There was a sailor on watch, who gave me a friendly greeting and then took me to see the chief steward: a short, rather stout Dutchman with an engaging, friendly demeanour. He asked me many questions about my background and previous employment. He was rather surprised to see how small and inadequate the bag of gear I brought for my first voyage was. I had no sea-boots or waterproof clothing and was poorly equipped for cold weather. I now learned that merchant seamen were not given any clothing for sea-duty, being expected to buy everything they needed themselves.

I was taken to the stern of the ship, where I was to be billeted. This meant a short walk over the deck which was festooned with steel ropes, hatch-covers and other miscellaneous items needed for loading. We descended a short flight of stairs, at the bottom of which were two doors. The right door led to the seamen's quarters and the left to the firemen's quarters. We went through the door on the right and entered a space containing twelve bunks arranged in two tiers on each side of the room (forecastle). There was a long wooden table down the centre flanked by wooden benches. The chief steward walked over to one line of bunks and pointed to one on the lower level which was for me. He then left me to settle in.

The forecastle (so called even though it was in the stern of the ship) had three or four portholes in the bulkhead adjacent to the quayside. The steel plates of the ship were painted white and were extremely wet from condensation. My bunk, I noted, had a straw mattress and pillow and, folded on top, two woollen blankets. There were no sheets or pillow-cases. All the items were clean and gave me no cause for complaint as my many years as a boy-scout and my numerous camping experiences had inured me to sleeping in strange surroundings. Indeed the ship's bunk seemed quite luxurious to me.

There were no men around at that point but there was a boy of my own age (17). We soon got to talking and I learned that he was from Newfoundland. He was extremely frightened and nervous. It appeared that his previous trip across the North Atlantic had been very eventful and this had unnerved him. He was hoping to sign off and go home again if we went to Canada on the forthcoming voyage. He was the sailors' "Peggy": the name given to the boy who cleaned the sailors' quarters, got their food from the galley, etc. There was a 16-year old Scottish boy who was the "Peggy" for the firemen and I would meet him later. Like me, they were both under 18 and therefore qualified to be paid £5 per month plus £5 "danger money."

As the day wore on members of the crew residing in our forecastle came in from their work and got themselves washed in preparation for shore leave in the evening. They were all Dutch, with one exception. He was an able-bodied seaman from Bristol. There were about six boys on the crew (i.e., under 18) and I asked why there were no Dutch boys included. The answer was obvious and made me feel stupid as I should have thought it out for myself. I was told that when Holland was overrun by the Germans in 1940 *Ganymedes* was at sea with a full crew of Dutch men and boys. From that day on they were forced to sail the seas without going back to Holland or having any contact with their families at home. Over the next two years the boy members of the ship's crew became eligible to be classed as adult seamen. Because they could not be replaced by Dutch boys, the shipping company adopted a policy of recruiting British boys instead. The account reminded me of the legend of the Flying Dutchman, doomed to sail the seas for life. He was only allowed to come ashore once a year and his redemption would only come if he found a lady who loved him so much she would die for him.

With regard to the catering staff I learned the next day that as well as the chief steward there was a saloon-steward, a cook, a mess-room steward, myself and the galley-boy. The chief steward was in overall charge of all the catering functions, including provisioning the ship when we were in port and specifically looking after the captain, who was rarely seen. At sea I was greatly impressed by the captain, who seemed to be available on the bridge at all times, especially in periods of danger. He never seemed to sleep.

The saloon-steward serviced the main dining-room, which was used by the captain, the first mate and the chief engineer. The mess-room steward attended the mess-room, used by officers of lower rank and over which the second mate presided; it was used by the third and fourth mates and engine-room officers of corresponding rank. There was also a wireless operator but no doctor. It was strongly recommended that you remained in good health at sea because no medical help was at hand.

My job in the pantry consisted of washing dishes, preparing cold meats etc, and carrying food from the galley to the pantry, where it was then served by the saloon-steward. As well as the catering staff there were about eight firemen, eight seamen and their officers. There was a gunner and about six boys. The grand total of those on board ship was forty.

On joining the ship I had to report to the second mate, who was responsible for all administrative duties relating to the employment and welfare of the crew. Although he had a stern face it soon became clear to me that he was a gentleman and I respected him throughout the nine months I was on *Ganymedes*. He had some difficulty interviewing me at first and I think he was baffled by my accent and sing-song Welsh voice. After some time he turned to me and said, "Are you an Indian?" Under the circumstances this was understandable, as I had a dark complexion and he was obviously unfamiliar with the South Wales accent. He talked reassuringly to me for some time and then he told me, with great seriousness, that when we were at sea it was most important that I should remember four things:

- Always be fully dressed even when you go to bed;

- Always have your lifebelt near you;
- Always have your identification papers on your body or in a place where they can be picked up easily;
- Never close a door but ensure that it is always tied open.

This last instruction puzzled me at first until it was explained that when ships get torpedoed bulkheads become deformed so that closed doors cannot be opened and seamen get trapped and cannot escape.

Because the ship was small all the cabins for the catering staff, the officers' mess-room, the galley and the connecting companion-ways (passages) were open to the flush-deck of the ship. This meant that in stormy weather waves breaking over the ship would bring torrents of sea-water in, flooding these areas since we were not allowed to close doors.

As one would expect, a total blackout was imposed when we were at sea or in port in the UK. Another restriction, imposed mainly on the galley, was that no rubbish should be dumped into the sea. This was because U-boats sailed on the surface in the daytime tailing convoys, which they would then attack at night. Floating rubbish could indicate the presence of a convoy over the horizon.

All this information started my education in the ways of the Merchant Navy. There was much more to follow it in the next four years.

Within a few days I found myself completely at home on the ship. The Dutchmen were happy to help and to answer my questions and the boys were friendly, calling me "Taffy" within a few days. The other boys on board were all from Liverpool, with the exception of a 16-year old lad from Glasgow. The galley-boy was a rough individual who had a tendency to bully the young Scot. I resolved to keep out of his way if at all possible.

A day or two after joining the ship I was confronted by a spectacle that had a profound effect on me. One of our Dutch seamen staggered aboard one morning looking suspiciously like someone who had been in a serious road traffic accident. His eyes were blacked and clotted blood was liberally spread over his face. His clothes were torn and I had the distinct impression that he would fall over on his face at any moment. Nevertheless he managed to stagger to the forecastle where he collapsed on his bunk. None of his shipmates showed any surprise or concern at his state and took the whole matter amazingly calmly. Later one of them said to me, "Taffy, let that be a warning to you." It turned out that our shipmate had gone ashore looking for ways to spend the large amount of money he had accrued from his last voyage. As so often happens, he was attracted by a woman who no doubt promised him a good time. Unfortunately for him she was acting as a decoy for one or more men whose intent was to beat him up and take all his money. This episode impressed me profoundly and was a significant part of my education. It later reminded me of the anthem of the Merchant Navy: a song called "Maggie May." It also reminded me of the parting words of my scoutmaster. When he knew I was going to sea he said, "Ray, always remember your mother is a woman."

Within a few days it was clear we would soon be leaving Liverpool. The ship was now fully loaded with a general cargo of items no longer vital to the survival of the UK such as whisky, which could still be produced without a great drain on the war effort. The cargo-hatches were covered and sealed with wooden covers and made watertight with canvas sheets which were pegged down. The decks of the ship were tidied up generally and made clear of any obstructions until we were "shipshape and Bristol-fashion."

We were now ready to go to sea and, sure enough, a day or two later we cast off and made our way slowly to the lock which would enable us to leave the dock and enter the River Mersey. I felt excited and proud to be on our way and would soon learn our destination. I had not visited Stan for a couple of days but realised that as a policeman on the docks he would know the *Ganymedes* had sailed and would tell my mother.

As we left the lock and entered the river I noticed that some of our seamen were slinging a lifeboat out on its davits. I was told not to worry as it was standard practice to get a lifeboat ready for a quick launching in case of an emergency. As far as I was concerned I was already in a state of emergency. It started as soon as we had entered the waters of the Mersey. The slight, rhythmic movement of the deck in response to the flow of the river was making me feel quite ill and very soon I became violently seasick. This was a new experience for me and one for which I was completely unprepared. My shipmates had previously gone through the agony I now felt and they offered me great sympathy, condolences and advice that did nothing to reduce my misery which was increasing with every minute that passed. I was told that it would probably only last for a few days until I got my sea-legs, but was also warned some men experienced it every time they went to sea. This did nothing to lessen my suffering or increase my spirit.

Everyone on board had his own particular remedy for the problem, with the most popular advice being to contact the cook and ask him for a liberal amount of fatty pork, to be eaten as often as possible. The mere thought of this made me feel far worse and the only course of action available to me seemed to be to jump overboard, as death appeared to be the only solution. Fortunately I overcame this yearning and resolved to see it through until I was better again. The chief steward was very understanding and did not press me unduly when I found it difficult to go on working. He did, however, encourage me to stay on my feet and learn to respond to the movement of the ship. This was getting more difficult because the sea was becoming more turbulent as we moved northward along the coast of Scotland. I was told we were making for Loch Ewe where we would join up with other ships to form a convoy to go to our overseas destination. As predicted, I got over my sickness within a few days and was soon walking around the deck with a modest western ocean-roll.

After a short delay we left Loch Ewe and headed west around the northern tip of Ireland. There were perhaps fifty ships in the convoy arranged in a pre-determined order, to be maintained for the whole voyage. This was not always easy to achieve because some ships were old and less manoeuvrable than others. We were to be escorted by four or five ships belonging to the Royal Navy or allied navies such as those of Canada and America. I think the ships were corvettes as they seemed very small to me. Shepherding the convoy was quite a difficult task because it was spread over a large area of sea and was arranged in eight columns with six ships in each. The time was pre-Christmas in December 1942.

When we finally lost sight of Ireland we were told we were heading for New York and then on to Trinidad. The old hands in the forecastle were definitely unhappy with the news and all agreed that this was the most dangerous voyage to make at this point in the war. They obviously knew what they were talking about because they had just completed the same run on the previous trip. I received this news with a great deal of apprehension but was reassured when I heard that the weather was expected to be extremely bad and that the first concern of both U-boats and merchant ships was to ensure they survived the storms. This forecast proved to be true and according to the Bernard Edwards book (see Introduction), *"January 1943 saw Atlantic gales with winds in excess of 120 knots (more than 120 mph)...fighting their way across the ocean eight merchant ships foundered, four ran aground and more than forty suffered serious storm damage... one rescue ship capsized and sank as a result of ice building up on her decks...during the month a third of the escort vessels were temporarily taken out of service by the sheer violence of the weather."*

The trip to New York would be about three thousand miles, plus whatever zigzagging we would have to do if we met up with a pack of U-boats. It was estimated that as our speed would at best be about seven knots we would not see New York in under two and a half weeks, possibly three or more.

I was called at seven o'clock in the morning and made my way across the deck to the pantry. It was still dark at this time of the day but I initially had no difficulty in reporting for duty. However as the weather deteriorated it became extremely windy and cold, and my morning trip along the deck became very unpleasant and dangerous. As I had no suitable kit for such bad weather I was constantly wet and cold and the crew members loaned me some suitable gear which helped me over the crisis. The weather continued to get worse. Every time the ship plunged into a large wave the stern would rise out of the water to such an extent that the propeller would be free to rotate at an alarming rate as it no longer had the resistance of the sea to slow it to its normal rate. This "racing" created a frightening noise which interrupted my sleep for some time, as our sleeping quarters in the stern were only a few feet above the propeller.

One morning I went on deck as usual and was instantly assailed by a ferocious wind which seemed to penetrate my entire body. It was dark and the ship was rolling violently with water breaking over its sides. I made my way amidships to the pantry, clinging to a lifeline rigged for the use of anyone walking along the deck. I got safely to the pantry and was asked by the saloon-steward to go to the galley for a plate of bacon and eggs for one of the officers who was to go on watch. This was a routine order and I set out to the galley along the open deck. Across the bottom of the galley door was a steel plate about twelve inches high that was supposed to keep out the water breaking over the deck and the door was tied back for reasons already explained. This was a feature common to all doors opening onto the open deck of the ship. Unfortunately the steel plates also ensured that when water got into the galley or cabins it could not get out again. On this occasion the galley was in a state of complete confusion. As the ship rolled in the heavy seas a torrent of water was thrown from one end of the galley to the other and could not escape. In spite of the situation the cook succeeded in giving me my plate of bacon and eggs. I then stepped out onto the open deck in complete darkness and groped my way to the pantry with the wind blowing so violently I had difficulty staying on my feet. I stepped over the 12-inch water-board into the pantry and offered my plate to the saloon-steward. He and I realised at the same time that there was nothing on the plate: it had been stripped of its bacon and eggs by the ferocious wind. With a look of disbelief he sent me once more to the galley for bacon and eggs. This time I was given a metal cover to protect the contents of the plate!

During times like this, when the weather was extremely rough, cooking became a very dangerous occupation. Everything on the cooking-range had to be secured by metal slats fixed to the top of the range. Even so, boiling water could easily be spilled and seriously scald anyone in the galley. In my view cooking was one of the most dangerous jobs on a ship, and also one of the most tiring, as the cook could be at work all day and often suffered from bad feet. In the dining saloon and the various mess-rooms for the crew all items on a table would be retained in wooden grids to prevent their sliding onto the deck in rough weather.

Back at school I had heard stories about storms at sea and attendant waves which could be fifty feet high and more. At that time my reaction was to dismiss such stories as a product of an over-active imagination. But on my first trip, before I was halfway to America, I realised the truth of such stories. In fact I can honestly say that we encountered waves considerably higher than fifty feet. One minute our ship would be on the crest of a wave and it was possible to see only the mast-tops of adjacent ships in deep troughs, then suddenly we would plunge into the trough of a big wave and could see nothing but a towering wall of water threatening to engulf the whole ship. At the same time the ship would be rolling violently to port and starboard in blinding spray in a seemingly endless display of perpetual motion. The whole experience was worsened by the icy blasts from a hurricane-strength wind and constant immersion in sea-water breaking over the ship. We always seemed to be wet and cold; on the plus side, we knew we would have no trouble with U-boats in such weather so we could take our clothes off to dry out. I was to learn later that the winter of 1942/43 produced the worst storms in the North Atlantic for more than a decade.

Eventually the hurricane grew calmer as we approached an area south of Greenland. This area was a black hole as far as merchant shipping was concerned because it was too remote for aircraft cover and therefore was an ideal area for wolf-packs to attack convoys. It soon became clear that our naval escorts were becoming active, particularly at night, and we started to hear thunderous noises from the depth charges that were being dropped. The crews on *Ganymedes* and the other freighters could only guess at what was happening as we had no sonar or other means of detecting the presence of U-boats. In fact we were defenceless and relied solely on our meagre naval escort for protection. We knew that depth charges indicated a possible U-boat attack and this would be confirmed by a call to action-stations. The first time this happened I had no idea what was expected of me and was relieved when a seaman told me not to worry but keep out of the way and put my life-jacket on. Although thousands of merchant ships were sunk in the North Atlantic no U-boat, as far as I am aware, was ever sunk by a merchant ship. We were sitting-ducks for the U-boat crews and we relied absolutely on the ability of the Navy to keep them at bay. I think that we accepted subconsciously that our fate was a matter of statistics; on average maybe four ships would be sunk in a convoy of forty, so our chances of survival were nine to one. These were pretty good odds, so why worry? But when you considered how many convoys you would be in during the period of the war then the worry really got to you. These figures are chosen to illustrate a point. I do not know what an accurate assessment would have produced but it is generally accepted that Britain's merchant fleet lost four thousand vessels during the war (*Britain's Sea-War,* a diary of ship losses 1939–45 by John M Young).

On the whole my first crossing of the North Atlantic was dominated primarily by the exceptionally bad weather which made life difficult for the crews of the U-boats as well as for the crews of the convoy ships. Although we constantly heard explosions during the night I cannot say if these were entirely owing to depth charges, or also to torpedoed ships.

As we approached Newfoundland we experienced the well-known peril of persistent fog which lasted for days. Because the ships were herded together there was always the danger of a collision. As radar did not exist on freighters we depended on constant blasts of the foghorn to warn ships of our presence. This created a ghostly atmosphere on board ship since we were continually reminded that we were not alone, yet we could not see who our companions were. The one point in the fog's favour was that there was no chance of an encounter with a U-boat.

We were now more or less across the Atlantic but we still had the fairly long run down the eastern coast of Canada and the USA before we reached New York. On the whole I think the crew members were more relaxed than when we were in mid-ocean. We saw we were getting near our first destination and that we were in less danger than we had been.

One day the chief steward called me from the comfort of my pantry and invited me to join him on deck as he had something to show me. He pointed to a spot in the ocean where a number of whales were visible and blowing columns of water into the air. This was my first sighting of whales, an experience repeated many times in the future.

When we left the UK it became obvious that the galley-boy had a compulsion to bully some of the other boys on board. He took a particular delight in picking on the 16-year old boy from Glasgow. I was anxious not to get involved with the galley-boy and decided to keep out of his way as much as possible. But as the days at sea went on it became clear that he would sooner or later turn his attention to me. I resolved that if a crisis was forced on me I would not stand idly by to be bullied. The crunch came one day when he stepped over the weather-board into my pantry and, without asking my permission, cut himself a large slice of bread before exiting without cleaning the crumbs from my bread-board. Since I liked my pantry to be shipshape and Bristol-fashion I told him to clean up the mess he had made. This simple incident quickly turned into a violent conflict as we got stuck into each other. The crumbs were forgotten as plates, cups, saucers and the like got smashed as a result of our fighting in the confined space. The conflict was quickly stopped by the chief steward, who separated us. I thought I would be in deep trouble but the chief steward took the view that I was provoked and the galley-boy had it coming to him anyway. The sequel was that I had no further trouble with the galley-boy and we became shipmates of a sort for the rest of the voyage.

One day, some two or three weeks after we had left the UK, the chief steward appeared in my pantry and asked me to step outside onto the deck to look at something. Puzzled, I followed him out and looked in the direction in which he was pointing. I could just make out a misty silhouette that grew larger as we got nearer. Soon it was recognisable as a building and it was shortly accompanied by other buildings apparently rising out of the sea. This illusion was caused by the effect of the earth's curvature on my field of vision. I was in fact experiencing my first look at the famous "downtown" skyline of New York. It truly was an awe-inspiring sight. Gradually the Empire State Building, the Chrysler Building and other skyscrapers became recognisable. On our port side the Statue of Liberty looked regally down on our convoy and straight ahead was the majestic Brooklyn Bridge. A pilot came aboard *Ganymedes* and proceeded to take us to a berth. For a boy from the mining valleys of South Wales the whole panorama was unimaginably breathtaking.

Slowly our ship was piloted into a berth in Brooklyn beneath the ramparts of the famous bridge across the East River. We were opposite the downtown area of Manhattan, about half a mile away.

Part 2 – **New York**

During my four years at sea I visited New York nine times. My recollection of the things I saw and did cannot always be identified with a particular point in time or a particular ship but I have done my best to place events in the correct order. For example, I recall there were times when the weather in New York was incredibly cold with strong winds and snow, and other occasions when it was warm and humid. Obviously my memory of arctic conditions must have been January or early March 1943 during my first sea trip.

We boys were all excited about our visit to New York. As this was my first visit to a foreign port my mates were all keen to show me the sights of the city. We were given permission to leave the ship every day after our work was done and were also given a modest but fair allowance for shore leave. My first act on getting ashore was to have a haircut. My mates didn't think this was a good idea but I went ahead anyway. I understood the reason for their disapproval when I was presented with the bill, which made a big hole in my meagre resources. I was cheerfully told by my friends not to worry because they had a ready solution to my problem. (I don't know why, but every time I was confronted with a problem on board ship there was always someone around to tell me, "Don't worry.")

We decided to take the subway to Manhattan. This was dead easy as it was but a short ride across Brooklyn Bridge. All rides were at a standard rate of five (or ten, I'm not sure) cents. For this small amount we were free to go as far as we wished on any single journey. On arrival at the other side of East River we made our way to the Blood Transfusion Clinic, which had been frequented by my mates on other occasions. Following their advice I presented myself at the reception area and offered a pint of my genuine Welsh blood. After taking a few details of my health they invited me to lie down while the requisite measure was drained from my arm. The procedure was quite painless and I was invited to rest for a short time. I was then given a cup of tea and released after being given five dollars. This was an easily earned five dollars: an exercise to be repeated on future visits to New York.

Probably the most enduring memory of my first visit to New York was our trip to Times Square and Broadway. After war-weary Britain it was a revelation to see the neon-lit shops with an abundant supply of goods that could be bought freely without ration-books. There were canteens for allied seamen to which we were cordially invited and given lavish hospitality. They were run by civilian volunteers who would give us free tickets for cinemas, theatres and other places of interest in New York. Sometimes we were given guides to show us around the city or to take us to their homes for an evening. I took advantage of a suggestion by Aunty Edith that I should visit her husband's sister if ever I had the opportunity to do so. She lived in the suburb of Yonkers and when I went along with two of my friends we were regally received and entertained.

In our exploration of the city we went to such places as the Rockefeller Centre, Radio City, Jack Dempsey's Bar on Broadway and so on. Sometimes the cinemas would have a floor show between films and I managed to see such celebrities as the Andrews Sisters and Alan Jones (the man of *Donkey Serenade* fame). We were always called merchant marines by the New Yorkers and I believe that their deep regard for us was because the war was really brought home to them by the sinking of merchant ships within sight of New York. The one thing difficult to understand was the fact that New York could be seen from miles out at sea at night as there was no blackout.

This made entry into the city by sea extremely difficult when U-boats were in the area, as often happened in 1942 and early 1943.

We were in New York for less than a week. Our main objective had been to refuel the ship and to take on board supplies of food etc, as all these things were readily available. All the crew agreed that the big advantage of going to New York was that for the immediate future we would have ample supplies of good food and access to articles of clothing not so easily come by in the UK. Many of the crew would buy ladies' silk stockings and other items much sought after for their girls and wives back at home. My most pressing need was for several items of clothing for my seagoing comfort, for example sea-boots, jeans and a white polo-neck sweater, that would be more suited to my requirements than the gear I initially had.

It was generally assumed that we would return to New York prior to making the return voyage across the Atlantic. With this in mind I resolved to have enough money put aside to buy a waterproof jacket and, of course, some silk stockings for my mother and a present for Pat and Dad.

As we sailed away from New York I was left with an impression of the kindness shown to us by the people of the city and a memory of a fabulous fairytale town where everything one could desire was available in abundance. It was a world away from Ebbw Vale.

It did not come as a great surprise to us when we were told that we were to go to the West Indies, probably for a cargo of sugar. It was rumoured that we would be going to Port-of-Spain in Trinidad, which proved to be true. Travelling there would take about a week and we would be sailing down the eastern seaboard of the USA. What I did not know at the time, but learned later from a BBC history programme, was that this coast was the scene of great carnage in 1942, just after the USA entered the war. During this time U-boats had been sinking merchant ships at will because there were no convoy systems in place. In fact in June 1942 the U-boats had succeeded in sinking 136 merchant ships, making it the worst month for sinkings during the whole war. About 1,000 were sunk along this coast in 1942 and it would have been worse had the U-boats not run out of torpedoes. The area at this time was known to the U-boat crews as the Great American Turkey Shoot. Most of the ships sunk would have been British or American, although some allied shipping were also lost. A significant proportion of ships lost were tankers carrying aviation fuel destined for Britain.

After we had been at sea for a day or so I asked the chief steward when we would join a convoy. He surprised me by saying that on this occasion we would be sailing without the protection of a convoy, but that we were not entirely alone as there was another ship going to the West Indies and it was quite close to us. Apparently we could not see it because of the curvature of the earth. This reassured me and I settled down to a period of sunbathing when I was off duty since the weather was much warmer as we sailed further south towards the West Indies. The sea was quite calm and I would lie on the hatches in the sun and think what a great life it was to be a merchant seaman.

One day I was alarmed to find some of the crew talking rapidly in Dutch, clearly troubled. I asked them what all the fuss was about and one of them told me that the radio operator was receiving SOS calls from a torpedoed ship nearby. I immediately assumed it was the ship near us that I'd heard about earlier. I was upset to hear about it and asked one of the crew how long it would take to rescue them. He then broke the devastating news that we would make no such attempt because captains of merchant ships were ordered to keep away from torpedoed ships. It was considered too dangerous to approach them because U-boats often stayed in the area submerged, hoping to sink any ship trying to rescue the unfortunate men in the water. I was very distressed to learn this and could think only of the men in the sea fighting for their lives. My immediate thought was that the humane thing to do would be to at least try and save them. It was so cruel to leave them to their fate. Later, when I was calmer, I talked it over with one of the crew members. He reminded me that our job was to ensure that our cargoes reached the people in Britain and the U-boat crews' objective was to sink as many merchant ships as possible, thereby starving the British people of food and our armed forces of supplies such as aviation fuel which allowed them to keep fighting. I could not fault this logic and like the majority, if not all, of the merchant seamen came to accept the fact that if we were torpedoed other merchant ships were ordered not to endanger themselves by effecting our rescue. Now, over sixty years later, I can see that this policy was sensible, but cannot forget the incident and still imagine those men in the water fighting for their lives. Nor can I forget that when a merchant seaman was forced to leave his sinking ship his pay stopped immediately.

The remainder of the trip was without memorable incident and we arrived at Port-of-Spain and tied up alongside the quay. There we prepared to unload our cargo of miscellaneous products not considered essential for the survival of the UK in the fight against Germany. The unloading of a cargo-boat using its own derricks is a fascinating sight and a tribute to men's ingenuity and the skill of the seamen who operate the steam-winches. Each hatch is served by two derricks (long steel posts). One is tied in position directly over the centre of the hatch being unloaded and the other is tied over the point on the quayside where the cargo is to be dropped. Each mast (derrick) acts as a simple crane and each item to be lifted from ship to shore is attached to the hooks at the end of each of the two derricks. The two winches, each operated by a seaman, are then co-ordinated in such a way as to lift the load out of the hold, swing it over the side of the ship and lower it on to the quayside. The whole process is simple, elegant and very effective. The unloading was done in exactly this way when we tied up alongside the quay in Port-of-Spain. The actual manual work in the holds was done by local labour, usually Afro-Caribbean in origin. Once the cargo was unloaded the holds were cleaned and work began on loading the ship with thousands of sacks of sugar. These sacks had to be manhandled in the holds to ensure they were safely stacked and secured so that no movement could occur in rough weather. Once again we were free to go ashore as soon as our daily work was done. This, however, was a completely different experience from going ashore in New York. It was my first visit to a tropical island and my expectations had been influenced by a song popular at the time in America and the UK. It was about Trinidad and its wonderful beaches and the much-publicised drink of "Rum and Coca Cola," and was one of the songs liked by the Andrews Sisters and one which they sang when I saw them perform in New York.

I was sadly disappointed with Port-of-Spain in Trinidad. I had expected a paradise and all I found was poverty on a scale far greater than anything I had experienced in South Wales during the years of the depression, and light years away from the affluence of New York. We did, however, enjoy the local drink of rum and Coca Cola but I don't remember anyone being intoxicated.

There was not a great deal for a seventeen-year old boy to do in Port-of-Spain, although no doubt adults with plenty of money found some wonderful beaches. My lasting memory of our visit was the wonderful and distinctive smells that filled the air in the evenings and the sound of crickets and other insects at night. I was to experience these many times in the future in tropical countries.

After a week or so in Trinidad we set out on our return trip to New York. This was uneventful except for a fight on deck between two of our Dutch crew. I don't know what it was about but it did scare me when one of them pulled out a knife and made to use it on the other man. Fortunately it all ended with no serious injury to either party and I concluded that it was probably a disagreement over one of the ladies they had encountered in Trinidad. It should be explained that it was common practice for the deck-hands to carry a sheath-knife while at sea. It could mean the difference between life and death in an emergency and was primarily used to cut ropes securing a life-raft when it was necessary to abandon ship.

After a week or so at sea we arrived back in New York. Once again we berthed in Brooklyn in our usual place near Montague Avenue by the bridge. The boys paid another visit to the Blood Transfusion Clinic and each received another five dollars. I wondered how often we could repeat these visits without serious consequences. This was, of course, before the comedian Tony Hancock became famous in the UK by appearing in a TV sketch where he donated "a whole armful" of blood in a similar clinic. We also went to the American Organisation, which issued us with free cinema tickets and suchlike. Finally we spent considerable time on Broadway looking for suitable presents to take home to our families. One shop that caught my attention had a flamboyant display of terrapins in a big tank in its window. These tiny tortoises, about an inch and a half in length, had their shells beautifully painted and when one was sold the buyer could choose a name to be painted on its shell. I bought two and had Ray and Pat painted on their shells. I also bought an abundant supply of chocolate, which was scarce in the UK, some silk stockings for Ma and bought duty-free pipe-tobacco on the ship for Dad.

After leaving New York we sailed north and followed the coast of the USA until we reached Halifax in Nova Scotia, Canada. We entered Bedford Basin, a large harbour used to anchor ships waiting to be assigned to a North Atlantic convoy to sail to the UK. There were scores of ships there, representing many countries united against Germany. All were fully loaded with essential war supplies—food, high explosives, aviation fuel, aeroplanes, tanks—an awe-inspiring sight.

We only stayed in Halifax for a short time, but long enough to be given shore leave. The town was quite small compared with New York but it was extremely important as far as the war at sea was concerned. It was the starting-point of the sea-link to the UK. Our short stay gave us the opportunity to mix with other British boys when we went to the Merchant Seaman's club in Hollis Street or the Green Lantern Restaurant and Soda-Fountain. They were all looking forward to the start of the 3,000-mile voyage across the North Atlantic and to seeing their families again. We did not know it at the time but many of these men and boys would sadly never see their homes again as we were to become part of *Convoy HX 229* and be involved in one of the greatest convoy battles of World War Two.

According to Martin Middlebrook and Jurgen Rhwer by the end of 1942 the Germans had increased their U-boat fleet to three hundred vessels, so that at any one time about a hundred U-boats were actively operational, with the majority in the North Atlantic. These were deployed in large groups (wolf-packs). In the first few months of 1943 they successfully attacked all convoys in the North Atlantic that were beyond the range of allied air cover,

At this crucial time the German Enigma machine was modified so that we were unable to break down their codes. The Germans, however, had cracked our naval codes. Thus we had no way of knowing the location of the U-boats, while they did know when our convoys would leave Halifax and the routes they would take. This was the position in mid-March 1943 when we left Halifax. The Germans confidently stationed forty-four U-boats in a line to contact and attack us. Even though we had naval escorts the U-boats succeeded in intercepting *Convoy HX 229* and sinking twenty-seven merchant ships from it and *Convoy SC 122*. The latter was a convoy from Sidney in Nova Scotia. Before I joined the Merchant Navy my friends sometimes commented on my phenomenal good luck, so much so that Tom Jones remarked to me with some annoyance, "You're so lucky that if you fell into a pool of sewage you'd come out covered in chocolate and smelling of roses." How right he was. When the ships were organised prior to leaving Halifax it was decided to arrange them in two groups. The slower ships would leave first as *Convoy HX 229* and the slightly faster ships would follow as *Convoy HX 229A*. The latter group was programmed to follow a route which the German naval intelligence expected to ambush with their wolf-packs. *Ganymedes* was instructed to join *HX 229A*, which surprised us as there was a high proportion of big tankers carrying aviation fuel in the group while we were just a small freighter with a cargo of sugar. Within a few days of our departure from Halifax there was a concerted attack on *Convoy HX 229* by the large pack of forty-four U-boats in mistake for *HX 229A*. By a miraculous piece of luck the Germans had attacked the ships in the less vulnerable group and our own group was diverted due north towards Greenland and missed the carnage by sailing into an extensive area of sea covered in ice-floes and icebergs. Once again I had been "lucky."

We sailed through this area for a considerable number of days to the accompaniment of continuous crashing sounds as the ship forced its way through the ice. To make our situation worse we ran into serious fog and were virtually blind. We had no radar but relied on visual observations, a practice rapidly becoming impossible. During the brief spells when the fog was less intense we could see enough to realise we were surrounded

Convoy HX 229A: Halifax (Canada) to UK, with the Dutch ship "Ganymedes" in the foreground. March 1943. Painted from memory by the author.

by icebergs. Our speed was drastically reduced in consequence and, as we were diverted so far north, we realised our voyage would take considerably more time than originally expected. As a result of the intensely cold weather a large amount of ice formed on the rigging of the ship, on ladders and other exposed parts. This made walking on deck treacherous. The escort vessels tried to help the merchant ships by using their searchlights to warn them of nearby icebergs. This was some comfort to us, who anticipated a collision at any moment. A number of ships turned back to Newfoundland for repairs. Near us in the convoy a big British oil-tanker, the *Svend Foyn,* ran out of luck and crashed into an iceberg, sinking with considerable loss of life; they would have survived about five minutes in the sea before freezing to death.

Among those lost was a sixteen-year old cabin-boy from Tyneside. In spite of the fog and ice one of our naval escorts managed to save some of the crew. It must have been a very tense time leading up to the crash for the crew of the 15,000-ton tanker as they were carrying fuel-oil and knew they had little chance of survival if they were torpedoed. How cruelly ironic to die in the end because they hit an iceberg—and how unjust for the survivors, whose pay was stopped when their ship was sunk and would only be reinstated when they got home and found another ship.

We finally sailed clear of the ice and fog and made our way east towards the south of Iceland and on to Scotland. Again we were lucky in avoiding the U-boat patrol in the area, which failed to spot us. After rounding the north of Scotland we sailed down the east coast of England and finally docked in London's East India Dock.

It is interesting to note that of the ships that sailed in convoys *SC 122, HX 229* and *HX 229A* and survived the crossing of the North Atlantic seventeen of them, according to Middlebrook, were sunk on subsequent voyages. My luck was to be with me again.

My first voyage was now over and I was back in the UK. My parents' fears were clearly unfounded as I had not been corrupted by the loose morality of the seamen I had lived with; in fact I had learned a great deal from such men and I am sure my education had taken a positive step forward. I recall an incident that happened on our return trip. The weather was extremely cold and ice had formed on many parts of the ship as we slowly made our way through a sea of pack-ice. As part of my daily tasks I took a mug of cocoa to the officer on watch, who was bravely resisting the inclement weather.

I noticed one of the Dutch seamen standing on deck staring intently into the blanket of fog that surrounded us. He looked very cold and lonely, so I returned to the galley and got a piping-hot cup of cocoa and gave it to him. He accepted it, turned to me and said, "Thanks, you are a gentleman and a scholar." His words were gratefully received at the time but it was only later that I thought how surprising it was that a common sailor laid such store on those two attributes. In fact I wasn't quite sure why he should address a seventeen-year old boy in those terms. At the time I couldn't, I think, have told the difference between a gentleman or any other kind of man, and I was definitely not a scholar. I now realise he had made a small but important contribution to my education.

Upon arrival in London all the crew were immediately signed off, the custom following a voyage, and then re-engaged as appropriate. I signed on for another voyage, this time as a mess-room steward which was an improvement on being a pantry-boy. I was given some leave and happily set out on my trip home. It would be exciting to see my parents and little sister again. I decided to surprise them by turning up without letting them know I was back in the UK. In the event, however, there was to be no surprise as the Dutch Shipping Company had sent a telegram to my parents to let them know I had arrived safely home and was fit and well. During the four years I was at sea this was the only time my parents were informed of my safe return and I think the unique gesture was down to the company's relief that the *Ganymedes* was not one of the ships lost in the convoy battle (there were five Dutch ships in that battle, two of which were sunk).

Everyone at home was glad to see me again but they knew I would only be home for a short time. Pat was pleased with the terrapin and chocolate I brought her. Ma, I felt, had aged considerably: no doubt from worrying about me. Dad had to warn me about using foul language as it seems I was having nightmares and in my outbursts gave vent to my feelings about German U-boat crews. When I was a schoolboy I would fantasise and dream of the adventures I would have if I left Ebbw Vale and went to sea. I would escape from my unfortunate environment and visit faraway exciting and exotic places. Now that I had completed my first voyage I realised my dreams had turned into nightmares. I was still only seventeen but was filled with doubt about my future. I looked forward to my next trip with trepidation and wondered if I would live long enough to see my eighteenth birthday. I can see now that I went to sea as an innocent boy. After one voyage I was transformed into a sceptical man. I was the same height and weight but had changed inside and I knew my life would never be the same again. I determined that if I survived the war I would make a success of my life and ensure I would never experience the unemployment that blighted my boyhood days in Ebbw Vale.

After this short period of leave I returned to the ship to find that I was the only boy retained for the next voyage. The new boys were all Londoners and were quite friendly. The pantry-boy, John, became a pal of mine and for a short time, while we were in port, I stayed overnight at his home. We were soon outward-bound, however, and learned we were to cross the North Atlantic again. This time I was not a first tripper but a seasoned member of the crew. I was not looking forward to what was to be a re-run of my other two crossings but we survived and arrived safely in New York once more. This time I was the veteran and soon found myself showing the other boys around the city; that is, after we had all earned five dollars-worth of "blood-money."

I should explain that in my new job as mess-steward I was now berthed in a cabin amidships with the saloon-steward. This was a great improvement on being berthed in the forecastle with eight others, where we literally had no room to swing a cat. When at sea we had two hours free time in the afternoon so I started to read regularly. My latest visit to New York found me wandering the famous streets looking for the first-rate bookshops to be found there. I was amazed at the reasonable prices of some of the books and usually came away with a bargain. One of my first purchases was a beautifully bound copy of the works of R L Stevenson—*Treasure Island* etc. I also bought *Descriptive Chemistry and Physics,* which I enjoyed reading.

After we left New York we were told that our next destination was to be Kingston, Jamaica. This was good news as the prospect of going to Trinidad again did not appeal to me. In Kingston one of my shipmates took me to a place called Springfield on one of the beautiful Jamaican beaches. It was a club of some sort where one could get a drink and dance provided you had a partner. It was select and definitely not a place to pick up loose women. My chum was friendly with a girl whose sister he thought I should meet to go dancing. I duly went and met the sister, who I thought was gorgeous. Her name was Sylvia Hue and she was of Asian origin, probably Chinese.

She was clearly well-educated—and well-chaperoned by her elder sister. I think her father was a businessman. Sylvia and I were about the same age and both of us were rather unworldly. We were mutually attracted but it was not a sexual attraction, but simply an enjoyment of being together as young friends. We were in Kingston about two weeks and we went dancing every night, but of course it had to end. Although I knew we were to sail the next day I could not warn her of our departure and she must have been very upset because she wrote to my mother to say she loved me and was desperate to get in touch with me again. I did in fact write to her to explain my sudden departure and told her how unlikely it was that we should meet again. I had no idea how long the war would last and I hadn't yet started on a career which could support me.

From Jamaica we went to Dominica for a cargo of sugar, which we collected at La Romana and San Pedro. When fully loaded we sailed to New York, where I was able to buy some silk stockings and other scarce items required by my family. It was very hot and humid and my shipmates and I spent some time on the beach at Coney Island. We were all greatly impressed by the fairground and my lasting impression was that it far exceeded the facilities of the Barry Island fairground where I was taken as a child. As before, the ship took on vital provisions in New York: mainly food and fuel but also some deck cargo. After leaving New York we stopped once more at Halifax to join a convoy for the UK. This time we did the 3,000 mile crossing without any serious problems and docked in London in September 1943. Upon arrival I signed off the ship before going home, which meant I would be assigned to a new ship at the end of my leave.

It is a sobering thought that the two voyages to the West Indies had taken nine months and the end result was the import of about four thousand tons of sugar. By the end of the century the trip could be done in under six weeks and one modern freighter could easily carry far more than a 4,000-ton cargo.

The next ship was a Dutch coaster called the *Vliestrom* and I joined her at Barry, a town I knew well. My new ship was coal-fired, as one would expect of a collier. She was used to carry coal around the British coast to the numerous coal-fired power-stations in the country. It was a dirty job insofar as we would be enveloped in clouds of coal-dust while the ship was being loaded. At sea the crew would spend their time washing down the ship before we got to the next port and the same thing happened again during the unloading process.

There were fewer than twenty men in the crew and my berth was with the deck-hands in the forecastle. Some of the crew were of non-white origin and I believe I was the only British national on board. It made no difference to me and I had no difficulty getting on with everyone as they were all friendly shipmates. However I was not happy just sailing around the UK. My heart was in the deep-sea voyages to faraway countries and I took the first chance I had to sign off the ship and look for another berth. This occurred after about three months when I was discharged and instructed to sign on at the Merchant Navy Pool in Newport for assignment to a British ship.

In Memory of the 16- and 17-Year Old Boys of Convoys SC122, HX229A and HX229—March 1943

The freighters and the tankers
Rest in Bedford Bay.
All have their sailing orders
And plan to sail this day.

Fort Anne, Baron Elgin, Zaanland,
Ganymedes and *Coracero*
Set sail for dear old England.
The crews all know the score.

Galley boys and coal trimmers,
Peggies, just a few,
Firemen, ABs and Officers
Make up a motley crew.

Some come from dear old England
And some from far away,
Norway, Greece and Holland,
Durban and Bombay.

Muslims, Hindus and Christians,
And some with no known God,
All from allied nations,
And some you may find odd.

All tightly bound together
With only one belief;
That by helping one another
None may come to grief.

In wind and snow they're set to go
Across the treacherous sea.
What lies below they cannot know,
The horror that's to be.

In innocence and fully dressed
They hit their bunks each night.
They dream of home and being blessed,
And then awake in fright.

The ship's alarm has sounded:
They can no longer sleep.
The young boys are confounded
But have their rules to keep.

They open sleep-starved eyes;
Their lips with fear sealed tight;
Their panic grows and terrors rise
Of facing death that night.

They cannot see the wolf-pack,
Whose silhouettes are too low.
They know they cannot turn back;
There is nowhere to go.

A deafening explosion
Means a freighter has been lost.
Its men are in the ocean,
All too soon to pay the cost.

Their lifebelt lights are blinking,
Their shouts are loud and clear.
We know they will be thinking:
There is no rescue near.

Five minutes they are given
Before they freeze to death.
They're on their way to Heaven
With one last worldly breath.

A thunderous ball of amber
Rises quickly in the sky.
"It's from a crippled tanker,"
We hear our shipmates cry.

There's little hope for the tanker's crew,
The sea's a roaring fire;
The price that's paid by the few
To sate man's war desire.

Carnage continues three more nights
'Til air support is in range:
Aircraft with their long-haul flights
Herald a welcome change.

The only things against them now
Are the hurricane winds and cold
And treacherous seas of ice and snow.
By fewer men the tale is told.

The final cost was counted:
Twenty-two ships had been lost,
As well as many crewmen:
A shocking, dreadful cost.

It's the price that's paid for petrol,
Sugar and meat and bread,
Guns and planes and tanks and oil—
For Britain must be fed.

But the story is not ended,
For in a week or so
The ships will be directed
To cross the sea once more.

Raymond Hicks,
cabin boy on the Dutch ship *Ganymedes*

Chapter 8

British Merchant Navy

At the end of 1943 I began a three-year period of service in the British Merchant Navy. All the voyages were deep-sea and covered service on six ships. Four of these were freighters and two were well-known liners. There is no point in detailing all my voyages and I shall restrict myself to brief notes on items of particular interest.

My first ship was a freighter called *Bolton Hall* and our destination was Oran in North Africa. We stopped en route at Lisbon for reasons unknown to me. We were visited on board by a party of Brits who, I believe, were attached to the Embassy. They gathered the whole crew on deck and gave us a lecture on the perils of going ashore in Lisbon because it was a neutral country and teeming with German spies. The lecture included a graphic account of the dangers of consorting with women, some of whom were employed by the Germans to prey on merchant seamen. During my stay I kept well away from women and restricted my activities to buying a very posh cigarette-lighter. I left Lisbon with two questions unanswered: why had we really stopped at Lisbon, as I don't remember any cargo being loaded or unloaded, and why did I buy a lighter, as I didn't smoke? My only worthwhile memory of the place was a photograph I had taken with a shipmate from Newport, showing us standing nonchalantly and eating bananas.

Enjoying a banana: the author (right) and a shipmate in Lisbon. (1943)

From Lisbon we sailed on to Oran for a cargo of iron-ore that was to be taken to Teesside for the steelworks. I was a little concerned by the reaction of the older hands aboard, who were not happy because the cargo was considered to be a dangerous one on account of its high density. I was told that other ships with a cargo of iron-ore had sunk in less than a minute after being torpedoed. From Oran we sailed to Gibraltar and stayed there at anchor waiting for a convoy to return to the UK. We were all nervous during this stay because a number of ships had been sunk while at anchor because of limpet-mines being attached to the underside of ships by saboteurs operating from Spain. They used chariots (miniature submarines) to carry out this kind of attack. After leaving Gibraltar we gained a homeward-bound convoy and docked at last in Middlesbrough.

My next ship was the *Queen Adelaide,* which I joined at Newport. She was a five thousand-ton freighter and we were bound for West Africa with stops at Port Harcourt and Sapele for a cargo of timber. Both stops were on the River Niger and in terms of poverty ranked lower than any other place I had been to so far. The natives loading the ship worked completely naked and when carrying the timber would chant in unison. It reminded me of the film *Sanders of the River.* The highlight of these visits was a challenge from the natives to a football match, a challenge accepted by our ship's officers. For some sadistic reason I was picked as one of the players for our team. This was probably the most unwelcome episode in my seagoing career, as I considered football to be a vastly inferior game to my beloved rugby. Our opponents did wear shorts but surprised us by playing in their bare feet. They were fantastic footballers and had no difficulty in beating our team.

After loading our cargo we went to the capital, Lagos, to await a homeward-bound convoy. We were awarded shore leave because we had to wait for several days before sailing. Lagos was not a place I should like to stay in longer than necessary and my memories of it are best forgotten.

I left West Africa with a big bunch of green bananas, a tom-tom and a small monkey. The bananas were gratefully received by my mother and sister, the tom-tom was presented to my old scout-troop but my monkey disappeared when we were in the Bay of Biscay. The general opinion of my crew friends was that my monkey must have been thrown overboard by one of our deck-officers, an opinion deriving from the fact that the officer's parrot had vanished a few days earlier and my monkey was blamed by him for the incident. I think I must have gone soft in the head on this trip—what would have happened if I had arrived home with a monkey?

During my voyages to North and West Africa we were well within range of enemy aircraft, which were constantly searching for allied convoys.

Despite our being detected and called to action-stations on more than one occasion my luck held out and I returned home unscathed.

It was now the summer of 1944 and the allies had invaded Normandy. After some leave I reported to the Merchant Navy Pool at Newport, wondering if I would get involved in the invasion in some way. I was soon relieved of my uncertainty. The Shipping Office instructed me to join a small freighter called the *Wild Rose,* located at Barry docks. It was about two months after the invasion and we were chosen as one of the ships to carry coal to ports in France as they were liberated.

"Wild Rose" on her way to Normandy after the invasion. (1944)
An impression painted from memory by the author.

There were about twenty-four men in the crew including officers, seamen, firemen, coal-trimmers, a cook and me as mess-room steward. The ship was coal-fired and the engine-room crew were of Indian or West African origin; I'm not sure which. Our first trip took us to Caen in Normandy. The town had only recently been liberated after heavy bombardment. One day a Frenchwoman somehow got on to our ship. She had a bucket and begged us for some coal—a distressing scene. War is hell.

We made regular trips to Normandy for the next six months. Two incidents stick in my mind. One morning we were in Barry docks fully loaded and ready to sail when it was discovered that the cook was not on board. I do not think he had deliberately deserted his ship; I had got to know him quite well by now and my guess was that he was still tucked up in bed with some woman he had met. The captain announced that, cook or no cook, we had to depart on time and asked for a volunteer to act as cook on this particular voyage. I realised, with some alarm, that all eyes were fixed on me and I had no alternative but to volunteer.

We set sail on time and made our way down the Bristol Channel. I had a fine cooked meal on the galley-stove and a huge pot of soup simmering nicely. The first customer in the saloon was the first mate: a grand old man with a face lined like a walnut after a lifetime at sea, a career which included sailing-ships as well. He sat down and shouted to me in the galley, "OK, mess, bring in the soup and make sure it's piping-hot." Full of pride at my culinary prowess, I thought I'd better add a bit more pepper since he was so insistent it was really hot. Now the pepper was kept in an old cocoa-tin with holes punched in its lid. I picked it up, innocently desirous of satisfying the first mate's wishes, but in my haste the lid of the tin came off and about half a pound of pepper disappeared into the soup-pot. I began to panic but then came up with the idea of stirring the pot vigorously so that the pepper was mixed in thoroughly. I went quickly into the saloon, served the first mate with a bowl of soup and retreated to the galley next door. Within a matter of seconds a loud noise came from the saloon and a string of colourful and imaginative nautical swear-words erupted from the first mate. I returned to the saloon and he showed me his dish, which had been drained of soup but contained a generous deposit of pepper in its bottom. By now the crew had also sampled the soup, with the same result. Christian and Muslim shipmates all agreed that they would throw me overboard if it was the only way to relieve me of my responsibilities. Although I'm not the greatest brain in the world it rapidly became apparent to me that I was in mortal danger and there was a strong chance my young life would end in an enforced suicide or simple murder. With a great deal of hurt pride I agreed that one of the older members of the crew should take over the job. This was accomplished and we sailed once more to France and continued to supply the allies with coal.

The other memorable incident occurred around Christmas-time in 1944. The ship had taken on a cargo of coal at Barry and once more we set sail for France. The weather was foul and deteriorated into a very strong gale as we slowly made our way down the Bristol Channel. As usual the firemen were having a difficult time maintaining a working head of steam in the boilers; a recurring problem due to the extreme age of the ship and no reflection on the firemen themselves. By the time I went to my bunk the ship was being pitched all over the Channel by a ferocious sea and hurricane-force winds. I had experienced this kind of weather several times before so I was quite unconcerned about the situation and was soon soundly asleep in my bunk. Sometime during the night my sleep was disturbed by a violent lurching of the ship to starboard and a sudden rush of water into the cabin caused, no doubt, by a heavy sea breaking over the deck. This again was not unusual but I was alarmed when I realised the ship was listing badly and did not roll back and right herself as expected. My alarm increased when one of the deck-hands came into my cabin and told me to get up and put on my life-jacket and get on deck. Once there I found that the ship was listing so badly that the deck on the starboard side was barely above the surface of the sea. Inadequate trimming of the cargo by the dockworkers in Barry had resulted in the coal in the hold shifting to one side of the ship and any further movement could cause the ship to turn right over. If that happened our chances of survival would be slim. That night became the longest in my life. For hours the firemen, helped by some deck-hands, did everything possible to nurse the ship into the nearest port, which happened to be Swansea. We made the docks the next morning but the whole episode had a deep effect on my belief in prayer, or was it just my luck?

During my six months on the *Wild Rose* we had no experiences associated with enemy action. The war on land was drawing to a close when I left the ship in February 1945. I could now look forward to a peaceful period for the remainder of my service at sea and I began to anticipate where I would be voyaging in the future. After a few weeks home-leave I was ready to go to sea again; I suppose I was getting restless.

One day I received a letter telling me to report to the pool at Newport and I was surprised to hear that Bobby Clubb had the same instructions. We went to Newport but were immediately told to report to Bristol, where we were to join an unspecified ship. When we reported to Bristol we were sent on to Liverpool, who were apparently short of available seamen. When we reached Liverpool we were told we were to join a ship at Gourock: none other than the *Queen Elizabeth*. All this moving about took several weeks, during which time we stayed in the Seamen's Mission in Bristol and then Liverpool. These missions could not be considered palatial but they were greatly appreciated by transient seamen and others who were survivors of ships sunk by enemy action. I recall living and sleeping in communal rooms whose occupants were of different skin colour and whose religions were certainly not Christian. Nevertheless we cohabited with no problems at all and talked of the sea and faraway places or played snooker etc. This was not considered unusual by merchant seamen for ship crews were similarly mixed. In the whole of my four years at sea I cannot recall any instance of ethnic or religious intolerance.

After a medical examination and interviews by representatives of the ship we were both accepted as suitable members of the crew. Following this Bobby and I adjourned to Scotland about the middle of March 1945. We made our way to Gourock on the Clyde and were ferried to our new ship, which was anchored some way from the shore. It was foggy and for some time we could not make out the shape of any ship until suddenly its huge form appeared as a ghostly shape in the mist. We went alongside and entered the towering grey structure through a doorway ten feet above the water-line. We went on board with a dozen or more new crew members. My first reaction was one of complete amazement. It was like being in the foyer of a large hotel and none of us knew where to go or what to do. It was quite bewildering and a completely different experience from going aboard a freighter. Eventually we were escorted to our quarters. I was taken forward to a forecastle on "D" deck containing two dozen bunks arranged in parallel. I had signed on as a plate-pantry steward, which is a posh way of saying I was a dish-washer. All the members of our forecastle had jobs in the galley and when I met them I found they were generally about my own age, that is nineteen or twenty. Bobby was a member of the engine-room crew and was berthed in another forecastle but we often met at sea and went ashore together when in port.

With 17,500 men to feed three times a day it's not surprising that the galley was extremely large and manned by a small army of cooks and supporting staff, including our team of dish-washers. The system on board was that the American army officers had normal china crockery for their meals while the ordinary soldiers used stainless steel trays with separate sections for different types of food. We were responsible only for washing the china crockery used by the officers and, as there must have been a thousand or more of them, each meal produced a mountain of dishes to be washed every day. Our team was divided daily into two groups. The first group worked in a section of the galley used as a station for collecting and sorting the dirty crockery. All the plates were given a preliminary scouring by hand to skim off any food residues and they were then sent by a dumb-waiter to the plate-pantry in the deck below for washing by the second group of our team. They would wash the dishes by loading them into wooden racks and these were sent through a hot-water cleaning tunnel. It was extremely hot work and the washing-room was constantly enveloped in steam.

I was working in the galley one day when we were approached by a party of military men who were being conducted around the ship. They stopped by our group of dish-washers and started asking questions which we readily answered. We were all pleasantly surprised when we realised that one of the party was none other than the famous actor James Stewart.

I should explain that I made five voyages to New York on the *Queen Elizabeth*. The first of these was in April 1945, a month before the war ended. We were making history on this trip because we were bringing home to the USA the first contingent of American troops who had fought in the liberation of Europe. I am reasonably sure that it was on this trip we had James Stewart as a passenger.

Our arrival in New York was unforgettable. As we sailed up the river to Pier 52 we were escorted by an armada of ships all blowing their horns and, in some cases, directing jets of water in the air. The quayside was tightly packed with people to welcome the troops home. There were bands playing and groups of people shouting. The decks of our ship were covered with thousands of excited GIs waving to the crowds on the quayside, who included Marlene Dietrich: lifted up to show off her famous legs. Hanging on the wall of my study is a photograph of our ship entering New York.

Photograph of the "Queen Elizabeth" entering New York with returning GIs before the end of the war.

Although it is difficult to pick me out in a crowd of 15,000 GIs and crew, I am there somewhere.

By coincidence my regular trips to New York resulted in my being in the city on several historic days: on VE (Victory in Europe) Day; on the day when President Roosevelt died; and finally on VJ (Victory in Japan) Day. On each occasion Bobby Clubb and I made our way to Times Square, where great crowds gathered to celebrate the victories or to mourn the loss of Roosevelt.

On two of our visits to New York our stay was prolonged by a few weeks, presumably for maintenance work to be carried out on the ship. This meant some of the crew had no work on board and were allowed to work ashore if they wished. I decided to take advantage of this chance to earn some extra dollars and presented myself to the immigration authority, seeking a permit to work ashore. On receipt of the appropriate documentation I got a job in one of the many quick-food restaurants (one called Bickford's, if I remember rightly). Needless to say I had no problem in getting a job as a dish-washer! Bobby and a number of my forecastle mates landed jobs in one or other of the big department stores. They were employed after closing-time to clean the floors of the various departments. Another time I had a job in a food factory, where my unique skills enabled me to pack boxes with doughnuts and other food items.

Bobby Clubb and the author (right) celebrating VE day in New York.

When we were at sea we had plenty of time to mix with American troops, who were mainly friendly and happy to be going home. My clearest memory is of their passion for gambling with dice and cards and their comprehensive vocabulary of foul language, vulgar in the extreme. This may have been the same among British troops for all I know. Sadly over the last sixty years I have witnessed a growing tendency to use these words and phrases on the television so that now even children use four-letter words quite freely. I fear that worse is yet to come.

As our main objective was to transport troops back to America, it follows that our return trips to the UK were very easy and gave us a lot of free time. During these periods of ease I was taught chess by one of my shipmates and played quite often. My greatest leisure pursuit was reading. Some of the lads were extremely well-read and were always giving reviews of quality books they thought would interest other members of our forecastle. As a result I read many books which had a profound effect on me in later years such as *Martin Eden* by Jack London, the English translation of Goethe's *Faust* and the poetry of Kipling, Longfellow, Omar Khayyam, etc. The beauty of poetry is that it sometimes reveals passages of great wisdom. I believe my education took a quantum leap forward when I served on the *Queen Elizabeth.*

Not all the seamen resident in my forecastle were interested in chess and good books. Some had more mundane interests and talked about their adventures ashore, particularly with the women they had met and the interesting bars they frequented when in port. Some were fond of enhancing their descriptive vocabulary by using familiar four-letter swear-words. I clearly remember one young man swearing quite unnecessarily and another member of the forecastle turning to him and saying, "To swear is a painful exhibition of vulgarity and a sure sign of the uneducated." Most of the other men present agreed with this sentiment although most of them had little schooling and, like me, had left school with no qualifications. I wonder how they would react today to the language used on television and by society generally, including children and professional people we consider to be educated.

At the end of our first voyage to New York the *Queen Elizabeth* berthed in Southampton, her first appearance at this famous port which was to be acknowledged as her home. There was little or no welcome for us when we docked as the UK was still very much affected by war austerity. All my future trips on the *Queen Elizabeth* were made from Southampton. In fact the port became very familiar to me as my next ship, the *Capetown Castle,* was also based there.

The *Capetown Castle* was a beautiful ship belonging to the Union Castle Line. When I joined her near the end of 1945 she was used as a troopship, serving areas associated with the war in Japan: that is, India, Malaya and Ceylon. This was a welcome change from the North Atlantic where I had spent the previous three years. Furthermore this was the first time I joined a ship in peacetime, so I could look forward to voyages without the uncertainty of danger from enemy action.

I was assigned to the ship from the Merchant Navy Pool at Newport. A number of other Welsh seamen were joining the ship with me. As far as I can remember we were all to work in the galley. I was employed as a scullion, along with Harry Stubbs from Cwm near Ebbw Vale. Harry and I had our little scullery attached to the main galley. We were responsible for cleaning the huge copper pots used in the galley. At the start of our first trip we took on board around a thousand Italian troops who had been prisoners-of-war in the UK. Our destination was Naples in southern Italy. Our trip to the Mediterranean was uneventful except for a very rough crossing of the Bay of Biscay. Both Harry and I were used to being tossed about in rough seas but this time we had the problem of lifting and scouring very large and heavy copper pots while the ship was rolling violently from side to side. We both saw the funny side of the situation, although we knew we would be seriously injured if one of the pots were to crash into us.

We were not allowed to go ashore in Naples, where we only stopped for a short time to offload our passengers who, no doubt, were very glad to be home again after being POWs in Britain. The first thing I remember after leaving Naples was one night when I was on deck and had a good view of a volcano belching molten lava which ran down the side of its cone. I wasn't sure which volcano it was, as there are a number active in this area of the Mediterranean. I consulted my shipmates, who all had their own theories, but I don't think any of them knew which volcano it was. I also clearly remember standing in the bow of the ship after leaving Naples to get some fresh air after being confined in the hot, sticky atmosphere of the galley. Suddenly I became aware of a shape in the sea rapidly approaching us and trailing a distinct wake. My instinctive reaction was one of terror. I thought it was a torpedo! In fact it was a porpoise, who was quickly joined by others. I watched them in fascination as they swam parallel to the ship and skylarked about our bows. This was the first of many occasions when I stood and watched the porpoises; in fact, I succeeded in taking a photograph of them with my simple camera. I still have that picture.

Our next stop was Port Said in Egypt, prior to entering the Suez Canal. This only lasted a short time and again we were denied shore-leave. There was, however, a multitude of bum-boats gathered around our ship as we dropped anchor. They were prepared to sell their wares, which included just about everything, to any member of our crew. They seemed to have more stock than any big department store in Britain. I was taken in by one trader, who sold me a most magnificent dagger with a handle in the form of a gorgeous woman. I thought it would make a good souvenir as a paper-knife and felt very proud to possess it. Unfortunately the blade bent into a banana shape the first time I attempted to use it.

After a short stay at anchor in Port Said we entered the Suez Canal and thence the Red Sea. We must have sailed over the spot where Moses led the people of Israel out of Egypt. Finally we sailed into the Indian Ocean. The weather was now really hot and we spent as much of our time as possible on deck. Our main objectives were Bombay, Ceylon and Singapore. As I made three trips to the area I cannot be sure of the sequence in which I visited these places, although I know we went to Bombay on each trip. We also made calls at Aden and Malta, but again I cannot be sure on which trips.

Bombay was a complete contrast to all the places I had visited previously. It was a very large city which seemed to be teeming with life. The streets were always crowded with people on foot or bicycles and there was a constant din from car horns as motorists tried to negotiate a passage through the crowds. Street-vendors were everywhere and always ready to sell trinkets and other mementoes of India. Beggars were always prominent and at night many people slept on pavements or in convenient doorways. The people for the most part were poor but

The author (right), very sunburned, on a beach in Bombay. With fellow crew members of the "Capetown Castle."

usually colourfully dressed and generally passive: we met no hostility when we went ashore. This is in contrast to our stay in Kingston, Jamaica, where we were in danger of being robbed when ashore.

While in Bombay we had a reasonable amount of time for shore-leave. The older members of the crew, who had been to Bombay before, gave us the names of various places worth visiting. One was a beautiful beach which, as one would expect, was well-known as a delightful place to lounge in the sun and go swimming. There was also a swimming-pool within easy reach but it was not as popular with us as the beach. We visited a number of markets. One that was very popular with the crew sold Indian carpets and many of us bought one to take home.

On one trip I bought an elaborately carved coffee-table whose legs were replicas of the head and trunk of an elephant. It was extremely heavy and bulky but I managed to get it home to Ebbw Vale. Sixty years on it resides in our lounge in Newcastle upon Tyne, along with other items such as a pair of beautifully carved elephants. I also found Bombay a good place to buy quality books, such as Wilde's *The Picture of Dorian Gray,* which were enjoyed by all my mates in the forecastle.

My third visit to Bombay coincided with my twenty-first birthday. To celebrate the occasion my parents told me to buy myself a good-quality watch as a gift from them. At this time it was still difficult to get such things at home in the UK.

On one occasion we went from Bombay to Colombo in Ceylon. I don't remember a great deal about this visit but I must have been greatly impressed with what I saw because the idea was firmly planted in my mind that after leaving the Merchant Navy my objective would be to get a job as manager of a tea-plantation.

The other place I visited during my three voyages on the *Capetown Castle* was Singapore. This was the furthest east we travelled and it was about a thousand miles from Bombay. We sailed south down the coast of India and turned east into the Indian Ocean and over to the coast of Malaya. We then sailed down the Straits of Malacca adjacent to Sumatra until we reached Singapore, which was almost on the equator.

Singapore was memorable because it had been captured by the Japanese in 1942. When we got there the only Japanese we saw were the ones who had been captured by our forces when we recovered Burma. These men were put to work labouring on the docks when we were there. Singapore was filled with British troops who had fought, and in some cases been prisoners, during the war with Japan. Our job was to bring them home on the *Capetown Castle*.

My great schoolboy friend, John Evans, was known to be in Singapore at this time and I went to the RAF camp to visit him. After a great deal of trouble finding the camp I was disappointed to hear that John was no longer there, having left it some days earlier to join a homeward-bound troopship. By an incredible stroke of good luck it turned out that John was one of the hundreds of RAF men who had embarked on our ship. We were both joyful at our reunion and with the help of my mates I managed to get John a bunk in our forecastle. He therefore had a more comfortable passage back home than the other RAF men. Sadly I have not seen John since that voyage.

The famous Raffles Hotel in Singapore was used as a forces canteen at the end of the Japanese war. We would go there when we were ashore and one day I had a surprise. I was sitting there talking to my mates when someone came up and started talking to me. It was Tommy Crump, a lad who lived three houses away from us in Ebbw Vale. This was the second

The "Capetown Castle" in Singapore.
Preparing to return British forces from the East.

surprise-meeting I had involving someone in Singapore—and there was to be a third. About fifty years later I joined an art class in Newcastle. One of the members told me he had been in Singapore in 1946. After some discussion I learned that he was brought home on the *Capetown Castle* at a time when I was a crew member.

After three long voyages on the *Capetown Castle* I was signed off when we returned to Southampton. I staggered home with my latest purchases from Bombay and settled down to some home leave. Subsequently I reported to the pool at Newport and was quickly allocated to a new ship, being sent to Barry to join the *Dalcross*. She was a freighter of about 4,000 tons and when I first saw her she was tied up alongside a dockside granary. I quickly learned that we would be going to Hudson's Bay in northern Canada for a cargo of grain. After a year on troopships I was looking forward to being on a freighter again. Although the *Queen Elizabeth* and the *Capetown Castle* were wonders of marine engineering they did not capture for me the raw spirit of the sea which one gets on a freighter. I know that these troopships could be violently tossed about like a cork in a big storm, but being encased between decks and surrounded by thousands of troops does not compare with the exhilaration of being on a rusty old freighter with the sea breaking over its deck and clinging to a lifeline to make your way to the galley.

My voyage on the *Dalcross* was uneventful but interesting, insofar as we were going to a remote part of Canada which was not visited by many ships. This is hardly surprising as it is not accessible for many months because the sea gets frozen over.

We were going to Port Churchill for a cargo of grain. To get there we sailed north along the western coast of Greenland until we were sufficiently far north to round the top of Canada and then sail south into Hudson's Bay and Port Churchill.

When we paid our visit in 1946 there was very little to see: a general store which proudly claimed to be "The Hudson's Bay Company" and a massive granary where the grain from the prairie provinces was stored. The grain was exported in freighters like the *Dalcross*. The railway station was of great interest to me. Its primary purpose was to bring grain from the provinces hundreds of miles away. It fascinated me to see its single track disappearing into the distance on a perfectly flat landscape, as if it led to infinity. I also recall seeing what appeared to be a small whaling-station.

In recent years Port Churchill has become well known through TV films. It is completely ice-bound in the winter and visited by polar bears, which are plentiful in the area and come to Churchill to forage for food. They become such pests that they are caught and put into polar bear "jails" until they can be flown to suitably remote regions. Sightseers are taken round the Churchill area in special buses designed to allow them to get close to the bears.

In the autumn of 1946 we arrived back at Barry in South Wales. When I had first told my parents I was going to join the Merchant Navy they were horrified. They had been warned by well-meaning neighbours that going to sea would lead to my downfall. There were clear warnings that I would be living with depraved men whose ever-constant aim in life was to get drunk in each port of call and consort with ladies of doubtful virtue. As if that were not enough I would meet all sorts of men with unchristian beliefs and from vastly inferior cultures. In short, I was on the verge of entering the portals of hell. I never accepted these views, being a great believer in thinking for oneself and not believing everything one is told. Furthermore I saw a spell at sea as a means of gaining experience of the world at large and a likely contributor to my real education. After four years at sea I realised my parents had nothing to worry about. I firmly believe it was the turning-point in my life and was the catalyst which kindled my dormant ambition to make a success of my life. I did find that some men went ashore and got drunk, while others got into trouble with the women who were always available in any port. It was sad beyond belief to go ashore in some countries and immediately be accosted by a small boy telling you he had a sister who was clean and readily available. As we spent more time at sea than in port many men tended to make up for lost time when ashore, particularly with drink, since there was no alcohol allowed on board ship. The one exception I found was the *Queen Elizabeth* where we could buy beer at the *Pig and Whistle,* the ship's pub. After they had made an unpleasant Atlantic crossing and knowing they would be doing it again in a week or two one can understand their desire to forget their problems in drink.

Many people know nothing of the life of merchant seamen in wartime. Actually all were volunteers and were not called up like members of the armed forces. They were men who chose to go to sea as a means of earning a living and keeping a family, very much like a steelworker or coalminer on land. Some were highly intelligent, some were not: like people everywhere. The difference was that at sea you all lived in the same home—all different kinds of men in close proximity. This was especially true of freighters where crews of under fifty were common. At sea the crew are united by one unchallengeable fact: that in war or peace they have to rely on one another in order to survive. This single fact overcomes all possible conflict over nationality, religion, colour, standard of education and so on. In my entire time at sea I cannot recall one incident in which any of these issues caused a problem worth mentioning. Merchant seamen complained that most people were ignorant of their role. In war they were classed as civilians, even though their death rate because of enemy action was considerably higher than that of the armed forces. If a merchant seaman lost his ship for any reason his pay was automatically stopped from the moment he abandoned ship. Torpedoed merchant ships were also abandoned by other shipping, which were forbidden to try and rescue the crews. Few people would recognise a merchant seaman as they generally wore no uniform ashore, which sometimes resulted in their being accused of draft-dodging. I would say that the Merchant Navy made a significant contribution to my education. For the first time in my life I came into contact with men from backgrounds vastly different from my own. It gave me the opportunity to understand their feelings and beliefs and also encouraged me to begin reading serious, thought-provoking books. Many of these books had been recommended by men who, although only simple merchant seamen, were very well educated in the ways of life. Who would have believed that a supposedly uneducated ship's fireman could recite long passages of poetry after spending his watch shovelling coal into a boiler? For example:

"I have felt a ship's deck heave under me and so
I know what gods and poets and sailor-men must know,
Why shiftless men go seeking what other men despise
Why broken men and cruel have beauty in their eyes."

(Author unknown)

or

"In peace, scant quiet is at sea;
In war, each revolution of the screw,
Each breath of air that blows the colours free,
May be the last life movement known to you."

(John Masefield)

I owe a lot to the Merchant Navy and the seamen I met. It played a major role in my education and my decision to go to sea as a boy was amply vindicated.

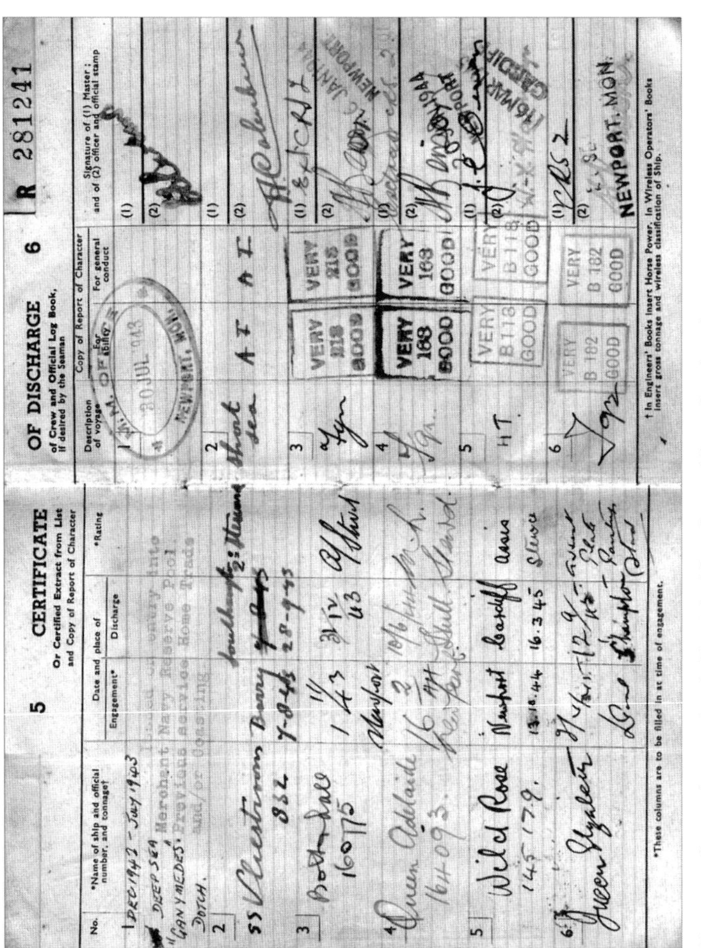

5 CERTIFICATE Or Certified Extract from List and Copy of Report of Character

OF DISCHARGE of Crew and Official Log Book, if desired by the Seaman 6

R 281241

No.	*Name of ship and official number, and tonnage†	Date and place of Engagement*	Date and place of Discharge	*Rating	Description of voyage*	Copy of Report of Character For ability	For general conduct	Signature of (1) Master; and of (2) officer and official stamp

*These columns are to be filled in at time of engagement.

† In Engineers' Books insert Horse Power. In Wireless Operators' Books insert gross tonnage and wireless classification of Ship.

Extract from the author's British Merchant Navy log book.

Chapter 9

McAlpine

By September 1946 I was twenty-one and realised I had to make some important decisions, since I was now eligible to be demobilised from the Merchant Navy. The first thing was to decide if I wanted to stay in the seafaring trade. I had sailed about 100,000 miles, which is roughly equivalent to four times round the world. I had in my time at sea visited many interesting places all over the world that I would never have visited under normal conditions.

After thinking about my options very carefully I decided that a future in the Merchant Navy would not give me the prospects of a significantly improved life, which I knew instinctively was what I was looking for. I therefore decided to take my discharge from the Merchant Navy and seek my fortune elsewhere. My next step was to report to the Resettlement Advice Bureau, which had been set up by the government to help war veterans re-enter a world of peace and particularly to give them advice on future careers. I applied for an interview and was duly given a date to be seen by a panel of men who were presumably knowledgeable about the opportunities that might be available to me.

I had in fact been giving a great deal of thought to my post-war career. The one factor I was clear about was that I did not want to live permanently in Ebbw Vale. My thoughts turned towards possible lines of advancement. I had visited a number of places which appealed to my imagination: for example Ceylon, India and Malaya, all of which I had visited in the last year. It seemed to me that an ideal situation would be as manager of a tea-plantation in one of these places.

I was duly interviewed by members of the advisory team, who wanted the history of my pre-war experiences. They were particularly interested in my achievements in the grammar school, in my hopes for the future and any ideas I might have concerning a possible career. I had anticipated this line of questioning and had rehearsed my reply in my mind. I explained that I wanted to be the manager of a tea-plantation in Ceylon or India. They thought it was a worthwhile objective but pointed out that as I had dropped out of grammar school I had not matriculated, and the key to any future career was to pass a matriculation examination.

They advised me to take a correspondence course to prepare for the matriculation examination that was staged annually by London University for external students. They advised me to register with the ICS (International Correspondence School) and gave me a donation of £5 towards the cost. I realised that these people were sincere in their advice and that they had some faith in my objective. I came away from the meeting determined to get a matriculation certificate.

I realised that to take a correspondence course I would need to stay at home for a few years and also get a job to support myself. My parents were happy with these proposals which, in a way, must have pleased them: particularly my mother after the disappointment she must have had when I did not live up to her expectations of me at the grammar school.

My first action was to report to the local labour exchange and hope to get a suitable job. As many men older than I were returning from their war service they were given priority for their old jobs in the steelworks. It appeared there were only two jobs that were available to me: there were openings at Milford Haven for sailors wishing to join the fishing-fleet; the other possibility was a labouring job on a house-building site only four hundred yards from my home. I had no hesitation in accepting the labouring job as it would give me the opportunity to study at home. With a job secured I then registered with the ICS to begin my studies.

Some of our neighbours were very sceptical about my possible success, particularly after my failure at the grammar school. In fact one lady teacher who knew my mother went so far as to inform her that, "Raymond will never amount to much, Mrs Hicks; he just cannot apply himself to studying." How wrong she was.

One day I met my old friend Tom Jones who suggested that I should join the Ebbw Vale Male-Voice Choir, which I promptly did. He also suggested that I go to the Saturday dances that were held in the local drill-hall where I had served some years earlier when I was in the Home Guard. I was mixing again with old friends I knew at school and in the scouts. The most important reunion was with Marjorie Wall, my future wife. We always seemed to gravitate towards each other at the dance. Her brother Ewart also joined the choir and started going to the Saturday dances. I would call

Ebbw Vale Male Voice Choir: the author's head can be seen towards the right of the very back row.

for Ewart at his home on choir nights, thus having added opportunities of seeing Marjorie.

Most of the music we sang in the choir was traditional and included choruses from many famous operas. Favourites were the soldiers' chorus from *Faust,* the song of the Hebrew slaves from *Nebucco,* the sailors' chorus from the *Flying Dutchman* and so on. We also sang choruses based on great poetical works by such as Longfellow. There were a considerable number of young men in the choir and on our way home we would sing some of the choruses, not because we were rowdy or wanted to make a nuisance of ourselves but for the sheer joy it gave us. This was the beginning of my passion for opera, which remains with me today. All this contrasted significantly with the hostile reaction of my school-friends and I to the well-intentioned efforts of the headmaster at grammar school, who went to so much trouble to put on a gramophone rendering of the opera *Tosca.* We were simply too young in our early teens to appreciate it at the time, but its beauty became apparent to, and was greatly appreciated by, me ten years later.

I was getting on quite well with my studies and my job on the building-site. I enjoyed being a labourer, spending my time outdoors with a pick and shovel digging foundation trenches. It made me quite fit and muscular but its greatest effect was on my appetite, which was hugely increased by all the physical work I did and the energy I used up.

One day while at work I had a visit from Tom Jones, who lived next door to the building-site. He said he had a friend who was a civil engineer with McAlpine on an opencast coal-site. It appeared that Tom had been discussing me with a friend, Emlyn James, who was of the opinion that if I met him at the site office he might find me a more suitable job than labouring. The coal-site was on the top of the mountain near Blaenavon, four or five miles and two bus-rides away from Ebbw Vale. Without any hesitation I decided to go at once to see Emlyn James. The only problem I had was how to get there. Unfortunately there was a dense fog over the whole area at the time and there were no buses running that day. Undaunted and determined I made my excuses to the site foreman and set out at once to walk—quite an undertaking as it was uphill all the way and visibility was poor. After two hours I finally found the site office, which was a large wooden hut. It was enveloped in thick fog and there was no-one about. I went into the building and after knocking on a few doors and enquiring for Mr James I found him in one of the offices clearly used by the site engineers. When I told him the reason for my visit he was amazed and impressed that at the drop of a hat I had left the job I was doing and walked all the way from Ebbw Vale to see him. After some discussion with me he left the office to see the chief engineer, who returned with Emlyn to interview me. The end result was that I was given a job as a student civil engineer at two pounds ten shillings a week and I was told to start at once. This was an enormous piece of luck and a big step forward. I had now succeeded in climbing onto the lowest rung of a ladder which would lead me to a professional job as a chartered civil engineer in the years to come.

I started my new job as soon as my previous employers furnished me with the statutory paperwork. On the first day with McAlpine I got up early to catch the first of the two buses I would need to reach the site. Journey times of 30–45 minutes each way meant a reduction in the time available for study.

My duties included helping the civil engineers to do the weekly site-survey, necessary because the excavator-drivers and the other workers were paid a bonus each week depending on the amount of overburden (topsoil etc) and coal that had been dug. The main skills needed to do the survey were in using the instruments and having the mathematical knowledge to evaluate the readings and, from the results, to calculate the volume of the material dug. Although it was six years since I left school I was surprised to find I could remember with little effort what I had learned, so the elements of surveying came easily to me. We spent one day a week making a comprehensive survey of the site, then returning to the engineers' office where we would set out the survey on a drawing-board and evaluate the results. We would also walk around the whole site examining the newly-exposed coal-seams, which could be about fifty feet below ground-level.

One aspect of my new job was the interest the civil engineers took in assessing my mathematical ability. They would give me problems designed to see how far I could get in attempting to solve issues unrelated to my day-to-day job. One such example sticks in my mind. I had to imagine a circular field in which a goat was tethered to the boundary by a rope pegged at the circumference. I had to calculate the length of the rope as a proportion of the diameter of the field so that the goat could graze in half the area of the field. I became obsessed with this problem and worked on it during my spare moments in the office. Although I failed to find a solution I did improve my knowledge of mathematics and was comforted by the revelation that none of the qualified engineers could answer the question (that is, find an exact solution as opposed to approximation). I pushed the problem to the back of my mind and stopped thinking about it as I had more pressing problems to solve. Forty years later, however, it came back to haunt me when I had retired and could enjoy the luxury of using my time in trivial pursuits. One evening I was out enjoying a leisurely walk when the unsolved problem of the goat and its pasture came into my mind. After some thought I came to the conclusion that I should attack the thing in another way, which I did as soon as I got home. To my immense joy I immediately got the full solution. This, no doubt, was down to the greater knowledge of maths and experience gained in the intervening forty years.

It soon became clear to me that my new job would be of immense help in my study for the matriculation certificate. My daily contact with two or three experienced civil engineers ensured I would be well prepared in engineering drawing and mathematics. My great concern was the need to prepare myself for the English and French exams. I knew that with dedication I could master the English grammar but my great worry was learning French. This subject had been my great failure in grammar school and I now realised this had been the result of a complete lack of interest and effort on my part. Now it was of supreme importance that I mastered the subject, at least to matriculation standard. My great handicap was the lack of a tutor of any sort. I realised that I would have no coaching, but on the other hand I would not have any oral examination. This was an immense help to me as I found it impossible to learn the correct pronunciation from a book. My difficulty thus became simply one of learning vocabulary and constructing sentences. Although I now spent more time at work and in travelling, resulting in less time for study at home, I realised I had the opportunity to learn French vocabulary whilst I walked around the coal-site every day. I now started to write well-constructed sentences in French in a pocket-book and learned them as I walked. I also referred to my old school textbooks and ICS books for French grammar. It came as a surprise that many of the things taught to me in school were still stowed away in my mind and surfaced with a little prompting. My method of learning

French by composing a notebook may have been common practice at the time, although I didn't know it then. Many years later when I did a lot of overseas travelling I bought records and phrase-books which served the same purpose and proved very useful to me.

An opencast coal-mine, as its name suggests, is simply a large hole dug in the surface of the ground to expose the coal-seams which, in our case, were twenty to fifty feet under the surface. Between the seams were layers of shale, which could be split into thinner layers. Above the first layer of coal would be a layer of something called overburden, consisting mainly of boulders, loamy soil and clay. The overburden was the first layer to be removed in order to reach the uppermost layer of coal. Although the coal outcropped on our site it was interesting to learn that the same seams were located some miles away in the Ebbw Vale valley at Cwm. At that location the seams could only be reached by sinking a deep shaft, perhaps several hundred yards deep. This tilting of the coal seams gives an indication of the geological upheavals which had occurred millions of years ago.

Examining the excavated shales was immensely interesting because they were usually rich in fossils. There were fossilised shells, ferns and some small creatures like snails. Sometimes we would find a large sphere of rock

Cousin Leslie and the author (right) enjoying a camping holiday after war service.

called a geode. When split open these would prove to be hollow and lined with beautiful crystals. The coal itself would also vary in colour and texture. Usually it was black but sometimes it would have other colours such as purple and even gold. Sometimes it was quite brittle.

It was amazing how quickly I settled into my new job and also into the leisure activities with my old friends at Ebbw Vale. I got involved with the scouts again and was pleased to find my old scoutmaster still as active as ever. It was not long before I became the cubmaster and found myself looking after a group of youngsters who seemed to enjoy some of the stories I told them.

My membership of the choir was going well and I attended a number of eisteddfods in which we competed. These festivals were common in the whole of Wales and were patronised by a whole spectrum of competitors, from the very young to those classified as pensioners. The only feature of the eisteddfods I didn't like was that the programme started with the performances of the very young and went on for hours before the male-voice choirs performed as the last item. It was not uncommon for them to be called to perform after midnight, by which time we were all feeling very tired.

Our public performances did not merit any worthwhile prizes during my membership. This may have been a result of my indifferent singing. However we all enjoyed ourselves immensely, which was evident from our impassioned singing in the bus on the way home.

There is a picture-book devoted to old Ebbw Vale and in it is a 1948 photograph of the male-voice choir. A modern-day viewer would be struck by the high proportion of young men in this picture (I'm standing in the back row). How sad it is that when we see a modern male-voice choir there are very few young members, only old men.

One day I was surprised when the chief engineer summoned me to his office. I had no idea why he wanted to see me and I grew a little apprehensive, hoping he wasn't dissatisfied with my performance. He told me gravely that he had been thinking about my future and felt that I would benefit from extra tuition in a technical college. The company was prepared to give me day-release for one day a week to attend Crumlin Technical College to study for a National Certificate in Engineering. He assured me there would be nothing to pay as my bus fare would be refunded and there would be no reduction in my pay. This was a terrific boost to my morale as it was clear I was doing well and was considered suitable material to join the company's staff as a fully-fledged civil engineer in due course. Although I was a little concerned about the extra studying I would have to do I felt sure I could cope and therefore accepted the offer.

My relationship with Marjorie continued to flourish and we were now seeing more of each other. We still went to the Saturday dance and started playing tennis together with her brother Ewart and Emlyn James, my boss and mentor at McAlpine. We went to each other's home and it became obvious there was a mutual attraction between us, which would eventually end in marriage.

In the autumn my interest in rugby was revived and I would go to most or all of the home games, usually accompanied by Ewart. It was most exciting to see our team win particularly when you could identify the players, who were all from Ebbw Vale or nearby and in some cases were personal friends or old schoolmates. They all played for the love of the game and their reward was to know they were playing for their own town.

In spite of all my leisure activities I was continuing with my ICS studies with great dedication. I found their study notes extremely good and was on course for sitting my exams the next year. I'm afraid my presence at home must have been a great burden to my parents and sister as I banned any background noise in the house when I was studying, which was most of the time. Everyone was committed to talking in whispers while I worked in the front room (parlour). The strain on them must have been enormous.

By now I had more or less decided that my future lay in civil engineering and my original objective of becoming a tea-planter was dropped. Arrangements were made for me to go to Crumlin Technical College for an interview with the principal. He came to the conclusion I would make a good student and I was told to start my studies at the beginning of the 1947 autumn session. Crumlin is a small town about ten miles down the Ebbw Valley from the estate where I lived. I was therefore committed to a further increase in my studies and a reduction in my available time.

The autumn session began and I took my place in a class of young men, who were mainly craft apprentices, and older men like myself, who had been away on war-service for a number of years. We were classed as mature students. My lessons were very much as expected, with a strong bias towards engineering. The range of subjects was greater than those I was studying for my matriculation. This meant that my academic workload increased considerably. Another problem was that in the college I was also getting homework, which added further to my commitments.

On our coal-site it was becoming clear that the current rate of coal extraction was coming to an end. I presume this conclusion had been drawn from the results of boreholes that had been sunk in the area, not by McAlpine but by government authorities. It was evident that we would have to move to another site. This was to Blaenavon about two miles away. All our equipment would have to be moved, including our very large dragline excavators. After considering the problem it was concluded that the only way to move them to a new site was to construct a dirt-road around the contour of the mountain and use it as a route for transporting the excavators, which could be made to walk under their own power. I was employed for some weeks surveying the proposed route: a welcome change from my weekly survey of the opencast mine.

By now we had a new member of our engineering staff. He was an ex-RAF post-war conscript and after serving his time in the forces was aiming to start a career. His name was Roy Key and he came from Bliana. He was taken on as a student engineer but received no pay, which was common practice before the war for boys indentured to learn a trade. Roy proved to be a very likeable chap and was readily accepted and liked by all of us in the engineering office. The plans to move to a new opencast coal-site in Blaenavon were now finalised and work began on building the dirt-road bed on the mountain. This was done fairly quickly and was not a difficult undertaking. Next it was necessary to build railway sidings for the time when coal extraction would begin. This job was the responsibility of Emlyn James, who arranged for me to work with him. As I was a great railway enthusiast it gave me great pleasure to help lay out and construct the sidings. We also had to design and construct various supporting equipment and buildings, such as a weighbridge for checking the tonnage of coal shipped, screens, workshops and so on. It was all very interesting work.

After I had been at the college for six months or so the teacher began to take a great interest in my performance and was keen to know about my plans for the future. He knew my history and the work I was doing to get a matriculation certificate. One day he asked if I planned to go to a university.

I told him I had no such plans because there was no way I could pay for a university education. He then explained to me that the Monmouthshire Education Authority had an annual competition for an engineering student to win a scholarship to a university and in his view I had a good chance of winning it. He said that my chances depended very much on my ability to prepare myself in the next six months prior to the competition. He offered to help me in applying for entry and would help and support me in any way he could, especially in advising me on areas of study. He assured me that the work I did at the technical college would prove very useful to me in the competition. I don't recall the name of this teacher but his help and experience were invaluable to me. I only wish I could thank him for taking so great an interest in me.

It was obvious that this was a challenge too important to ignore, so I promptly agreed to enter the competition and gratefully accepted his offer of help. By now I was feeling the pressure of my various commitments to study. Firstly, I had my ICS studies for matriculation; secondly, I was going to college for one day a week to get a National Certificate; and thirdly, I was now to prepare for a competition to get a university scholarship (n.b., members of the armed forces who served during the war were guaranteed a place in university at the government's expense. This facility was not offered to merchant seamen as they were not deemed to be in the armed forces, in spite of the fact that the Merchant Navy had the highest rate of men killed during the war, over and above all three armed forces).

I talked over with Marjorie the idea of a university scholarship; we had reached the stage of talking of marriage but she felt that I should concentrate on winning the scholarship first and not think about marriage at that time. She did say that if I succeeded she would wait for me until I had a degree. Her general view was that the higher I got with my technical education the more secure we would be when we finally got married. I was not surprised to hear her views and I had no doubt that she would encourage me.

It was now the beginning of 1948 and the time was drawing near when I should sit both my matriculation examinations and the competitive exam for the scholarship. I don't know for sure which came first or where I took them, although I think that I sat for the matriculation exam in Cardiff Technical College.

Some time later I was at a Saturday dance with Marjorie when we were approached by a girl who did secretarial work at Crumlin Technical College. She was very excited and told us with glee that I had passed the mathematics exam for my National Certificate with a mark of 100%. This gave a big boost to my morale, although of course she should not have told us.

The time came when I was scheduled to take my two examinations. In a way they were equally important as I didn't know whether, if I won the scholarship, I would be accepted at university if I had not matriculated. I knew that at least one other student from Crumlin Tech. was competing for the university scholarship. He was in my class and I had a great respect for his academic ability. I had no idea, however, how many other students from other schools and colleges had entered the competition.

I now entered a period of acute anxiety, as my exams were over and I eagerly waited for the results to be published. All this brought back memories of my efforts to win a scholarship to the grammar school when I was eleven. The matriculation exam went as well as could be expected, although I was concerned about the French paper. I succeeded in completing it but was unsure whether I had done well enough to pass. I had no idea of the scholarship result but I did feel I had done well. Also, of course, I had no idea of the performances of the other competitors. I just had to be patient and wait for the results.

The first letter I received was from the University of London informing me that I had passed in all five subjects of my matriculation and was placed in Division Two. I was delighted and immediately told my parents, who must have felt very relieved and satisfied. I had at last succeeded in doing what I had failed miserably to do when I was in the grammar school.

I had been discharged from the Merchant Navy near the end of September 1946 and had sat the matriculation exam in January 1948, so the ICS course had enabled me to get my matriculation certificate in sixteen months even though I had dropped out of the grammar school seven years earlier. I felt that this was a very gratifying performance and it greatly increased my self-confidence.

A while later I received a letter which had the unmistakable mark of an important communication. With great trepidation I carefully opened it. I was almost afraid to read the enclosed letter, but its contents were unbelievable. I had been awarded the senior scholarship to study for four years at a university. The award consisted of an annual stipend for living expenses and the cost of all my tuition fees. My parents and sister were delighted by my success, my mother especially as all her dreams for me were coming true. Friends of my mother who had predicted that "Raymond will never amount to much" were now proved to be wrong.

When looked at objectively my failure in the grammar school was a stroke of great good-fortune; if I had I stayed in school and passed my matriculation exams at sixteen my future would almost certainly have been to get an apprenticeship in the steelworks or a job in the bank or an office of some kind. There was no way I could have gone on to a university because my parents could not have afforded to send me there and my chances of winning a scholarship would have been nil.

As could be expected, Marjorie was very excited by my success. She was not surprised, however, as she had always had great faith in my ability to do well. Marriage was now out of the question if I was to concentrate on my university studies and we realised we would have to wait for four years. The big decision was Marjorie's. She said she would wait for me and cheered us both by reminding me I could come home for weekends and holidays.

My colleagues at work were also pleased to hear of my achievement and came forward with some useful offers of help. It was assumed that I would choose Cardiff for my degree course and my friends pointed out that as there was no accommodation available at the college I would have to find a suitable place to lodge. The chief engineer told me that McAlpine's could help in this respect as they had previously lodged some of their own men in the area. This was a great relief to me.

My next action was to ask the university if they could admit me as a student in September to begin my first year. It was suggested I should pay a visit to the engineering department to see Professor Norman Thomas, an authority on surveying, and discuss my options with him. This I speedily did. I found Professor Thomas to be a kindly man who was most impressed by my past experiences. He said he would be delighted to have me as an undergraduate but there was a problem. Apparently a limit was placed each year on the number of admissions and in my case the threshold had already been reached, places having been taken up by a large influx of men who had done their National Service. Professor Thomas told me that I could, if

I wished, take the first part of my degree as an external student of London University by enrolling at Cardiff Technical College and take the Inter BSc exams at the end of the first year. If I did this Professor Thomas assured me he would guarantee a university place for me at the start of the following year. This arrangement would still allow me to complete the course in four years as originally envisaged, a very important consideration for Marjorie and me.

I was disappointed with the proposal because having already done one external course I was very aware of the extra work they entailed. This new one would be more difficult than being an internal student at Cardiff University but I was so anxious to start that I finally accepted the Professor's proposal.

I duly applied to Cardiff Technical College as suggested and was accepted to start in September 1948. My next problem was to find suitable lodgings in Cardiff. McAlpine recommended that I stay with a Mrs Mahoney in Splott Road, who already had one of their civil engineers lodging with her. She had never had students as lodgers but was prepared to take me as an ex-McAlpine man. So I moved into Mrs Mahoney's house and started an amicable arrangement which was to last for four years. She was a Roman Catholic, as one might expect with a name like Mahoney and an address in Splott Road, and she had a wonderful smile which always seemed to be on display. She looked after me as if I were her own son. She had three daughters about my age but no son and I guess that I filled the gap for her. I owe a great deal of gratitude to Mrs Mahoney for her constant help and for always making me feel at home.

Chapter 10

Technical College and University

I started my studies for a London University external degree at Cardiff Technical College in September 1948. It was an impressive building situated in a prime position in Cathays Park. The park was one of the showpieces of the city of Cardiff. Essentially it is a collection of grand buildings around the four sides of a large rectangular area with lawns and flower-beds forming an open space in the centre, complete with an imposing statue. Cardiff Museum and City Hall were two of the buildings on one side adjacent to Queen Street, a shopping centre. Along the other sides of the park were modern buildings for the university, technical college and students' union. The whole area was well laid out and a delightful place for students to work.

The city itself was compact with a very good shopping centre. The castle and Arms Park rugby ground were all close by. To me it was a far more desirable place to live than Ebbw Vale. One of the attractions it held for me was the local swimming-pool that was near the college and ideally situated for me to visit at lunchtime, which I did every weekday during term-time for the next four years. My digs on Splott Road were about a mile away and gave me a reasonable walk to and from my college. My landlady, Mrs Mahoney, provided me with a good breakfast and a large traditionally cooked meal every evening at around six o'clock which allowed me a few hours of study each night. I did this in the main Cardiff library because there was no suitable place in the house; I also felt the exercise was a good idea. My course of study consisted of maths, mechanics, organic and inorganic chemistry and physics. We had the same teacher for maths and mechanics and I found his lessons very well-presented with a series of useful notes and examples for me to follow. I even consult them today, more than fifty years later. Our teacher in chemistry was also excellent, but the subject was not as interesting to me and we had a massive amount of notes that was difficult to cope with. I did work diligently, though, to master the subject, even though I knew it would be of limited use to me in the future. The physics lessons—heat, light and sound—became a worry. The subjects were important to me but I found the lecturer uninteresting and I began to feel my progress was unsatisfactory. Because of the way the examination system operated the whole syllabus had to be covered in equal measure and my problem with physics was that I felt the teacher would never cover the whole syllabus in enough depth to ensure I had a good chance of passing the exams. I therefore embarked on a programme of teaching myself in areas I thought necessary, using textbooks to supplement my lessons as appropriate.

Life in Cardiff soon developed into a routine of study during the weekdays and a bus on Friday to Ebbw Vale, where I stayed until Sunday evening. I spent as much time as possible with Marjorie, despite my still having to do a considerable amount of homework. Saturday evening was always spent at the drill hall dance and on Sunday we would perhaps go for a walk before I returned to Cardiff. I had by now given up my involvement with the scouts and the choir but I still enjoyed going to the local rugby match on a Saturday.

During the Christmas holiday I had sufficient time to take a job to supplement my scholarship allowance. My first one was as a temporary postman in an area near my home. I remember with pleasure the occasion when a dear old lady gave me threepence as a Christmas gift. I am sure she had little income, which made the gift all the more important to me. Later, in the Easter holiday, I got a job labouring on a building site between Ebbw Vale and Tredegar. I quite enjoyed this arrangement as it paid more than the postal job and the manual work was beneficial to my health—it certainly improved my appetite!

While I was at Cardiff my sister Pat was training as a nurse at Llandough hospital, about three miles from Cardiff. I was able to see her occasionally, a welcome bonus, as I had seen very little of her in the past. I had been at sea when she was in school and then she started work at Harrow School when I was demobbed. She was at the famous boys' school as an assistant in their medical department, a precursor to her nurse training.

After Easter I realised that very soon I would be taking my Inter BSc exams. I was not exactly looking forward to this as I had found the studying very demanding and I was not entirely confident of success. When the time came, however, and I had sat the exam I felt a little better. I was reasonably sure that I would pass but kept my thoughts to myself. Eventually the letter arrived informing me that I had passed. This gave me great pleasure because I knew I would be going to Cardiff University at the start of the next academic year. My first action was to call at the university to tell Professor Thomas of my good fortune and to remind him of his promise to accept me as a student for an honours degree course in September 1949. He repeated his offer and said he expected me to do well in my studies. I took my leave of Mrs Mahoney, who said she would be delighted to see me back for the next year. I now felt I was truly on the way to forging myself a worthwhile future. By this time my ambition to become a tea-planter had completely evaporated and I now anticipated a career as a civil engineer.

I returned home for the three-month vacation period and my mind turned to getting a temporary job. I knew I would benefit enormously if I could get work with a civil engineering company. After a lot of enquiries and some offers I accepted a post with Gee, Walker and Slater, a well-known company in South Wales. They were building a factory in Brynmawr, two miles from my home, and it was of great interest at the time because of the factory's unique design. The main floor space was spanned by nine vaulted sections joined together to give a large floor area. Each section was like the top sliced off a boiled egg and trimmed vertically to give a square-plan view. The factory was later to become world-famous and caused an uproar when it was demolished fifty years later.

My first priority on being home for three months was to see Marjorie, which I did as often as possible. In those days there was a strict moral code in the Welsh valleys and, I suppose, in other parts of the country too. Sex was strictly forbidden until you were married. Marjorie and I both accepted this as sound common sense and never questioned its validity. We would wait until we were married. It was during this summer vacation, I think, that Marjorie's father died quite unexpectedly. He was in good health as far as I know but one night he woke up with a pain in his chest and within minutes had collapsed and died. Marjorie was devastated, as were her mother and two brothers. While such a sudden death seems a good exit for the victim it can traumatise those left behind. The death of Marjorie's father came only a short time after that of my Uncle Will. It is recorded that Will committed suicide in one of the works feeder ponds near Waunlwyd but his sister, Aunty Flo, always believed there was something sinister about it because when his body was found his hands had been tied together. I was upset to hear the news about Uncle Will as he had meant so much to me when I was a boy and I could never understand why he would have committed suicide. I really don't know what happened.

Although I no longer played an active role in the scouts I was always pursuing scouting activities on my own. I was keenly interested in natural history and in particular collected butterflies and beetles. These could be found in vast numbers in 1949 but are much rarer nowadays. I was also very interested in the small creatures which lived in the ponds dotted across the area. I often went off on my own and usually camped out. I loved the country on the north-western side of Ebbw Vale, outside the coal-bearing strata area, in the region of Llangyndr, the Brecon Beacons and the Black Mountains. Although I mix well with people I can be quite content to be alone in quiet places.

My mother and sister always looked forward to my return from a ramble with a good deal of trepidation. It was always dangerous to go through the pockets of my clothes. Matchboxes were likely to contain a Dor Beetle or a Devil's Coach Horse Beetle which I'd brought home to add to my collection. If I returned with a jar of water it almost certainly held a Great Diving Water Beetle or some other pond specimen.

In September 1949 I returned a few days early to Cardiff to prepare for my first term of the three-year course. It was a pleasure to see Mrs Mahoney, who still had her perpetual smile. In my absence David, the McAlpine engineer who had been a lodger with me the previous year, had left and I understood that Mrs Mahoney would like his replacement to be another student. So I decided to see if I could find another engineering student for her.

I presented myself at the university on the first day of term and was a little surprised to learn that Professor Norman Thomas had retired and his position taken by Professor Gurney, who came from Cambridge University where he was well known for his research work in applied mathematics. He was particularly concerned with stress distributions in steel plates and had done a considerable amount of work for the Royal Aircraft Establishment at Farnborough. He had covered the effect of various types of loading on aircraft structures, especially the wing and pressurised fuselages. His colleague at Cardiff was Dr Ashwell, who had worked with him at

Cambridge. Although I did not realise it at the time the arrival of these two eminent academics would be a significant influence on my future career.

The engineering department was based in Newport Road. It occupied what was the old university building and was clearly of Victorian vintage. We shared the building with the medical department appropriately enough, as both departments were committed to rugby football by virtue of their male undergraduates. Engineering had extensive workshop facilities and test laboratories which were mainly industrial in nature. With its eye-catching brick-built that -stack and the like the department would have been out of place in the new university buildings in Cathays Park.

The university teaching methods were quite different from those of the technical college where students sat at desks in classrooms and copied notes written on a blackboard. In the university we attended lectures, sometimes in a lecture theatre, and although a blackboard was used we usually made up our own notes ad hoc. There was more discussion with the lecturer and we were encouraged to put forward our views. We also had tutorials in some subjects, with Dr Ashwell being my tutor, which became more frequent as we drew near to our final exams.

The first two years of the course covered a spectrum of engineering subjects taken by all regardless of career choice. In the final year the course concentrated on one branch only.

I was only a day or two into my studies when I met Jack Lord, a civil engineering student who also came from Ebbw Vale. He was a few years older than me and had been in the forces during the war. When I first met him he was looking for digs so I suggested he might like to stay with Mrs Mahoney. He was delighted with the idea so I mentioned it to Mrs Mahoney, who immediately agreed to take him as a lodger. So Jack joined me in my digs, where we were to stay until our final exams three years later. We had single beds in the back part of the house. These were very comfortable but every night Jack would wake up between two and three A.M. with an urgent need to visit the toilet, which unfortunately was situated outside in the garden. With my head snugly covered by my blankets I would listen to Jack quietly swearing to himself as he put on his clothes for the necessary trip. This was not so bad in summer but in the middle of winter it was torture.

I continued to visit the swimming pool every lunchtime: the pool was only about two hundred yards from the engineering department. Although there was a canteen for undergraduates I rarely went there. My normal lunch was a simple sandwich which I made myself from a Marks and Spencer sliced loaf with ham or jam as a filling. I had my own drawer under a table in the drawing office and kept my food there. This hiding-place was used for three years and was never discovered by man or mouse.

About half the students in my group were ex-servicemen who had served in the war or done national service and the other half were boys who had just left school.

Although there were lots of activities available for students—political and other debates for example—these were usually more popular with students of other faculties. Engineers seemed to be more interested in sports like rugby which provided more relaxation after study.

In my first year I joined the boxing club but discovered that although it was a great way to relax and escape from studying I simply did not have enough aggression to become a member of the college team. I also played rugby sometimes but my performances did not impress the team selectors so I played only the occasional game. In the end I concentrated my sporting instincts on basketball. With my height and weight I had about the right physique for the game. I played regularly and was soon picked for the university team, appearing in more or less all their games for the next three years. In 1952 I was awarded full colours by the University Athletes Board.

In our group of undergraduates we had a number of male students from overseas, such as Indians and Arabs. At this time they had their tuition fees paid by the British government and paid for their living and accommodation costs themselves. They were readily accepted by the British students and I have no recollection of any adverse comments or feelings. On the whole they were polite and well-behaved. This practice of free tuition was later stopped, presumably because it was considered unfair to British students. Many years later when I was selling British capital equipment overseas I was impressed by the advantage we had over our foreign competitors. Many of our Indian and other customers were favourably disposed to us because they had been educated in British universities and were consequently pro-British. This advantage must in my opinion have been significantly lessened when we stopped giving help to overseas students.

During the whole of the time I was at Cardiff University I went home every weekend to visit Marjorie and to see my parents. On one of these weekends my mother told me of an encounter she had had with one of the neighbours. The conversation went something like this:

Neighbour: Hello, Mrs Hicks—and what is Raymond doing now?

Ma: He's in Cardiff University studying to get a civil engineering degree.

Neighbour: Is that so? Well, it's better than being on the dole, isn't it?

I tell this story to illustrate how the spectre of unemployment dominated the thoughts of people in Ebbw Vale. Like so many others this poor woman was haunted by the consequences of joblessness. She knew my history as a young dropout from school and the worries this must have caused my mother. She genuinely thought she was giving her some words of comfort.

I had no serious difficulties with my studies although I found some subjects more enjoyable than others. There was little or no homework, unlike the grammar school, but it was necessary to study the notes taken in lectures and put them into a written form that could be understood at a later date. Any problems this threw up could be researched personally or taken up with your tutor. We also had a very good library in the department with tables and chairs for use by any students seeking a quiet haven to do some work. One of my most difficult problems was finding enough time to do my homework and subject research. As I had no facility for study in my digs and only about two hours each evening to work in the city library I had to organise my spare time as profitably as possible. One way to increase working time was to use the time we had between lectures, which could be as much as an hour or so on some days. I studied in the departmental library, my general aim being to keep up to date in understanding my lecture notes and not have to rely on swotting it all up just before an examination.

My practice of working during the holidays continued as I was anxious to save as much as possible for our wedding. Even though it was two years ahead it was always on our minds. Once again I became a temporary postman at Christmas and did a labouring job at Easter, but in the long summer break I looked for a job which would have some relevance to my future career. I therefore got a post as student engineer with Simon Carves, who had a contract to build a large boiler plant in the Ebbw Vale steelworks.

Coincidentally it was on a site near the blast-furnaces and stores where I had worked as a sixteen-year old boy.

My second academic year was an extension of the first with added emphasis on field work. To further our knowledge of surveying a group of us went to a camp for a week and spent each day surveying the surrounding countryside. This was most interesting and also familiar to me in consequence of my time with McAlpine. On another occasion we congregated at night on the roof of the engineering department, the object of the exercise being to take readings on certain celestial bodies; with the use of astronomical tables and a clock we were instructed to identify the exact position of the university on the surface of the earth. The whole thing degenerated into a farce with a multitude of different results from the students. My own answer pinpointed the university as being in the middle of the Irish Sea.

One outside activity I enjoyed was our regular outing to sites selected to improve our knowledge of geology. This would usually be to a cliff on the edge of the Bristol Channel or to an inland quarry. My interest in the subject had started with my employment on the opencast coal sites when I worked for McAlpine. During our lectures on geology we were given interesting facts about the erosion of cliffs on the shores of the Bristol Channel. It occurs to me that these frequent visits by geology students to chip away busily at the cliff face must have had a significant effect on the speed of erosion. Some people consider geology to be a boring subject but I find it fascinating. It is of great practical relevance in civil engineering. Our lecturer, Mr Trigg, became known nationally some years later. He was a consultant on the Aberfan coal-tip disaster in South Wales where about 120 people, mostly children, were killed.

I was now approaching the last year of my undergraduate studies, leading to an honours degree in civil engineering. My main areas of study were the theory of structures, mathematics and the strength of materials. All of these subjects interested me greatly and I found it great fun working on problems thrown up whilst studying them. These subjects were the ones my professor and tutor had researched while at Cambridge and consequently they took particular interest in my progress. One day, after a lecture on the design of suspension bridges, I became absorbed in the calculations for the structure and developed a method of simplifying the work. I showed it to the professor, who was most impressed, and he urged me to send it to an appropriate magazine to see if they would publish it. I was very sceptical about this but I sent the article to the *Engineer* magazine. I was astounded when they accepted it for publication and sent me a proof to check. This was the first time I had attempted to publish work I had done and I was delighted and surprised to receive a cheque for my efforts.

By the time I had got to my honours year I was rather assuming that I would end up going into the colonial services and getting a posting to one of the African colonies. This was the route taken by many civil engineers embarking on their career after leaving university. On the other hand the more I studied for my honours degree the more absorbed I became in the mathematical theory of elasticity, the same field researched by my professor, and I began to have doubts about joining the colonial service. I decided to wait until I knew what grade I would get in the forthcoming examinations. I talked it over with Marjorie and found she felt as I did. Finally the great day arrived when I was to face the prospect of learning whether all the work I had done since leaving the Merchant Navy had been worthwhile. The exams on all subjects were of three hours duration and at the time I was a little disappointed with my performance. I was sure I would get a degree but I knew I would only be satisfied if I earned first class honours. I need not have worried for in a short time I received a letter saying I had passed in all subjects and was awarded first class honours. Furthermore, I was informed by my professor that I had been awarded the Page Medal for my performance as best student of the year. Until that moment I had no idea such an award existed! My mind was now in turmoil. I abandoned all thoughts of working overseas and started to apply for a job as a stress analyst in a number of aircraft companies. Marjorie was delighted with this because she was not keen to move abroad as her mother was unwell. We were now at the stage where we could get married as soon as I found a suitable job and our hope was to get married at the end of August. Predictably, all this exciting news was extremely gratifying to my parents and sister.

Again Fate intervened. Before I had attended the graduation ceremony for my degree the professor approached me and said that in his view I should stay on at the university to do research in the subject we both loved. I explained that we were getting married shortly and that to date I did not have a job. He then revealed that he had been in contact with people at the Royal Aircraft Establishment in Farnborough and they had agreed to fund my research for an initial year to enable me to get a MSc degree. He also told me that my income would allow us to get married and that I had been chosen to attend the Conference for the Advancement of Science in Belfast near the end of August. I would be able to take my wife with me, so we could treat it as a honeymoon. Marjorie and I discussed the matter fully before deciding to accept. This meant I would have to find a flat in Cardiff as soon as possible: a bit of a problem as I would normally be at home in Ebbw Vale doing vacational work. The solution was simple. I took a vacational job in the engineering department of Cardiff City Council and stayed with Mrs Mahoney until I eventually found a flat near Roath Park. We rented the upstairs rooms of Mr and Mrs Sullivan, where we happily stayed until I finished my work at the university. It is interesting to note that Mrs Mahoney and the Sullivans were of Irish descent and that a large proportion of the inhabitants of Cardiff also had Irish connections, mainly the result of an influx of Irish people to provide labour for building Cardiff Docks (and later Barry Docks) around two hundred years earlier.

Actually Cardiff was only a small town of little consequence before the mining of coal in the South Wales valleys and the manufacture of iron and steel in the towns at the heads of the valleys. Much of the materials produced was shipped to Cardiff and Newport by canals especially made for the purpose. The products were then shipped abroad from Cardiff, Newport and Barry.

Finally the great day arrived and, on 28th August 1952, Marjorie and I were married at last after the long, agonising four-year wait while I studied for my degree. We were both very happy and looking forward to an exciting future. We had been sweethearts since I left the Merchant Navy in 1946 and would remain sweethearts until she died in 1991. We had also known each other since we were infants in the same school class. After a reception in the Westgate Hotel in Newport we went to Porthcawl for three days before embarking on a boat for Belfast, where we stayed for two weeks. We visited Dublin and places of interest in Northern Ireland and I attended the science conference as planned.

We returned to Cardiff and settled into a domestic routine. Basically this meant that I spent most of each day at the university and Marjorie would do her household chores. She also did all the typing for preparing my research papers that were published in various journals. Her mother's poor health caused Marjorie to go to Ebbw Vale each week to monitor her condition, usually staying one or two nights with her mother. This didn't affect my ability to carry on with my research but it was a constant worry for Marjorie.

I think I was looked upon with some curiosity by the support staff of the engineering department such as the workshop manager and the lab personnel. Apparently there had not been any research students in the department for as long as anyone could remember. My work was mainly concerned with the solution of various stress problems in elastic (e.g., steel) plates. What it really meant was research into the use of maths to solve these problems and I was therefore spared the necessity of doing complicated experiments with expensive apparatus, although some simple experiments were made to check aspects of my calculations. During this time my work was supervised by Professor Gurney and, of course, any published material

Our wedding, at the Blackwood Methodist Chapel on 28th August 1952.

would be checked by professional people who had an expert knowledge of the subject.

As an undergraduate I had spent a lot of time playing basketball: an effective way of keeping myself fit. But now I was married I felt it only fair to Marjorie to offer to give it up. She, however, felt this would be wrong and urged me to carry on as before, which I duly did. We agreed that when I was playing away at another university she would seize the opportunity to stay with her mother for a day or two. Some members of our team were doing research in other subjects and lived near us. We therefore had some social life when we were invited to their homes. One of them, Peter Coates, was married and his home was very close to us. We often went there and had enjoyable evenings watching game-shows such as *What's My Line?* on their television. We also went to the theatre quite often, particularly when a new play was being performed and we could get seats in the gods at a much reduced rate.

It was in the first year of our married life that I came to the conclusion Marjorie's health was rather fragile. This was a sudden development as for some years we had played tennis together but when we were in Belfast she had been ill with a chest infection which needed the attention of a doctor and several days in bed. At the time I did not take it as a bad omen as we all get ill from time to time but in Cardiff one day she complained of feeling hot and unwell. I immediately took her temperature and was horrified to find it was 103°F. I said nothing to worry Marjorie but contacted the doctor, who diagnosed erysipelas. I had no idea what this was but became very concerned when her hair started to fall out. As I had no family in Cardiff and knew no-one with experience of the complaint I was obliged to do what I could for her with the sympathetic help of the lady doctor. Marjorie was confined to bed for some time, so I was unable to go to the university—but I was in no mood to concentrate on my research in any case. Of course she did get better in the end and her hair grew again, but I could not help feeling grateful that I had not pursued my original idea of getting a job with the colonial service.

As my first year of research was coming to an end I had to concentrate on writing a thesis for my Master's degree. This was duly completed and expertly typed by Marjorie, who was a great help in suggesting a number of improvements in the layout of the work. It was, however, clear that I would have to think of what to do next because my grant was for one year only. My immediate thought was to begin looking for a job but Professor Gurney advised caution. He thought I should stay for a further two years to get a PhD and promised to look into the possibility of another grant from an unspecified source. My thesis for a Master's degree proved successful and I was now in a position to look for a job if that proved necessary. I did not have to wait long before Professor Gurney saw me again. He looked like someone bringing good news so I waited patiently for him to enlighten me. He informed me that I had been awarded a senior research scholarship (now fellowship) by the Royal Commission for the Exhibition of 1851, which had been initiated by Queen Victoria and Prince Albert. Apparently its description said *"not more than four of these scholarships are awarded annually within the British Empire (now Commonwealth) to students of exceptional promise and proven capacity for research in any branch of science."*

I was dumbfounded. I had no idea that such an award was available and certainly did not know that Professor Gurney had entered my name and submitted details of my research. I was, however, very pleased that he had put my name forward for the award and remain deeply grateful for all that he did for me. In the year 2000 a list of all winners of the award since 1922 was published. There

Cardiff Student's Royal Commission award

Mr. Raymond Hicks, a research student at the University College of South Wales and Monmouthshire, Cardiff, has been awarded a senior studentship by the Royal Commission for the Exhibition cf 1851. Not more than four of these are awarded annually within the British Commonwealth to students of exceptional promise and proved capacity for research in any branch of science.

Mr. Hicks graduated at Cardiff in 1952 with 1st class Honours in Civil Engineering, and he received the M.Sc degree in 1953. For the last two years he has been engaged in research into the design of structures under Professor C. Gurney, during whic period he has written a numb of important research papers.

The award will enable him continue his research for a furth two years.

Extract from a South Wales newspaper (1953): believed to be the "Western Mail."

were six winners in the seventy-eight years covered who were from Cardiff University: four in botany, one in biochemistry and myself in engineering. Strangely, the first winner in 1927 was a botanist named Phyllis Hicks. As far as I know no relation of mine.

With the unexpected receipt of the Royal Commission award I was now in a position to concentrate on my research with confidence. We would have sufficient income to see us through the next two years. Although we were by no means well off we had enough income to afford a short holiday. We decided that we would go to Torquay and, because we had no car, we went by train. The holiday did us both good and I came back to Cardiff fully prepared to do my best in my research studies. My programme was very much like my first year and I concentrated on the effect of reinforced holes in stressed plates. I should explain that this interest came about largely from experiences gained during the last war. Some American all-welded ships failed catastrophically owing to the concentration of stresses in certain areas. Those stresses produced cracks in the metal plates forming the hull of the ship, which then spread across large areas of the hull. In ships produced before the war the hull and decks were instead made by riveting individual plates together and this tended to prevent cracks running further than the ends of individual plates affected. But in all-welded ships there were no natural barriers to arrest a crack, which would run unchecked across the welded joints and result in catastrophic failure. Such failure was usually due to a brittle fracture in the metal. A similar problem occurred in commercial jet aircraft, such as the Comet, which flew at a high altitude and required their cabins to be pressurised. This resulted in the body of the cabins being highly stressed so that windows had to be designed to reduce stress concentrations and so minimise the chance of metal fatigue. The next two years were mainly taken up by my research and producing and preparing papers, each of which had to be typed by Marjorie.

In my final year I was joined by a Polish student who did research on the strength of furniture. We became quite friendly and, on days when Marjorie visited her mother, we usually went to the local cinema: noted for its films of well-known operas. I think these trips to the Globe in Cardiff fuelled my love of opera.

By the end of my final year I had completed all the work necessary for me to submit my PhD thesis. This meant there was an enormous amount of work to be checked and typed. There were also some articles to prepare for publication. Marjorie was kept continuously busy over this period and did a great deal of the editing of the text. The thesis in its entirety then had to be professionally bound: a job carried out by a firm recommended by some of my university friends. In due course I was told that my thesis had been accepted and I was now a PhD. Armed with this achievement I started looking for a job. My search was directed to companies where my research experience would be useful. My efforts to give occasional lectures

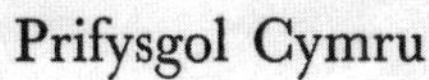

Prifysgol Cymru University of Wales

REPLIES SHOULD BE ADDRESSED TO THE REGISTRAR

Telephone 22656

UNIVERSITY REGISTRY
CATHAYS PARK
CARDIFF
CF1 3NS

THIS IS TO CERTIFY that Mr Raymond Hicks (30,679) was a full-time student of this University at the University College of South Wales and Monmouthshire.

Having attended approved courses of study and having satisfied the Examiners he was admitted on the 25th July 1952 to the degree of Bachelor of Science with First Class Honours in Civil Engineering.

In October 1953 Mr Hicks presented a work entitled:-"Reinforced holes in end loaded plates and concentrically reinforced laterally loaded circular plates", in candidature for the degree of Master of Science of the University.

The Examiners approved the work and Mr Hicks was admitted to the degree of Master of Science at a Degree Congregation held on the 17th December 1953.

In June 1955 Mr Hicks completed a scheme of study for the degree of Philosophiae Doctor of the University on the presentation of a work entitled:-"Reinforced holes in laterally loaded and end loaded plates".

The University approved the said work and Mr Hicks was admitted to the degree of Philosophiae Doctor at a Degree Congregation of the University held on the 19th July 1955.

Academic Secretary

21st April 1969

Notification of the author's success in obtaining his PhD.

to undergraduates convinced me that I would never be a success in that field; putting it briefly I lacked the talent and motivation to be a lecturer. In fact industry was in my blood—unsurprising in view of my earlier life in Ebbw Vale.

I had interviews with a number of companies but my preference was to work for Simon Carves, for whom I had worked as a student. Simon Carves and GEC (General Electric Company) were jointly responsible as a consortium for designing and building nuclear power-stations sponsored by the government. They were in competition with three other consortia chosen by the government. It seemed to me that nuclear power was a new industry with a great future and would need people with my knowledge to tackle the many new problems which were bound to arise during the design of the first power-station.

I was interviewed at Simon Carves and offered a job subject to my satisfying certain security conditions, as required of all staff. I was also seen by a panel of medical men, presumably to assure them of my mental stability. The upshot was that I was offered a job in the engineering department of the GEC-Simon Carves Atomic Energy Group. At this time the Group was in the throes of recruiting a team of highly qualified engineers, physicists and atomic energy scientists, all of whom were to be based at the Group's headquarters at Erith in Kent.

After due consideration and discussion with Marjorie I accepted the post on the basis that I would go immediately to Erith and start work while Marjorie would follow me as soon as I had found suitable accommodation.

At school I was considered to be a failure and a dropout: voted the pupil least likely to succeed in later life. But events had shown the prophets of gloom to be wrong. I believe I had at last given my parents, and especially my mother, all that they hoped for me. I had finally got the good "academic" education that they wanted me to have. I stress "academic" because I am sure that this is only a part of a well-rounded education: something which I think is only be achieved with a sound knowledge of life as a whole, and which can only be obtained from experience. The end result of all my studying more or less ensured that I should never experience the poverty and unemployment that had surrounded me as a boy.

Before leaving this section of my narrative I believe it's worth considering some of the factors which contributed to my academic success. Firstly, I was well motivated to succeed as my youth had shown me the soul-destroying effects of unemployment: something which I was determined to avoid at all costs. Secondly, my seven years of working in industry and at sea during the war had convinced me that to succeed in life I had to get an education. Thirdly, my desire to marry Marjorie gave me an incentive to do well and forge a career for myself. Probably the most inexplicable reason for my success is the uncanny way I always seemed to be lucky with the people I met and how events seemed to develop in my favour—as, for example, with Professor Gurney.

Professor Gurney was an acknowledged authority on the theory of elasticity (a branch of applied mathematics). Research in this area could be pursued without the need for complicated and expensive equipment: all that was needed was a fertile imagination and the tenacity to solve basic mathematical equations. Professor Gurney started his new job at Cardiff University at the same time as I started my first year of study. He brought with him from Cambridge Dr Ashwell as a lecturer in the subjects of research he had himself followed. I don't know why, but it soon became apparent that I had a passionate interest in the research work of these two men and I began developing my own modest fields of research. They were both very supportive and did a great deal to encourage me, particularly after I had graduated and embarked on the three-year programme of research for my higher degrees. On a number of occasions I accompanied them on visits to Cambridge University, where they were Fellows of Trinity College. While there I was a guest at their High Table. Everyone treated me very kindly but I was deeply aware that I was the product of the Welsh mining valleys and didn't fit in with the polished atmosphere of Cambridge college life. This was purely a personal shortcoming and in no way reflected on the people I met. Although by now I had a first-class technical education I realised I had to improve my performance as far as public speaking was concerned and I resolved to do so.

There is no doubt that Professor Gurney had a profound effect on my educational development and I was extremely lucky to have been tutored by him at such an important time in my life.

Photograph at the University College: the author can be seen at the extreme right of the front row.

Chapter 11

Nuclear Power

In September 1955 I left Marjorie at home with her mother, said goodbye to my parents and took the local steam train to Newport. From there I took the London express and then the suburban train to Dartford in Kent. This was the place where I was to make contact with the Simon Carves representative, who was staying in a private hotel. When I arrived there I was surprised to find other recruits to the company, and learned that we would all be accommodated there until we found more permanent quarters in a day or two. The lady who owned and ran the hotel was clearly well educated and at times would join us in conversation in the evening. One such discussion stands out; she had been putting forward her views on the possible outcome of developing nuclear power and her general feeling was that it was a scientific advance we could well do without. After some thought I offered a view that nuclear power could be a force for good or evil and that the development of television could also be turned to one or the other. In fact I felt that television was more likely to harm society, bearing in mind the trouble fomented by Hitler through the propaganda he spread via radio and films, and that it was a far more effective way of promoting undesirable views than radio ever was.

Our stay in the hotel lasted for only a couple of nights before we were transferred to the Royal Victoria and Bull Hotel in Dartford, where we joined a new group of colleagues who had been staying there for the past few weeks. The idea was that we should reside there temporarily while we looked for and bought houses so that our families could join us in our new life. Simon Carves offered a deal whereby the employee could choose a house up to a set value, the company would then buy it and rent it back to the employee. Some people preferred to buy their house but in my case there was no reason to do so, the necessary cash not being available for such an expensive investment.

The Bull Hotel was of great interest to all of us. It was a facsimile of a page from a Charles Dickens novel and is actually sometimes mentioned in his works. It was built around a rectangular courtyard, which was approached through an arch under the first floor at the front of the building. There was an open-air balcony around the courtyard used to access the bedrooms on the first floor. With the exercise of a little imagination it was possible to hear the clip-clop of horses' hooves as the stagecoach rattled into the courtyard after its journey from London. I could imagine Mr Pickwick as a passenger.

We registered at the Royal Victoria and Bull Hotel then reported to the Atomic Energy Division the next day. It was situated in the Fraser and Chalmers works at Erith which were actually a component company of GEC. Security was very tight. We all had to wear identification discs prominently displayed on our chests. My number was fifty-something: an indication of the number of employees recruited by this time. As the number would eventually soar into the hundreds it is clear that I had joined the company early in its evolution.

I should explain that the marriage between Simon Carves and GEC was brought about because of their complementary expertise. GEC was a very large and well respected company with wide experience in electric power generation. Simon Carves, on the other hand, was well known in the field of steam-generation plant. Both areas of expertise were necessary for the design of a nuclear power-station. People recruited by GEC were generally experts in their particular subject, such as electrical engineers and physicists. Simon Carves recruited people with expertise in heat transfer and like topics associated with steam-generation and civil engineering. My own expertise was very relevant to both companies. The managing director of the Atomic Energy Division was Bob Miller, a Cambridge graduate between 35 and 40 years old. I was assigned to the engineering office presided over by Keith Mitchell, who was about my own age. He started with GEC as an apprentice and had worked with them all his life. Although he was not university-educated he had an extremely extensive practical knowledge. He studied all new technology which he thought relevant to a problem in hand. Keith was about the only one in the design department who wasn't a BSc, MSc or PhD but we all had the greatest respect for him because he was an exceptional practical engineer. He became a great friend of mine and remained so until he died in his late fifties.

To assist me in my job I had a UMIST graduate called Stan Gregory. Stan was a mechanical engineer of the highest quality and I was very lucky to have him. He stayed with me for most of his career and is still a great friend whom I visit every year at his home near Aberdeen. There were about twelve of us in our office covering the design of the reactor containment vessel, the support for the reactor core and fuel-rods loading equipment. The people involved were mainly GEC personnel as this part of the project was GEC responsibility and the only exceptions were Stan Gregory and myself. I think this was because of my research experience at Cardiff which made me the ideal person to evaluate the stresses in the reactor pressure-vessel and its support. Later I would do similar work for Simon Carves when the steam-raising boilers were being designed.

Simon Carves had an office housing their civil engineers. They were responsible for the reinforced concrete containment shield, which was seven feet thick, and for other civil engineering projects on the site. They also had a team of engineers working on heat transfer problems which involved a great deal of testing to determine the heat transfer characteristics of certain components of the reactor and the steam-raising units.

Our first project was to design a nuclear power-station for a UK site as yet unspecified. We were to submit our proposed design and our quotation for commercial consideration. I was working particularly on the stress analysis for the design of the steel sphere which housed the reactor. This sphere was to be seventy feet in diameter and made of steel plates three inches thick. When it was completed it would be pressurised to 250 pounds per square inch and would hold the nuclear reactor core weighing about five thousand tons. My job was to analyse the stresses in the sphere and its support. This was a very difficult problem in applied mathematics and would not be easy to solve within the accuracy required to ensure stress concentrations were within acceptable limits. At this time we were not sure what effect irradiation would have on the welded steel joints and were guided in our assessments by the work done by the UK Atomic Energy Authority. I knew from incidents during the war that in cold weather welded ships sometimes failed disastrously owing to stress concentrations causing a brittle fracture at a welded joint. We also knew of incidents after the war of aircraft with pressurised cabins failing because of stress concentrations leading to metal fatigue. The one thing we didn't know was the effect of irradiation on welded joints. It was therefore imperative to get an accurate assessment of the stresses in the reactor pressure-vessel and keep them as low as possible.

With my prior knowledge of stress distributions in steel plates I felt fairly confident of the way to tackle the problem but I was sure it would require extra manpower to deal with the numerous calculations necessary. Stan was of great help to me but he was already engaged in work on other problems and could only devote part of his time to the pressure-vessel calculations. Although the design of the reactor and its containment vessel was essentially GEC's responsibility I assume I was chosen because of my relevant research and my receipt of the Royal Commission Research Award.

There was regular contact between the technical staff housed in the Bull Hotel. We were allocated a special dining-room where we could talk freely. We were all looking for houses. As the single men had no difficulty finding flats or digs they were not resident in the hotel but the rest of us talked mainly about the various properties appearing on the market. There is no doubt that the local estate agents had a very profitable time satisfying our needs. Most of us wanted houses within easy reach of the works as many did not have a car; although highly qualified most of us had not worked in industry after research and consequently were not well endowed with cash.

There was a steady flow of new recruits to the Atomic Energy Division and we always welcomed them with great interest as their expertise was of vital importance to us: our combined effort directed towards a single goal. One day we were joined by a new arrival. He was a Scot and highly qualified as a physicist, with a PhD in atomic physics. Interestingly, we all had the same impression of this fellow, feeling that he was behaving oddly and not in touch with the rest of the team. But we knew that he had been cleared by security, as we all were, and had passed the psychological tests so we accepted him accordingly. Then one day we were all surprised to see the headline in a London newspaper which read "Atomic scientist guilty of shoplifting," and even more astonished to learn that the culprit was none other than our new Scottish colleague. I think we all lost faith in the validity of the expert screening as a result. Our scientist did not appear again on the premises. I cannot recall any other examples of a misfit in the organisation.

As those of us living in the hotel saw a great deal of each other in the evenings and weekends we conspired to enjoy our leisure together. One member of our civil engineering department was the proud owner of a car and once a week a party of us would pile in it to go to Woolwich and take in a show at the famous Empire Theatre. I believe this was one of the last remaining theatres in the country to stage vaudeville shows. They were usually very entertaining and we were glad to be able to go there before the theatre was closed to vaudeville forever. Another time a group of us went to the West End and enjoyed a meal in a Chinese restaurant, something I had not experienced before. I was induced to try sweet and sour pork, and I liked it immensely. During my early days at the Bull Hotel in Dartford I was constantly looking for a house with a view to setting up home as soon as possible. I saw a few in Bexleyheath but they failed to meet the required standards of the firm, who would be the purchaser. Marjorie was in touch with me regularly about the situation as we both wanted to be together as soon as we could. Another problem I had on my mind was my status in the Institution of Civil Engineers. To become a chartered civil engineer one had to pass a written exam and do at least three years practical work on site. The latter was not a problem as I had worked on site for McAlpine, Gee, Walker and Slater and Simon Carves. The part I was not happy about was the exam. As I had just completed seven years in a university, emerging with a PhD among other things, another exam was the last thing I wanted. After I had wasted a good deal of time trying unsuccessfully to get an exemption I decided to bite the bullet and take the exam. I passed and was duly registered as a chartered civil engineer.

New specialists were recruited as the Atomic Energy Division evolved and our numbers increased significantly. Consequently we were split into different groups to form new departments, the buildings allocated to us were increased to accommodate the new staff and facilities provided for test work in areas such as heat transfer and metallurgy. My team expanded over the years in line with the demand: Ralph Bailey, a New Zealander, was recruited—he was a Cambridge PhD and an expert on computer programming (at the time computers were massive machines which had to be housed in special air-conditioned rooms); Michael Bayer, a South African with a Cambridge MSc also joined us as did Noel Murray, an Australian PhD from Sheffield University. Eventually there were also a dozen others, all with a BSc in their particular field. My group formed what was known as the Structural Development Department. We were given our own offices and I became Head of the department. These changes took place over a number of years as the nuclear power business increased.

In the Atomic Energy Division practically every department was headed by a PhD research graduate except for the civil and mechanical engineering departments. These PhD graduates were specialists in certain fields such as atomic physics, metallurgy, heat transfer, stress analysis and so on. As there were four consortia set up to design and compete commercially for nuclear power-station contracts the drain on technical specialists must have been enormous. At this time the government predicted a steady growth in the use of nuclear power and the industry was working on the assumption that one such station would be required every year for the foreseeable future. The inference drawn was that each consortium could expect to get a new contract every four years and would also be eligible for overseas contracts. These predictions heralded the dawn of a bright future for the industry and its employees. In the event, however, they were far too optimistic and the industry would soon be struggling for its life and its specialists seeking alternative employment.

One day I received a message from Marjorie saying she was unwell and wanted to see me. I had no idea what her illness was but, assuming it was something quite serious, I asked the Simon Carves manager for some leave to visit her. He was very sympathetic and advised me to go at once and not worry about my work. I took the first train I could get to South Wales and reached Marjorie's home. It was obvious she was ill and on the verge of a nervous breakdown. She insisted I took her to Kent even if it meant living in an hotel. To pacify her I agreed to take her the next day, which I did. Such was her haste we did not even go to see my parents half a mile away. The trip to London was a nightmare; she was so ill I took her into an empty first-class compartment so she could lie down. When the conductor came round he told me not to worry about the excess fare. He was so kind. When we reached London I realised that I needed help so I phoned Marjorie's brother Howard, who lived in Wandsworth, and told him of our plight. He immediately told me to bring her to his home where he and Marian, his wife, would look after her for the time being. It was an offer of help that I desperately needed and I will be grateful to them for the rest of my life.

Howard and Marian were true to their word and they got their doctor to take Marjorie as a patient. She was a very good doctor and a specialist in psychiatry and it wasn't long before I could detect an improvement in Marjorie's health, although it would be a long time before she was completely better. I made it a practice to visit her once a week even though, lacking a car, I had a difficult rail journey. In the meantime I was busy with my work and getting on reasonably well with my analysis of stresses in the reactor pressure-vessel and its support. I realised it was only a matter of time before the analysis was complete. My objective was to find a general solution to the problem and get the work published. To do that I needed the approval of GEC and Simon Carves, who might feel the need for secrecy on commercial grounds. My view was that if the work were published it would have the benefit of checks by many competent people in the field of analysis, including those in our rival consortia, and I was sure they would sound an alarm if I had made any fundamental errors.

I was still looking for a house and had examined quite a number before eventually finding a suitable one on Long Lane in Bexleyheath. It was viewed by the Simon Carves general manager at Erith, who deemed it suitable for the company to purchase. This they did and then asked me to accept it on a rental basis. By now Marjorie had made sufficient progress to come and look at the house, which she did. We immediately agreed to take the tenancy and, although Marjorie was still living with her brother, we were sure that when the formalities had been completed she would be fit enough to join me. When she did in fact do so the house was in my possession and we were faced with the task of furnishing it. Our savings did not amount to a great deal and we had both been brought up on the belief that one should never go into debt. This meant that we only bought things that were absolutely necessary. One item above all, however, was proving to be essential: a car. I had no problem getting to work by bus or getting a lift in someone's car but a difficulty was looming which would make having my own car a necessity. Marjorie had been told it was imperative she should attend regular group therapy sessions to enable her total recovery, and arrangements had been made for her to go to a London clinic once a week for the foreseeable future. It was clear that I would have to take her, and for this I needed a car. The upshot was that I bought a second-hand Ford

Popular for £295. We then began weekly evening trips to London that were to continue for many months.

In the design office more time was spent on the design of the steel grillage to support the reactor proper. It was to be of plate-girder construction supported on a short steel cylinder inside the pressure-vessel housing the reactor. This supporting cylinder would be of the same diameter as that supporting the reactor. In general it was approached by similar methods to those used in plate-girder bridge design but with the difference that it had members going in two directions intersecting at right angles. Because we were designing to minimise stress concentrations we had to find a way to ensure the load transmitted to the support cylinder was equally distributed around it. I was strongly aided in this work by Stan and through the good offices of two Cambridge structural experts. It should be recognised that throughout the design of the nuclear power-station the work of the various departments was closely monitored in one way or another by experts representing the Atomic Energy Authority and governmental safety bodies. Furthermore, when we won the contract to build the station in Hunterston, Scotland, we had endless discussions with experts acting on behalf of the customer. There were also numerous codes of practice which had to be considered. The one for pressurised vessels was BSI 1500 and the Committee responsible for its implementation was made up of representatives from various organisations involved in the design and use of pressure-vessels. I was myself a member, representing the GEC/Simon Carves Atomic Energy Group.

After completing the stress analysis the company game me permission to publish my findings in a reputable British journal. I chose the Institution of Mechanical Engineers and, after a lot of work preparing the article for publication, I sent it to the IME in February 1957. It was published in 1958 *(Vol.172 No.31)*. Subsequently I received a number of technical letters from people interested in the problem. These were of great interest to me and I was especially pleased that no-one had any fault to find with my analysis! The company's consent to publication of the article was part and parcel of its policy with regard to employees' research. I was also free to publish other research done at the university which had not hitherto been made public and which included the following papers:

- 1957 *Journal of the Royal Aeronautical Society*
- 1958 *Institution of Mechanical Engineers*
- 1958 *Journal of the Royal Aeronautical Society*
- 1959 *Journal of the Royal Aeronautical Society*
- 1959 *Journal of the Royal Aeronautical Society*
- 1959 *Institution of Mechanical Engineers*
- 1960 *Journal of Mechanical Engineering Science*
- 1960 *Journal of Mechanical Engineering Science*

The last two papers were written jointly with Dr Ralph Bailey. The basic mathematical research to find a solution was done by myself and the ensuing computations done by Ralph using a state-of-the-art computer. As well as the above I also published a number of other papers in lesser outlets and, as co-author with Ralph Bailey, wrote a number of chapters for books.

As Marjorie's health improved our social life expanded. We regularly played bridge with Scottish friends Anne and Hamish Sims. At weekends we went rock-climbing with Stan and Doreen Gregory and Noel and Sheila Murray. The venue was Harrison's Rocks in Tunbridge Wells. I should say that the climbing was done by the men only. Noel (Dr Murray) was, as I have said, an Australian and eventually returned home to become Professor of Engineering at Melbourne University. He was a very talented rock-climber and did a number of difficult climbs when he returned to Australia.

One summer Marjorie and I went for a holiday to Sennen Cove in Cornwall. This made a welcome change for both of us, although we were amazed how far it was from Bexleyheath. More than 300 miles in my old Ford Popular was more a trial of endurance than a holiday and in those days the roads were very slow indeed. Probably a year later we toured Scotland in the same car: an even longer trip as we went as far as Glencoe, Ben Nevis and Loch Ness. The whole tour of the Highlands was greatly enjoyable and made a lasting impression on both of us.

At work my big challenge was to evaluate the stresses in the perforated plate that covered the top of the grillage and contributed significantly to its strength. The perforations were needed to allow spent fuel-rods to be ejected from the reactor core. As I explained previously, the grillage was a large plate-girder bridge used to support the reactor. Its uniqueness lay in it being circular in plan and supported around its boundary. After a great deal of mathematical analysis I finally found a general solution to the problem.

By now Ralph was on my staff and able to program my solution to get numerical values for specific cases. My team of specialists had also grown significantly and we now had facilities for testing my research. Ralph Bailey did a lot of work on testing my theoretical predictions by using a strain-gauge analysis and in due course we published a joint paper of our results in the *Journal of Mechanical Engineering Science*. By now we had been awarded a contract to build the nuclear power-station at Hunterston and work on site quickly began. I had virtually nothing to do with it except when design changes were made on the junction of the reactor sphere and its supporting skirt. I then had to evaluate the new stress concentrations. There was still work to be done by my team of stress analysts on the Simon Carves heat-exchangers. This was relatively routine work and was in no way comparable to the problems associated with the reactor sphere.

My most important responsibilities for 1957 were directed to the problems of a possible design for a nuclear power-station in Japan. We had been informed that Japan planned to build a station in Tokia-Mura as part of a network for the Tokyo-Yokohama area of Honshu. It was to be operated by members of JAPC (Japan Atomic Power Company). An enquiry for a simple (i.e., single) reactor station of the Calder Hall type was issued in February 1958, with tenders to be submitted the following July. Possibly the most interesting feature of the power-station was that it had to be designed to resist an earthquake. Initially the Japanese sent a delegation to visit the four groups in the UK who would be competing for the brief. In due course we met the delegation and got to know the individual members with whom we would be working if we were appointed. Our next step was to send a delegation to Japan in September 1958 to convince them of our ability to meet their requirements. The delegation consisted of: Lord Lindley, Chairman of GEC; Mr Leo Brooke, Director of Simon Carves; Mr R Miller, MD of GEC/Carves Atomic Energy Group; and a supporting technical staff, including me. My inclusion was doubtless down to the fact that the station had to be earthquake-proof, at least insofar as it came up to the design criteria supplied by the Japanese.

Our party arrived at Heathrow Airport to begin our journey to Japan. We were clearly expected as we were met by a senior official who led us to a special lounge set aside for our delegation. We settled into our comfortable chairs and waited for an announcement calling us to our flight. However the first announcement over the loudspeaker called for Dr Hicks to report to the information desk. This came as a great surprise to me and, I suspect, to my companions. I made my way to the desk and was astounded to see an immaculately dressed official, resplendent in a gold-braided uniform, waiting for me. It was none other than my cousin Leslie, born in the same house as I was but three months later. We were like brothers. It transpired that he was responsible for the wellbeing of customers and had singled me out for special treatment. Before I realised what was happening he escorted me to an airport car and drove me out to our plane, which was standing in the parking bay completely empty apart from the crew. I therefore found myself alone in my plane waiting for the other passengers. In the meantime the other members of my party were getting concerned about my absence, particularly when they were escorted to the plane as VIPs. They all expected to board an empty plane but instead found it already occupied by a very junior member of their own party. It took me some time to explain my presence there!

We travelled to Tokyo on a flight from Copenhagen lasting twenty-eight hours, with an hour on the ground for refuelling in Alaska. The plane was a SAS DC7C propeller aircraft and our route was over the North Pole. SAS (Scandinavian Airway System) were proud of the fact that they were the first airline to exploit this route and later we were all given a certificate to commemorate our journey.

An interesting thing occurred while we were in flight and which I remember with a smile. Our delegation was travelling first-class and as a result we were furnished with bunks to ensure we had a good night's sleep. As usual, I fell asleep almost immediately but was violently shaken in the night by a stewardess who wanted to inform me that we were "now directly over the North Pole." With great difficulty in keeping my eyes open I peered through the cabin window adjacent to my bunk but failed to see any sign of land, let alone the North Pole. I was not amused and turned over and went to sleep again. On arrival we were all very tired after being in the air so long and were very happy to be safely on the ground again.

Our stay in Japan was a mixture of work and pleasure. We were housed in Tokyo's finest and newest hotel and were regally entertained and escorted on a number of sightseeing tours. We were told that the Imperial Hotel was built to withstand earthquakes. They were understandably obsessed with the need to make their buildings earthquake-proof. To illustrate their point they showed us the effects of the great earthquake of 1923, which devastated Tokyo with a loss of more than 100,000 lives. From their visit to the UK their personnel knew that I was the person who would be mainly responsible for the earthquake-proof design and structural analysis of the proposed station. So I was often singled out with Keith Mitchell (our chief mechanical engineer) to have meetings with their earthquake specialist engineers and university academics whose interest was in that field. One

Geisha party during Typhoon No 22, Japan.

memorable visit was to an earthquake research building where we witnessed a demonstration of the effect of an earthquake on a tall structure. The result was devastating and convinced Keith and myself that we would be taxed in the extreme when we came to the detailed design of the proposed power-station for Japan.

On 26th September 1958 we were invited by the Japanese to join them at a geisha party they were holding at Suiho-En Tokyo. I had become very friendly with the Japanese interpreter, Mr Otsuki, who was also a civil engineer. He told me that the programme would not embarrass us in any way. It consisted of innocent games, dancing and musical entertainment from the girls. We were all paired off with our own geisha, whose job was to attend to all our needs (not sexual!) and partner us in the games that were to follow. All the girls were dressed in traditional Japanese kimonos and had lavish hairstyles. The party began with an invitation for our group to sit down at a table which spanned the whole room and was beautifully laid out for a feast. Unfortunately it was only about ten inches high and we were clearly expected to sit on the floor, although we were allowed to sit on cushions specially provided for the guests. We were served during the meal by the geishas, who knelt beside each of us to ensure we were properly wined and dined. After a magnificent meal we were told we would now play some games. This was accepted by our group with some misgivings, since we had no idea what to expect. We needn't have worried as most of the games would have gone down well in a UK primary school. It was amazing to see the Japanese top executives and our own top brass joining in these games with glee. One game consisted of placing a cushion on the floor and standing back-to-back with your geisha, with your respective heels on the cushion. Other geishas would then start playing their stringed instruments while the two protagonists rotated their bottoms without touching each other. The

Geisha dancers during Typhoon No 22, Japan.

object of the game was to lash out with your behind when the music stopped and dislodge your partner from the cushion. Since I was six feet tall and weighed fourteen stones and the geishas were all short and petite I had no difficulty in becoming the Japanese bumps-a-daisy champion! During the party the rain we were experiencing became extremely heavy and the wind increased to gale force. Apparently we were enjoying Typhoon No. 22 for 1958 and we were therefore forced to stay at the geisha party until the early hours of the next day. The typhoon was responsible for the death of many people and was reported in the British press. Unfortunately my wife read about it and became very worried. She contacted the newspapers for more details, concerned for my safety. I was not very popular when I finally got home and she heard about the geisha party!

The author playing the "Cushion Game."

Before we came home we were treated to a grand tour of the country around Tokyo. We visited Lake Hakone and stayed in the hotel facing Fujiyama over the lake. We also went to Kamakura and saw the Great Buddha. One of my highlights was a visit to the top of Tokyo Tower, which is higher than the Eiffel Tower in Paris. I was escorted by Professor Naito, the designer of the tower, who took me to a level higher than that allowed to the general public. Professor Naito was one of the academics whom I saw on each occasion I subsequently visited Japan. During my stays at the Imperial in Tokyo two incidents occurred which gave me an insight into the Japanese character. They were intensely proud of their hotel and the service they gave to their guests. Each evening a smiling Japanese girl would call at my room to ask me what I would like for breakfast; for several evenings I told her I would like bacon and egg but she would always deliver bacon and two eggs. After a great deal of effort on my part I finally reached the stage where I thought she understood my request and she left my room bowing gracefully and smiling. Next morning she appeared at my door bowing and smiling and obviously pleased to have obliged me at last. To my amazement she placed before me a plate of bacon—with a double-yolked egg. I immediately had visions of the hotel kitchen being awash with discarded single-yolk eggs!

The other incident occurred about ten years later on a trip to Tokyo with Stan Gregory for Winget Refrigeration. It involved the maid who cleaned my room each day while I was away at work. I had bought a present for Susan, my daughter: a toy gorilla which I was sure she would like. I had left the gorilla carelessly on the dressing-table but when I came back he had been carefully put in a sitting position with one of his hands holding a cigarette in his mouth. I had a good laugh and was pleased to see once again an illustration of the Japanese sense of fun so nicely displayed at the geisha games ten years earlier.

In general the Japanese people I met were all friendly, with the exception of one youth who clearly resented the fact they had lost the war. He was the son of one of our hosts. I myself had helped to bring home from Singapore British troops who had been POWs in Japanese camps and it was difficult to believe the camps had been run by the same people I now knew.

At last we got back to the UK and settled down to serious work on the Japanese project. Our overall task was to design a nuclear power-station to satisfy the Japanese requirements, the most important being earthquake resistance. The two people most involved were Keith Mitchell and myself, for reasons already covered. I now had a very good team working for me and adequate facilities to test various assumptions. The problems thrown up by the unique design requirements were many and varied. The core of the reactor had to be dropped to minimise the effect of horizontal forces arising from an earthquake. For the same reason the core of graphite blocks was based on a hexagonal lattice instead of the normal square pattern. The vertical loading on the reactor support was increased by a factor specified by a Japanese code of practice for buildings at risk of earthquake. Similarly a horizontal load was assumed to be in place during an earthquake. In general all parts of the plant were designed so their relative displacements during an earthquake did not interfere with operation of normal control devices, which were themselves designed to maximise safety. It was appreciated that the additional loads imposed on a structure could not be predicted accurately; the dynamic behaviour of any particular structure depended on such intractable factors as the inherent degree of damping, foundation conditions and so on. We also had to consider vibrational effects on ducting and structural parts, such as bridges carrying vulnerable components. The stress concentrations in the reactor support had to be deduced for earthquake effects and for the Simon Carves heat-exchangers—and so it went on. Over the next two years Keith and I were frequent visitors to Tokyo, mainly because of the need to deal with mechanical and structural problems. We always found ourselves surrounded by ten or more engineers and academics who carefully noted everything we said. They seemed to believe everything we proposed could be substantiated by mathematical analysis, which in some cases was impossible.

I had now been with the GEC/Simon Carves Atomic Energy Group for about five years. In that time we had obtained one contract in the UK for a nuclear power-station. According to the government we should get a new contract every four years but this seemed unlikely given the way the industry was developing. The initial euphoria surrounding nuclear power-stations was now gone and we were starting to think we would run out of work in the design offices at Erith. Of course we did have the contract for Tokia-Mura but there were no signs we would obtain other contracts abroad. Being very much a realist I decided to look around for a job elsewhere. It was evident to me that if the atomic energy industry failed to expand as initially predicted a lot of highly qualified engineers and scientists would be looking for jobs. I convinced myself that it was better to get a new job as soon as possible before others had the same idea. After I had told the company of my decision to leave as soon as I had a new post I was told by management that my place would be taken by Ralph. I thought that this was a good choice and said so. They then asked me if I would do one thing before I went. They wanted to know if I would make one more trip to Japan. They felt it would be a good idea for me to introduce Ralph to relevant engineers and management. I was delighted to do this as Ralph had been a faithful colleague and I was pleased to be of assistance.

We arrived in Japan and I duly did all I was asked to do but before I left I was asked if they could do something for myself and for Ralph. As a token of their appreciation of my work for them, and the development of our friendship, they wanted us to take a short holiday in a typical small seaside resort. The intention was to give us an idea how people lived in small towns and villages remote from Tokyo. We were told we would not be accompanied and the people in the resort would not be able to converse with us in English. They did assure us, however, that with the instructions they gave us we would manage comfortably. Ralph and I thought it was a splendid idea and an adventure not to be missed. So we were escorted to Tokyo Railway Station and put on a train to our destination. We were given detailed instructions about the resort and the hotel where we were to stay. We finally arrived at the station stop and were very impressed with the view of the sea and beach, which were just a short walk from the station. We took a taxi to the hotel and it was clear the receptionist was expecting us. We were shown to a large spotless room and introduced to the girl who would see to all our needs—neither of us could imagine what these might be. The room was completely bare except for a television placed on the floor in one corner. Our friends in Tokyo had failed to tell us we were going to a hot spring resort where it was the custom of residents bathe in one of the springs. We had seen a spring outside the room and before dinner we were approached by our lady attendant and friend, who made it clear with signs that we were expected to take a bath. Normally we would have accepted this as good advice but we had not expected the ladies to undress and bathe us, which apparently was the custom in Japan. Ralph was very shy and I had already been in trouble with Marjorie as a result of the geisha party some time earlier. So we bravely resisted the attentions of the ladies and bathed ourselves. At dinner-time our young lady laid out a small primus stove on the floor and proceeded to cook some thin slices of beef, which proved to be delicious. Ralph and I sat on the floor with our legs crossed in the traditional Japanese way. We both found this posture very uncomfortable and after a while quite painful. Our young lady saw the problem and got some cushions to ease our pains. We dined off a little table about ten inches high. After she had cleared the table and made everything neat and tidy she opened a cupboard door and extracted two mattresses which she unrolled on the floor: one for me and one for Ralph. She then disappeared for the night, walking backwards and bowing herself out of our room, all the time wishing us a good night's sleep in Japanese. She reappeared in the morning, once again bowing and talking sweetly in Japanese. She was constantly smiling and Ralph and I concluded she was saying something quite nice.

One other thing worth mentioning was that we were both provided with distinctive kimonos by the hotel. We were expected to wear them at all times: indoors and out. Apparently it was the custom of hotels in the resort to issue their customers with these kimonos, the design of which was unique to a particular hotel and thus afforded them free publicity.

There was one other problem on my mind at this time. Marjorie was now free of any medical problems and we were both very anxious to have children. Although we had been trying for some considerable time nothing happened and we decided to seek medical advice. We saw our own doctor who was very knowledgeable about our case and after some investigations found that Marjorie had some internal problem which could be rectified by a simple operation. I am a complete ignoramus on medical matters so I do not know exactly what the problem was; Marjorie, however, was unconcerned and agreed to have the recommended operation. This was carried out successfully and Marjorie and I worked on the assumption that sooner or later she would become pregnant.

I now began to look seriously for a new job and found that my preference was for a post as Development Manager with Head Wrightson and Company,

The author (right) in traditional kimono, Japan.

who were located in Thornaby-on-Tees. We were a little worried about the prospect of leaving Kent to work on Teesside, which was very much an area of heavy industry. The company had a broad range of subsidiary companies and this appealed to me as I would be involved with all of them. The end result was that I took the job and was scheduled to join Head Wrightson as soon as my link with Simon Carves was severed.

I was reluctant to leave a team of men who had served me loyally but it was gratifying to learn that they all did well in the future:

Stan (Gregory)
soon after I left the Atomic Energy Group he joined me at Head Wrightson and stayed with me for most of his future career

Noel (Murray)
returned to Australia and became Professor of Engineering at Melbourne University

Michael (Bayer)
returned to South Africa

Keith (Mitchell)
got involved in consultancy work for a company in which he was a shareholder. Ultimately he came to work for me

Most of the other members of my department went into academic jobs.

Ralph (Bailey)
did well in taking over my job. He conducted pressure tests on the Hunterston reactor vessel and confirmed stress concentrations predicted by my published analysis.

Regrettably some four or five years later Ralph was killed when an aircraft he was on crashed into Mount Fujiyama. He was on his way to visit the Tokia-Mura power-station after taking on my job. I often wonder if the plane crashed as a result of metal fatigue in the fuselage at a point of high stress concentration. Both Ralph and I did research on this kind of problem and it would be ironic if this was the cause of the crash. Some time before he died Ralph contacted me to let me know that the reactor pressure-vessel had been successfully constructed at Hunterston. It had been fully pressurised in accordance with the design requirements and he had been responsible for a full survey of the predicted stress concentrations. The tests were witnessed by various representatives of the customer. He was pleased to tell me that they were in line with my predictions. It was good to know that all the hard work done in my research years had proved to be correct and useful when applied to the design of the nuclear reactor vessel.

The Japanese power-station did not succumb to any earthquake effects, which is most reassuring, but I cannot actually say whether it was subjected to any significant earthquakes in any case. I assume that by now it has been decommissioned. This is a great relief to me, as I would certainly have been called to account if any disaster had occurred.

One highly significant event occurred during my visits to Japan. My Japanese friends knew of my passion for model railways and one day I was taken on a visit to a jeweller's shop in Tokyo. To my surprise the company concerned had expanded their business by making models of American railway engines, no doubt with an eye to selling them in the USA. They marketed these locomotives under the name "Tenshodo," which is now known the world over by model railway enthusiasts for its excellent quality and for the fact that its engines are handmade in brass. As a result of subsequent visits to Japan I have managed to make a collection of these models which forms the basis of the extensive model railway I now have. The first locomotive I bought forty-five years ago is still working perfectly today.

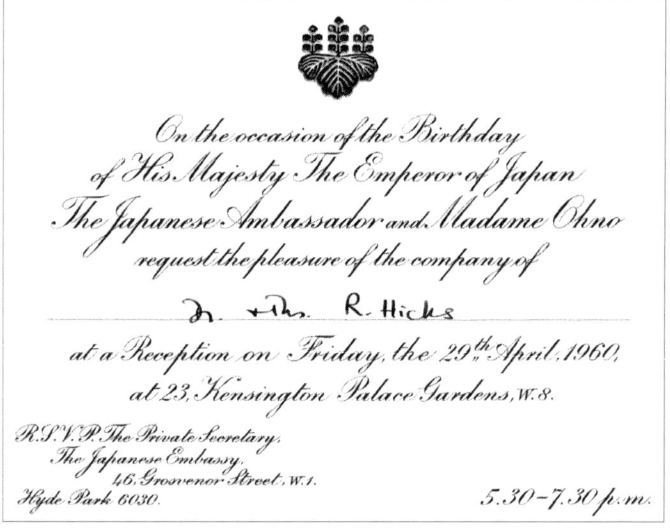

On the occasion of the Birthday
of His Majesty The Emperor of Japan
The Japanese Ambassador and Madame Ohno
request the pleasure of the company of

Dr. & Mrs. R. Hicks

at a Reception on Friday, the 29th April, 1960,
at 23, Kensington Palace Gardens, W.8.

R.S.V.P. The Private Secretary,
The Japanese Embassy,
46, Grosvenor Street, W.1.
Hyde Park 6030.

5.30–7.30 p.m.

Invitation to a reception at the Japanese Embassy in London, in celebration of the Emperor of Japan's birthday.

Chapter 12

Head Wrightson

Because our house in Kent belonged to my old company, Simon Carves, the move to Teesside would entail us buying a house for the first time. My new employer was prepared to make a furnished house available for up to six months, so our own furniture had to go into store. We bade goodbye to Bexleyheath and set out for Stockton-on-Tees, where the company house was located. The journey was about 270 miles so we decided to drive carefully and stay overnight somewhere. By this time we had acquired a dog—a West Highland terrier called Robin—and he, of course, came with us. We arrived on Teesside the next day and immediately went to our new house: a traditional semi-detached, very common at that time. It was built sometime after the First World War and was within a hundred yards of Ropner Park.

Before we left Kent we saw our immediate neighbours, who apparently went to the North-East every year to visit friends. They were very impressed by the friendly nature of people in the area and said that two of their friends would call in to see us when we arrived. We had been in the house for only a few hours when we were suddenly surprised to find the two aforementioned folk arrive at the door. We invited them in and sat them on a settee directly in front of the fireplace. They were, indeed, very nice people and we soon became great friends. We immediately tried to make them comfortable and get them some light refreshment. Seeing that the fire was all set up ready to be lit, we struck a match and applied it to the paper, sticks and coal, after which we explained that it might take a little while for us to provide tea as we were unfamiliar with the house, and vanished to the kitchen. Half an hour later we emerged to join our guests in the living-room. I carried the tray and Marjorie and the dog accompanied me. When we opened the living-room door we were met by a wall of smoke, which filled the whole room and enveloped our new friends, who were sitting valiantly in front of a fireplace belching smoke trying to pretend nothing unusual was happening. Marjorie and I were very embarrassed but we were soon all laughing at the absurdity of the situation. A blocked chimney was the root of the trouble.

This was my introduction to our stay in Stockton: a period destined to bear very good and very bad news.

Head Wrightson was a well-known Teesside company which was comprised of a number of subsidiary companies servicing specific industries including coal, steel, nuclear power, chemical and heavy machinery. These companies all had their works and offices in the Teesside area in places such as Thornaby, Middlesbrough, Stockton and Yarm. Their Head Office and centralised research and development facilities were located on a large site at Thornaby. On this site they had their substantial heavy fabrication works, known as Teesdale Engineering.

I reported to Dr Young, who was a metallurgist, and my research colleague was Dr Rounthwaite, who specialised in heat transfer. Dr Young reported to the Main Board of the company, which was chaired by Sir John Wrightson and included Mr Peter Wrightson. It was obviously a family concern run by very competent gentlemen. In the nuclear power field they competed with Simon Carves and this no doubt was a factor in my appointment as Development Manager. It soon became clear to me that one of their most pressing problems was to develop and find an outlet for their very large fabrication facilities at Thornaby.

With me in the development department was Dr Lawson, who was primarily a mechanical engineer, together with a number of university graduates. I was also responsible for the drawing office. One of my engineers, John Pictor, was an experienced mechanical engineer with practical experience. Our first objective was to consider the future requirements of the subsidiary companies. In furtherance of this I had discussions with the management of the individual companies to agree with them the areas where we could develop equipment and machinery which they could exploit in due course. The most urgent need was to develop new outlets for the Thornaby works. After a great deal of thought and research it was concluded that such a development could be found in the field of composting domestic rubbish and sewage. After many visits to rubbish disposal sites and sewage works, John Pictor and I decided that we should concentrate on a system for composting domestic rubbish. John was the prime mover in the research and did a great deal to show that such a project was feasible. We were given permission by Mr Lake (the Board member responsible for research and development) to examine various schemes for such a development.

About the time all this activity was going on I received some wonderful news. Marjorie suspected she was pregnant, a suspicion which was confirmed after a visit to our doctor. This was indeed fantastic and we immediately began to consider whether the baby was going to be a girl or a boy. In the end, of course, we decided it did not matter: all we wanted was a healthy child. This prompted us to take action to buy a house of our own and we increased our efforts to find something suitable. The company house we were in was badly in need of renovation, or perhaps resuscitation would be a more appropriate word. One day I heard Marjorie releasing the water in the kitchen sink. I was outside and noticed no water was flowing to the appropriate drain. On further inspection I concluded that the water was finding its way into the gap in the cavity wall!

We had by now started to explore the countryside near Stockton and found the North Yorkshire moors irresistible. In many ways they reminded me of South Wales. The coastline was beautiful and exciting, particularly in places like Robin Hood's Bay and Whitby. Stockton was interesting and had a certain Yorkshire charm, with its large cobbled street in the centre where the market was held.

At work our plans for a domestic composting plant were going ahead. The basis of the plant was a large rotating drum about thirty feet long with an eight-foot diameter. This was to be a test plant and was considerably smaller than a full-size commercial plant. The actual composting was done in the drum through the constant rotation and mixing of the organic material contained in the domestic rubbish. Ancillary equipment also had to be designed to sort out the refuse before it was put in the drum. For example, undesirable materials such as tin cans could be taken out by magnets placed over the rubbish as it was fed to the main drum via a conveyor belt. The drum itself was an ideal piece of equipment to be fabricated in the Teesdale heavy fabrication plant.

After a good deal of effort by John Pictor and members of the drawing office a proposed design was completed, costed and finally submitted for approval to the Board. Consent was duly given and work started on the pilot plant to our great delight. A site was selected on one of the town's refuse-tips and within a few short months the pilot plant was installed and ready to start its test programme.

Our search for a house was successful and we moved into a new semi-detached property at 2 Tunstall Road on the outskirts of Stockton. The garden was a complete mess, which is usually the case with new houses, and I resolved to get it done as soon as time permitted. We had not been in our new home for more than a few weeks when Marjorie came home from a visit to our doctor. She was in a dreadful state, sobbing uncontrollably, and could not speak. I was very alarmed and naturally assumed she had been given some bad news about the pregnancy, but this was not the case. She had been diagnosed as having a diseased kidney which would at some point have to be removed. This was devastating news, particularly as we had waited nine years for a baby, but Marjorie soon recovered her composure and, remarkably, seemed reassured about the baby. The doctor thought the kidney problem would not affect it at all and Marjorie was assured that the loss of a kidney would not affect her life expectancy, as it was perfectly possible to live normally with only one functioning kidney. It seemed that she had TB of the kidney and she was put on a regular diet of pills and antibiotics (possibly M and B tablets, I'm not sure). To me they looked massive enough to cure a horse. The only thing we could now do was to wait for the birth of our first child and pray it would be healthy and perfectly formed. We discussed the forthcoming birth of the baby and felt we could manage without family or other help apart from when Marjorie was in hospital for the kidney operation and when convalescing at home. Our plan was to ask my mother if she could come to Stockton to help us when the baby was born and Marjorie was in hospital. It was a lot to ask, as my mother was about 55 at the time and had my father to look after. Furthermore the car ride to Stockton from Ebbw Vale would be arduous, to say the least. As expected, however, Ma promptly consented to come and Dad was quite happy to look after himself in an emergency. He was very good at keeping the house shipshape and Bristol-fashion but I have no doubt his cooking would have been rather restricted.

I carried on working as usual, although I obviously had a lot on my mind. The composting plant development programme was proceeding under the competent hand of John Pictor. Ken (Dr Lawson) was working on an idea of conveying steel strip on a cushion of air instead of normal rollers. The application would be in a strip-mill in a steelworks, a scenario I remember well from my young days as a steelworker.

As well as overseeing these projects, I was making tentative research into the design of a mini steelworks. A normal integrated steelworks has to operate on a very high tonnage output in order to be commercially viable. I felt that with new ideas for plant and machinery a steelworks could be designed to be commercially successful even if its annual output were relatively low. These were early days and it would take me a year or so to reach any positive conclusions. By now my drawing office was fully engaged in producing the required plans for our developments. I should add that during my first year and subsequently Peter (Dr Young) did a first-class job in getting the Board to support us in our development work.

One day in June Marjorie told me the baby was on its way. She had everything planned for the great event and her little case was packed ready for transport to the hospital in Middlesbrough where the birth was to take place. As soon as she was safely settled in the hospital I was dismissed. Those were the days when fathers were not admitted to see the birth, so I went home and began the long wait for news. Ultimately I had a call to say I was the father of a fine healthy boy. My immediate reaction was one of relief that the child was safely born. I was so proud and pleased to be a father. Later that day I was allowed to visit Marjorie and our son. We decided to call him Michael Anthony and within a matter of days Marjorie and my little son were home in Stockton. I was relieved to hear that the doctor had seen Marjorie in hospital and assured her that Michael was quite healthy in spite of the fact that his mother had a TB kidney. It was now clear that our next problem would occur when Marjorie had her kidney removed. We realised that this was urgent and would have to be done as quickly as possible. A date was given for the operation and I arranged to go to Ebbw Vale to pick up my mother and bring her back to Stockton by car, as a long cross-country rail journey would have been too much for her on her own. The trip to Ebbw Vale was long and tiring but I was determined to get back to Marjorie as soon as possible, so we started back the next day and after a very long drive arrived back home. My mother was delighted to meet Michael and was proud to think she would be looking after him while Marjorie was in hospital.

Marjorie was duly admitted to Sedgefield hospital where her kidney was successfully removed. We were assured by the surgeon that she would manage quite well with her remaining kidney, an assurance which was fully vindicated. After a few weeks in and out of hospital Marjorie recovered enough to look after Michael. Once again I did the round journey to Ebbw Vale to take my mother home. Marjorie and I were very grateful to her for coming to our rescue at this time of great need. She was to do so on several other occasions in the future.

During the next year we settled down to a normal married life. I joined the Stockton Male-Voice Choir and Marjorie joined a local ladies' choir. We were able to be with Michael at all times as our respective choir evenings were on different days.

About a year after our move to Stockton I was joined at Head Wrightson by my old friend Stan Gregory. He moved into the company house we had initially occupied. Doreen, his wife, came too, of course and so did his little son Steven, who must have been about three years old. Stan was a good help to me in the development department and got involved with our mechanical engineering problems. I make no claim to being of any use when mechanical problems came our way. Because I was more inclined to applied maths and civil engineering, particularly structures, we complemented each other nicely.

I was continuing my research into the feasibility of a mini steelworks and had reached the stage where I had a good idea of how it could be achieved. My main difficulty was getting the information that would enable me to evaluate the capital involved in such an operation and consequently the costs of production. Our composting plant had been erected and John Pictor had it working to produce a useful-looking compost. In fact it was being used in my garden at an incredible rate, the whole of the back being covered to a depth of about six inches. Ken Lawson had his steel strip running on a cushion of air and had installed a tall column to test the circuit. Ken was also working on the design of a novel rolling-mill for the steel industry.

Shortly after Michael had passed his first birthday Marjorie told me she was pregnant again. We were delighted at the prospect of another child and this time hoped for a girl. The doctor said there was no reason to worry about Marjorie's health or the future of the baby as both were fit. He did say, however, that after the birth it would be prudent to plan for no more children and we both accepted his advice. Our only concern was that the new addition to the family should be strong and healthy. We had decided after the birth of Michael that it was not a good idea to have a dog around where there was a baby and so we gave Robin to a close friend, who gave him a good home.

We thought I was doing well in my career and perhaps it was a good time to move to a bigger house. We were thinking of a detached property in a more exclusive area rather than a building development where the houses were identical. So I began to look around, finally spotting a suitable house in Fairfield Road, Stockton. After the usual negotiations we bought the property and moved in, planning to be there for a reasonable time. The house had an attic which could be boarded over and used as a model railway room, much to my delight.

The time of Marjorie's confinement was rapidly approaching and we looked forward to the event with great pleasure. We realised, though, that as Michael was still a baby and I had to continue in my job we would need to get some assistance. Although I had some trips abroad during my time in Stockton, they did not inconvenience the home situation with just the one baby and it wasn't too difficult to arrange my commitments so that I would be at home during the confinement and for several weeks afterwards. With two babies to look after however, and with her medical record, Marjorie would clearly need a helping hand. We knew my mother was always ready to help but it seemed too much to expect her to come to Stockton again after only a year or so since her first visit. In any case she would need to stay longer, assuming she could come at all. As my father was still working in the steelworks and would have to look after himself if she came, his position had also to be considered. We concluded that if we lived nearer to South Wales our problems would be a little easier. I was still happy with my position at Head Wrightson but I could see that my future there had its limitations and I knew that my ambition was to reach the higher echelons of management: that is, managing director of a substantial engineering company. This could not happen at Head Wrightson as it was so much a family concern.

With another baby due soon and Michael still only a year old I had no intention of changing jobs at this time, but quite by chance I saw a big advertisement by a top-rate news agency in a newspaper, who were looking to fill a post in a well-known engineering group. The job was for a group technical director and offered a very attractive starting salary: about double what I was currently receiving. The successful candidate would be based in Gloucester and be on the Board of Directors. The position was way above my present one and the responsibilities far greater than at present. I discussed the advert with Marjorie and we agreed no harm would be done if I applied for the job, but we felt I probably had little chance of getting it. Still, I followed my chosen path and applied. In due course I was invited to the London office of the agency for an interview. This was an in-depth assessment of my career to date and an enquiry into my plans for the future. The interviewer was greatly interested in my progress from builder's labourer to Royal Commission scholar and seemed to have difficulty in believing it, although he knew it to be true. Following this interview I was asked to attend for a second one with the Group Managing Director, John Buckley, again in London. He explained that the Winget Gloucester Group consisted of a number of companies based mainly in Gloucester and Rochester. They covered a very wide field of industrial activities from constructional equipment to complete design projects, such as mechanical handling for steelworks. As I was a chartered civil engineer with, by now, a wide knowledge of different industries John Buckley thought I was an acceptable candidate, despite being fairly young for such a big job. He said that the long-term aim was to train the successful candidate for the post of managing director of the Rochester group of companies. The whole concept greatly appealed to me and I returned home to Marjorie to await the result of the interview. I was then invited to meet Norman Staff, the present MD of the Rochester group. I should say that Norman was in his late fifties and I liked him at once. He was an accountant with a very broad knowledge of engineering and had been with Winget Ltd for a very long time. He was, in fact, a very well-known member of the Medway Society. I had the feeling after our meeting that he approved of me and I was sure I would like working with him. I approved too of the other people I met. It seemed a good place to work. Shortly afterwards I was offered the job of Group Technical Director at the Gloucester Head Office.

It was agreed that I should join the company as soon as it was practicable to leave Stockton after the birth of our baby in about two months. I would be given a company house at first to allow us time to find and buy a house of our own. I told Peter Young, my boss at Head Wrightson, that I had a new post and would be leaving in a few months. He was most understanding and of the opinion that I was doing the right thing. Peter himself was to leave a few years later to take up a job in Australia. My research into the viability of a mini steelworks was complete and was handed over to the appropriate people. I had concluded that it was feasible but too big a step into the unknown for Head Wrightson to take. The idea was subsequently adopted by others and was successfully completed.

We did not know the exact arrival date of the new baby and had only the doctor's approximation to go on. To be on the safe side we decided it would be prudent to get my mother up to Stockton a week or so early. She was quite happy with the idea and Dad, as expected, was certain he would manage in her absence. So I set out once more on the long drive to Ebbw Vale. Ma was excited about nursing Michael while Marjorie was in hospital but she did express some concern about her ability to do the job as it was more than thirty years since my sister Pat was born. We settled down calmly to await the great day. We did not have long to wait; Marjorie went into Middlesbrough hospital and I was duly contacted with the news that I was the father of a beautiful baby girl and that both Marjorie and the baby were doing fine. I quickly drove to the hospital to see my new child. She was perfect and fulfilled all my dreams. We now had a complete family and Marjorie later submitted to the operation that ensured we would have no further children.

At home things were not going quite so well. Ma was doing a fine job looking after Michael in the daytime but at night he clearly missed his mother and would not settle down to sleep. At one point I thought I had an answer. I made a little bed on the lounge floor and lay down beside him while he continued crying. Far from this little ploy resolving the problem Michael was still crying when I fell into a deep sleep. Both my mother and I were delighted when Marjorie returned with our little girl, whom we decided to call Susan Patricia. Michael recognised Marjorie at once and reacted with obvious delight and we had no further trouble with him going to sleep at night. We agreed that my mother had done a marvellous job in looking after Michael in Marjorie's absence and she stayed with us for about two months, after which we thought Susan was fit enough to make the trip to Gloucester. Ma was getting worried about Dad as he had been on his own for so long. We knew he was quite capable of looking after himself but it must have been difficult for him as he was working on a three-shift basis at the steelworks.

I said goodbye to my colleagues at Head Wrightson and wished them good fortune in the future. Some of them would soon leave because there was a feeling of uncertainty about their future. The company depended on industries which were themselves in difficulties: for example, the nuclear and steel industries were not doing as well as predicted. Sadly, when I returned to the area some fifteen or twenty years later the company had gone and the site cleared for future development.

We arranged for our furniture to be put into store because the company house to which we were going was fully furnished. Then, after loading the car as much as possible and strapping Susan's pram to the roof, we set out on our long drive south. I had been given the house address and was told to report to the company HQ the following Monday.

My service with Head Wrightson had only lasted about two years. Nevertheless my life in Stockton had an important effect on my future for reasons not recorded in this narrative. In many ways it prompted me to consider the difference between life in the North-East and in the southern part of the country. Generally the people in the south-east were more affluent than those living on Teesside but this desirable state came at a price. There is no doubt that chances for young people to gain progressive employment in the south are greater than in the north. After all, I got started on my professional career by working in the south-east. On the downside I found life more hectic down south than up north. Anyone who has experienced going into London on a commuter train will know what I mean. On Teesside it's a simple matter to leave your house in the town and enjoy the beauty of the North Yorkshire moors within half an hour or so. There it's possible to roam freely over many miles of moorland covered with heather, just as I did as a boy on the Welsh hills and moors. There are many beautiful seaside places to see, like Robin Hood's Bay and Whitby which are full of charm and historical interest. On the moors themselves there is an abundance of ruined abbeys such as Fountains and Rievaulx. There are, of course, many good places to visit in the south-east but the problem of coping with the large population and voluminous traffic reduces its appeal as far as I am concerned.

Chapter 13

Winget–Gloucester

After a long and stressful journey from Stockton-on-Tees with two babies, we finally arrived safely in Gloucester. We had no difficulty finding the house and thought it would be quite a pleasant house in which to live. It was situated fairly near the company's offices, which could be reached by a short car ride.

Understandably, as soon as we arrived in Gloucester we would have visits from our respective families. They were all excited about the two babies they had not as yet seen (except for Ma, of course, who had nursed them). On our first weekend we had as visitors Marjorie's mother and brother, my sister Pat and her husband Cliff and Cliff's ageing father. My mother was also there, as she had come with us from Stockton.

We were now only sixty miles from Ebbw Vale, which could easily be reached by car as the route was serviced by a motorway and a dual carriageway. I had absolutely no doubt that we would be making this journey often. It was acknowledged that I had to get some help for Marjorie with the babies so that my mother could return home. It also seemed important to me to buy a house as soon as possible and recover our furniture and other belongings.

At the arranged date and time I presented myself at the Group's Head Office on Gloucester Road. I was surprised to find that on the other side of the road was the factory of the famous company who made England's Glory Matches. Our factory was equally well-known and once belonged solely to the Gloucester Railway Carriage and Wagon Company. On my arrival at the factory I met Mr Buckley for a friendly but lengthy introductory talk. He explained that the individual companies located on the site were:

- *Muir Hill Dumper*
- *Slater and Walker Dumpers*
- *Gardiners of Gloucester*
- *Moxey Ltd*
- *Gloucester Railway Carriage and Wagons*

- *Poclain Hydraulic Excavators*
- *Redler Cranes*

They were all autonomous commercial units which had been acquired by the parent company and in some cases were registered companies in their own right: for example, Moxey Ltd, who specialised in the design of complete mechanical handling plant for the steel and other industries. My job was to assess the technical viability of each of these companies and to recommend development programmes. I had to ensure that they developed products which kept them in the top ranks in their particular line of business.

There was another diverse range of companies at Rochester with which I was not as yet acquainted. Clearly one man could not be expected to be technically competent in all the activities covered and so it would be my responsibility to make sure that each company or unit was led by an expert in that field of interest.

My office was in the executives' block, which housed the Group Staff—for example, the Group MD, Group Production Director, Group Accountant, Group Secretary and so on. Staff were allocated to work in individual companies and were located in the main works premises of each. My time would obviously be divided between Gloucester and Rochester, which meant I would have duplicate offices in each place and spend half my time at each in turn. The Rochester half would entail overnight stays in hotels in the town or in London as appropriate.

I was allowed to buy a top-of-the-range Wolseley car which I kept at Gloucester, using the train for my trips to Rochester. There were also chauffeurs in each place whose services I could call on when necessary.

Initially I spent most of my working time at Gloucester so that I could make a reasonable assessment of the work I would need to do there. Rochester was not, however, totally neglected as I paid some preliminary visits to get to know Norman Staff. I soon had a healthy respect for him. He had a sound grip on all aspects of the Rochester operation and was palpably a great stabilising influence on the top management of the Winget Gloucester Group. It was evident that John Buckley and Norman Staff were the two people who controlled the Group's fortunes. They were completely different but complementary in character. Metaphorically speaking, John Buckley was an artist who produced the imaginative broad outline of a painting and left the details for others to add; Norman Staff, on the other hand, was like Constable, who knew exactly what was wanted and saw that it was done perfectly down to the last brush-stroke.

Another important member of the Group was Mr Ducas, the American founder of the Winget side of the Group and a major shareholder. He was a man with an inexhaustible flow of ideas for the future of the company. Many of them were, I have to say, impracticable but now and then he would come up with a gem. He was the initiator of many profitable meetings with American companies which resulted in long-term commercial arrangements.

One of my most pressing objectives was to find a house. I wanted something in or near to Gloucester to ensure it would be easy for Marjorie to get to essential services by bus and for me to have easy access to London. Many of the executives in the area lived in attractive Cotswold villages but this did not appeal to us. We were quite content to visit the Cotswolds at the weekends. We finally settled on a four-bedroomed detached house in Cheltenham, a few yards from Hatherley Park and about half a mile from Montpellier Gardens in the town centre. It was an ideal area in which to bring up children.

We moved into our house as soon as we could and were lucky to find a young lady to help Marjorie with the domestic chores and to look after the babies. We also had a gardener as the house stood in a large garden that was too much for me to deal with by myself. It was easy to drive the ten miles to my work in Gloucester and the train journey to London was relatively straightforward, although it was a nuisance having to go right across London to Victoria for a train to Rochester.

The Group also had offices in Bond Street, which I visited once a month to attend Board meetings.

My involvement with the component companies in Gloucester was progressing. I made it a practice to visit each of them and tour the premises, getting to know all the MDs well, and I was soon accepted as a necessary part of the organisation. We held development meetings and formulated programmes for developing new plant and machinery. There were some areas where it was clear we would need new executives to achieve our objectives and we set about rectifying this situation. In one instance I induced Stan Gregory to join us at Gloucester, where his presence was a great help. The one big problem was the development of the Muir Hill range of earth-moving dumpers. I discussed this with John Buckley and we agreed that we should make an attempt to engage the best designer available and we decided on David Brown. David was well-known in the industry and had a working arrangement with Caterpillar, the giant American earth-moving firm. I arranged to meet David, who was interested in our proposal, and after some discussion he agreed to join us at Gloucester. When he joined us at Muir Hill the company was destined to have a new range of dumpers, which were a great success.

I was now spending most of my time at the Rochester factory in Kent. Normally, I would leave home on Sunday evening and not come home until Thursday or Friday evening. The remainder of the week would be spent at the Gloucester factory. All this was hard going for Marjorie but she accepted it without any serious complaint. On occasion we were able to have weekends in Ebbw Vale, where we stayed at Marjorie's home but nevertheless always found time to visit my mother and father.

Stan and Doreen had bought a house in the Cotswold village of Minchinhampton and would sometimes visit us at the weekends. We often went to Bourton-on-the-Water with Stan and Doreen and their small son Steven. The main attraction was the cream teas.

Occasionally I would go overseas with John Buckley or another of our executives, usually in connection with possible business agreements for marketing or acquiring new products. On one such occasion I came back from Germany to find Marjorie in a very unhappy state. We had decided to have a new gas-fired central heating system installed and unfortunately the work was done while I was away. It appeared it had been necessary to raise some of the floorboards and Marjorie had had great trouble preventing the children from falling into the holes.

We were getting occasional visits from Mr Ducas, who was still living in New York. His latest idea was that we should develop a refrigeration system that could be installed in the numerous shrimp-boats which fished off the coast of California. His idea was that with such a system the shrimps would be frozen as soon as they were caught and could therefore be landed in a fresh condition. The idea had been prompted by the fact that one of our Rochester companies (Winget Refrigeration) made refrigeration plates for installation in refrigeration vehicles in the UK. The idea of going to

California to research this proposal did not appeal to me as I felt we had a number of more pressing problems to be solved at Rochester and we should concentrate on those; consequently the shrimp-boat idea was dropped.

Before my arrival one of the problems at Rochester was that they had a brilliant technical director, Mr Pullin, who ran a development facility isolated from the main works: an ideal way of doing development provided it was agreed by top management to be worth pursuing. Unfortunately Mr Pullin was prone to shut himself away in his workshop and produce new equipment which was not actually needed. No doubt in some cases his ideas may have been given to him by Mr Ducas, who was always ready to launch a new development. On one occasion he worked secretly for many months and finally produced what must have been the first mini-car. This was about 1962. The company made a batch of four of these cars for testing. The tests were very successful and a factory was procured for commercial production of the car but, unfortunately, there was a fire which prevented production. I assume the fire had a sobering effect on the management as they dropped the project forthwith. Mr Pullin's son was in possession of one of these cars and he used it continuously while I was in Rochester.

On another occasion Mr Pullin developed a hover-barrow for use on muddy building-sites. It was a wheelbarrow with no wheels, instead supported on a cushion of air. It was tried out in the company car park and found to work perfectly. A decision was taken to produce a batch of twenty-four. But when these were made it was found that although they worked in the car park, on a muddy building-site they remained stationary and showered mud on spectators. I was told that the batch of twenty-four was eventually sold to the army. All these events happened before I arrived at Rochester, by which time Mr Pullin had retired.

I never met Mr Pullin, who retired before my time. His successor had already started when I began going to the factory. He was about my age (38) and was an ex-Army officer who had been wounded in Normandy on D-Day. When I first started going to Rochester it soon became clear that the new technical director was not very popular with his fellow executives because they thought he had a superior attitude, which rubbed everyone up the wrong way. This was probably the result of his army career and public school background. On the whole I rather liked him and was sure he was very intelligent. I sincerely hoped he would prove to be an acceptable replacement for Mr Pullin. My general conclusion was that this was an appointment to be monitored closely.

The main activity at Rochester was the design and manufacture of concrete-making machinery. The name Winget was synonymous with the type of equipment found on all sites where concrete was used. It was generally accepted by all the staff at Rochester that Winget needed to design a new range of concrete-mixers. Such new designs would result in simplified manufacture and include elements of modern thinking, such as interchangeable parts as far as possible throughout the range, simplified fabrications and a reduction in the need for castings where they could be replaced by fabrications at a lower cost. This was the main objective of the new technical director. Incidentally, Winget had its own foundry on the works site and traditionally made its own castings.

The other major business located at Rochester was the manufacture and sale of a range of wire-drawing machines. They were made under a licence from the American Syncro Company obtained by Mr Ducas and it was the means by which Winget Syncro was started after the war. The development of new machines was thus dependent on the American company but they were not as progressive as our German competitors, to whom we were losing our share of the market.

Winget Refrigeration was another company based at Rochester, also formed by the taking of a licence from the Dole Company in Chicago courtesy of Mr Ducas. I knew that a lot of work would have to be done to improve our range of equipment at Rochester.

One day I returned home to Cheltenham after spending the customary days in Rochester to find that Marjorie, although as happy as ever to see me, clearly had something on her mind. When I prompted her she said it was the question Michael had asked of her, "Where does my Daddy live?" I was greatly shocked, and realised I had been concentrating on my job to the detriment of my family. Although I was ambitious and took my job very seriously my real priority was the welfare of my family, their happiness and security. I obviously had to do something because I could not continue to live my life in two places at once, so I saw John Buckley and explained the position and suggested an alternative means of working. I had been taken on with the idea that I would be groomed for a top post that would see me working mostly in Gloucester, where my usefulness was now actually decreasing. The Group's major difficulties were at Rochester and it would make sense if I were to live there on a permanent basis so I could concentrate my efforts in the place where I could do the most good. He agreed with me and said he would consider the idea.

When I saw John Buckley again he confirmed that he had talked the matter over with Norman Staff and they had decided I should go to Rochester permanently as the Assistant MD reporting to Norman. The basis of my work would be to resolve of the engineering problems there but I would at the same time be groomed by Norman in the company's commercial activities. This suited me perfectly as I was fed up with the weekly absences from home and felt I was missing out on my home life. Marjorie was delighted although, like me, she wasn't looking forward to another change of house and location. We were sorry to leave the Gloucester area because of its proximity to our families but decided we should move as quickly as possible. I would initially spend the week in Rochester and look for a rented house as an interim measure so the family could join me and we could then spend time together while we looked for a house to buy. Michael was fast approaching school age so that had to be taken into account as well. After a lot of fruitless searching I finally found a modern house to let for six months in Maidstone: about eight miles from work, so I could easily drive there each day. Marjorie was pleased with the arrangement and we planned to move in January after the busy Christmas season was over.

The day we actually left Cheltenham was cold and there was a certain amount of ice on the roads. I was confident, though, that with careful driving we would come to no harm. This was in the days before we had the motorway from South Wales to London which services Cheltenham and Gloucester, and well before the M25 was built as a ring-road around London. We negotiated London via the South Circular Ring-Road, the cause of endless confusion to people unfamiliar with the route. This included me, who had a great deal of trouble following the route!

After arriving in Maidstone we made ourselves comfortable in the house and started looking for a suitable school for Michael. We found one, and I was soon reporting daily for work at Rochester. Our search for a house to buy now began. We had decided that we would prefer to live in Rochester near a good school for the children and near enough to the Winget factory for me to walk there if necessary. One other condition was that the house should have a large loft where I could build my model railway.

We were greatly helped in our search by Norman Staff. He was well-known in the area and had many good contacts who could keep him informed of property going onto the local market. After two or three false starts we finally viewed a beautiful Georgian-style house in a prime location in Rochester called Priestfields. The house, called Camden House, backed onto extensive fields. Its front was on a select crescent of houses and it was about half a mile from a private school suitable for Michael and Susan. Lastly, as if to convince me of its desirability, the house had a large loft which was fully fitted and eminently suitable for a model railway. We had no doubt that this was the house we had been looking for.

We moved into the house in due course and one little incident remains with me. I saw Michael and Susan together, Susan crying and unhappy about living in the new house. Michael's words of comfort were, "Don't worry, Susan, we won't be in this house long." I could understand her tears and sympathise with her. After all, this was her fifth home and she was still too young to go to an infants' school. We had lived in Stockton, Gloucester, Cheltenham, Maidstone and now Rochester: surely a record any gipsy would be proud of. Actually it was Michael's sixth home, as he was older than Susan.

I could now concentrate seriously on the task facing me at work. The top priority was redesigning our range of concrete-mixers. Unhappily, I concluded that the new technical director was not up to the job in hand. We needed someone with a practical turn of mind as well as a good technical education. I discussed the matter with Norman Staff and he agreed with my view that the man would have to go. It was my responsibility to break the news that he was relieved of his post and he took it with great dignity, even seeing my point of view. I was sorry to see him go but I knew I had done what was necessary in the company's best interests. In my industrial career I had to make people redundant or even sack them: a task I hated doing. I always remembered my youth in Ebbw Vale and the years of unemployment there in the 1930's.

One day Marjorie, the two children and I were having lunch at home when there came a knock at the door to interrupt our family's chat. What happened next was completely unexpected. Marjorie turned her head in the direction of the door, toppled over and fell off her chair to the floor. I got up and found she was unconscious. I alerted the neighbours, who rang for an ambulance and took the children next door to play with two of their friends in the hope it would divert them from the shock they had just had.

I got in touch with the hospital and after some time they told me that Marjorie had had a major stroke. All of one side was paralysed, her sight had been affected and she was unable to talk. They were unsure of the future effects of the stroke but it was clear to me that they had doubts about her survival. I was devastated. I was left with two very young children and no nearby help. My immediate thoughts were to contact my parents in South Wales. As expected, my mother said she would come at once and stay as long as necessary. As my father had recently retired she said he would come too. This would be a great help and I now waited anxiously for their arrival and for further news from the hospital. When I was eventually allowed to see Marjorie she had recovered sufficiently to speak a little but it was obvious she could talk only with great difficulty and her voice was slurred and hard to understand. I could see she wanted to say something to me, and after a great deal of effort she managed to tell me she was worried about the children and asked me to promise that I would remarry for their sake. She was doubtless convinced that she would die. To pacify her I agreed to her request but deep down I was sure that she would pull through and there would be no need for me to remarry. Although Marjorie was a gentle and loving soul, I knew that she had enormous reserves of courage and would not give in to her latest misfortune.

Some weeks later she was let out of hospital to be cared for at home, mainly by my mother and father. My father was largely responsible for the household chores. Although he had spent all his life as a hard-working steelworker he was incredibly domesticated and could be relied on to wash dishes, dust around the house, etc. My mother attended to Marjorie's personal needs and was extremely good with the children. I continued with my job at Winget, although Marjorie was always in my mind. As the weeks went by she continued to improve and slowly recovered her faculties except for part of her vision. I saw the doctor who had attended her and he explained that the main artery to the brain went through the neck and because Marjorie's spine was not perfectly aligned the artery had been pinched when she turned her head. This had stopped the flow of blood to her brain for a split second and caused the stroke. Marjorie would have to have treatment from an osteopath to straighten her spine. This meant many months of professional treatment on a weekly basis and I had to have regular periods off work to accompany her.

Amidst all our troubles it was a great help to me that Norman Staff was completely understanding of my difficulties and did everything possible to help. I was soon able to put all my effort into doing my job as my parents stayed with us for many months. We could not have managed without them and were forever grateful for their help.

I was now able to turn my attention to finding a new technical director for Winget. Bearing in mind the nature of the job I considered that the ideal person would be none other than Stan Gregory, who had worked with me since he left Manchester University. I had been responsible for his being employed at our Gloucester factory and I wasn't sure how the management would react if I took him away. As a matter of plain common sense I discussed the idea with John Buckley to see if he would support it before approaching Stan himself. I need not have worried. John readily accepted my view that Stan would do more good at Rochester than Gloucester and suggested I broach the matter with Norman Staff as soon as possible. This I did and Norman agreed with my proposal. I therefore approached Stan with an offer of the technical director's post at Rochester and he accepted. He and his family would have to move to Kent as soon as possible, which meant he and I would be back in the area in which our association had first begun. The thought of Stan's move pleased Marjorie very much since she and Doreen were very good friends and were both going through the trauma of bringing up babies. I was happy because I had absolute confidence in Stan's ability to design the new range of machines Winget badly needed. I realised that Winget would have to diversify its activities and find new products and my thoughts turned to Peter Norrish, who had been with me at Head Wrightson. Peter was a metallurgist with an agile mind and the ability to identify opportunities for acquiring new businesses and products. I contacted Peter and explained what the company wanted and offered him a job with a free hand to follow up new ideas in engineering which could be of interest to Winget. As I expected, Peter accepted the job and started at once.

Part of my work at Head Wrightson had been to examine the possibility of developing a small-production steelworks which would still be commercially viable. One feature was a machine which could continuous-cast steel in an endless strip. Peter had helped me in my research and thereby informed me of a small company who had developed a process for continuous casting of non-ferrous metals. He took me to see them in Beckenham and I was impressed. The company also had a thriving business making sophisticated instruments for geophysical studies. I agreed with Peter that the company was worth looking at in depth. Consequently, after considerable study of its commercial strength, we made an offer and bought it. Peter was made managing director and therefore spent most of his time at Beckenham. The company, which employed about a dozen men, proved to be very profitable.

My association with Norman Staff was also proving to be very rewarding. He was a first-rate accountant and had an instinct for evaluating the commercial implications of everything we did in the way of new designs and design changes. I began to get a very good feel for the effect on the company's profits from reducing overheads, changes in staff numbers or machine prices and the expected reduction in sales associated with an increase in price. In fact, I was beginning to think and act like an accountant!

Norman was considered by some to be tight and penny-pinching but I began to see that our business was of the dog-eat-dog variety where every penny counted when you were trying to make a profit. We were making concrete-mixers by the thousand for customers who were close with their money because they in turn were selling their end-product in a highly competitive market. This business was light-years away from the design and sale of nuclear power-stations with which I was initially involved. There, safety was the overriding consideration for everything we designed and sold and our competitors were subject to the same stringent conditions. Although I am a dedicated structural engineer and applied mathematician, I was beginning to find accountancy interesting and in many ways challenging.

Because so much of our production was done under licence from American companies it was important for me to visit them from time to time to get a clear picture of their plans for future development. The largest item in our concrete machinery armoury was a range of truck mixers based on the designs of the Challenge-Cook company in Los Angeles. I visited this company but came away disappointed and feeling that any improvements we wanted would have to be done by ourselves. Our series of wire-drawing machines came from the Syncro Company in Perth Amboy, New Jersey. As I felt we were falling behind the Germans in this field, I visited Syncro to see if they were doing anything to improve their designs. The answer was quite simple: they were doing very little to fight off the threat from German competitors. Again, Winget Refrigeration traded under the design patented by the Dole Company of Chicago and I paid them a visit too. As I expected, they were also doing almost nothing to safeguard their market. I concluded that our American licensors were doing very little in the way of developing new machines and equipment to help us compete in the European market.

One day we got the unexpected news that Winget-Gloucester had been taken over by the well-known British firm of Babcock. This was a bombshell as far as we executives were concerned. We had no idea how it would affect us and we looked forward to the briefing we were to have from the Babcock representative. We were told that John Buckley had resigned as MD of the Winget-Gloucester Group and his post was to be taken over by Archie Thompson, a Babcock executive who had been with the company since his days as an apprentice. He was about my age (40–45). We were assured that there would be no significant changes in our areas of responsibilities and we were to carry on as usual. This implied that Norman Staff would remain as head of the Winget activities at Rochester, a piece of reassuring news.

Archie was to be based in Gloucester but would be making regular trips to Rochester. We soon met him and the general reaction was favourable. We all liked him and in time he became a good friend of mine and of my family. Susan was particularly fond of him as he always made her laugh. The end result of the takeover was that I carried on as usual with my Rochester job with the added help of Archie, who proved to be a very sound adviser.

One of the problems we had at Rochester was making two ranges of products, each needing different manufacturing facilities and skills. Our main product range was concrete-making machines, which were relatively simple to manufacture compared with the wire-drawing machines, that were more of a precision machine manufacture. This resulted in the Winget works being split into two distinct manufacturing units under different managers who had different views on many problems such as pay and conditions of working. We, that is Norman Staff and I, were not satisfied with the manufacturing performance of the wire-drawing side and I resolved to look for a new production director. After much searching and interviewing I finally decided to appoint Ron Lovesey, who had extensive practical experience of sophisticated machine manufacture. Although Ron came from South Wales, not far from my home in Ebbw Vale, it had not influenced me in my choice. After a short time Ron moved to Rochester and quickly settled into his new job. It soon became evident that I had made the right choice and Ron became indispensable. Furthermore he and his wife Margaret became good friends of Marjorie and me during the time we worked together.

Peter Norrish continued to look for new products for his company and he acquired a machine to butt-weld non-ferrous wire without using applied heat. This butt-welding machine was small enough to be carried comfortably by hand. It had great appeal in the wire-mills where we sold our machines. We had no competition from other companies because of the butt-welding machine's uniqueness and this remained so for the next few years so that we were able to make a good profit on its sale.

By now it was clear that our little factory in Beckenham was not big enough to meet our future manufacturing requirements. Consequently Peter was instructed to look for new premises. Owing to the sophistication of the products the new premises needed to be remote from Rochester. Peter eventually found a new factory in Ashford and many of our people were transferred there from the Beckenham plant.

Winget had a factory in Warrington that made machinery for making ropes. It was well established in that industry and had a good share of the available market for new machinery. The managing director reached retirement age and was succeeded by his second-in-command, who had to be removed after a short while as he was not suitable for the job. A new man was selected to become the MD but Norman Staff felt that I should become the Chairman of the company, which was called Hanson and Edwards.

This additional responsibility involved me in regular visits to Warrington. The company caused quite a stir in the rope industry when it developed a giant machine to make ropes up to seven inches in diameter. We saw outlets for this machine in countries where there were deep mines and large opencast sites where very large excavators were in use. In the next few years Bill Street, the new MD of Hanson and Edwards, and I visited the USA a number of times to obtain sales of the machine.

A couple of memorable things happened when Bill and I were staying in Durban in South Africa in a very posh Edwards hotel. A very nice white lady met me at the reception desk and called for a black boy to take me to my room. He took my key and then called another boy to carry my bags. The latter was a Cape coloured lad who was obviously inferior to the black African who was himself too superior to carry my bags. Such behaviour is quite absurd. On another occasion, we had checked into the hotel on the morning of our arrival and we found that we had no official engagement until the evening. We were, in fact, due to take some important customers and their wives out to dinner. Because our hotel was on the seafront, adjacent to the magnificent Durban beach, Bill and I decided to spend the afternoon taking life easy by renting two deckchairs. Now Durban is on the east coast of South Africa and faces the Indian Ocean. As one would expect, it is famous for its intense heat and endless sunshine. To take full advantage of these marvellous conditions we took off our shirts and lay back in our chairs. In no time at all we both fell fast asleep. The result was immediate and catastrophic; we woke up after a very short time and found we were badly sunburned. Our suffering was predictable and we decided that to relieve the pain we should get some calamine lotion. We knew that under no circumstances could we cancel the evening with our guests and I at least managed to ease my pain by covering my whole body with calamine and putting on my pyjamas under my evening suit. The whole ensemble was rather warm and uncomfortable but at least I got through the evening without revealing my secret. Bill was less fortunate: he had a fair complexion and his face was horribly burned so he had to smear calamine all over it in consequence. He looked like an African witch-doctor in full war-paint. Our guests understood what had happened and were very sympathetic, which was a good thing.

We also made a sale of our giant rope-making machine to British Ropes on Tyneside. I was involved in a number of visits to the factory before the sale was achieved. This incident is worthy of note since it heralded my first visit to Newcastle upon Tyne. It seemed a good place to live as it was near the sea and the Northumberland hills and there was good fishing in the area. Newcastle itself was an interesting and attractive city.

We had got to the stage where we had found two other areas of development. Firstly, we came across a man who had been developing a machine for making ice-cubes. This machine had been tested and was shown to work. A decision was made to buy the patent for the machine in the hope that it could be developed to a stage where it could be commercially exploited through the Winget Refrigeration Co. I agreed with Norman Staff that we should give it to Stan Gregory to foster as his new designs for concrete mixers were more or less complete. The original designer of the ice-cube machine agreed to join Winget to give assistance in developing it further.

The other area which came to our attention was a partly-developed machine for use in a brickworks to stack bricks into the patterns required for firing them. This was an extremely complicated piece of computerised equipment and it was unsuitable to be developed further by any of the Winget technical staff. It was therefore agreed that I approach Keith Mitchell (ex-chief mechanical engineer for the GEC/Simon Carves Atomic Energy Group) to see if he was interested in joining us to work on the machine. Keith was a great friend and he agreed to join us for this particular project. With hindsight the development of this machine was not one of my better ideas: it was too big a step into the unknown for exploitation by Winget.

By now Babcock had decided to buy the Blaw Knox Company based in Rochester. They specialised in the design and manufacture of tar macadam paving-machines and were well-known in this country and overseas. The logic was sound as they complemented the interests of Winget in the building industry. We had been interested in paving-machines some years before and I had in fact visited a company in Oregon in the USA to consider buying their designs. The designs were essentially for relatively small areas to be treated with tarmac, for example: pavements and drives for individual homes. The visit, however, was not productive and the idea was dropped.

With the coming of Blaw Knox it was acknowledged that some rationalisation of the two companies was inevitable. As the managing director of Blaw Knox had considerably more experience than I, it was a foregone conclusion that he would be responsible for the constructional equipment part of the new business when Norman Staff left. On the other hand, I would be managing director of a general engineering division consisting of a number of unrelated businesses based at Rochester and other parts of the country: for example Hanson and Edwards at Warrington, Winget Syncro and Winget refrigeration at Rochester, Blaw Knox transmission towers and Blaw Knox Steelworks equipment.

There was a big drawback with this arrangement because it would mean there would be two unrelated manufacturing facilities in Rochester reporting to two different works directors. This, in my view, was a recipe for disaster as it would create conflict during negotiations for pay etc with the workforces. This would undoubtedly be exploited by the trade unions, which were strong in the area. I therefore felt I should seriously consider my future. Archie Thompson knew of my concerns and gave me the news that Babcock had bought the well-known Tyneside mining machinery company, Huwood Limited. He also told me that the managing director was due to retire as he was over 65. Huwood was now the second biggest manufacturing company within the Babcock Group and had a workforce of nearly 2000.

A number of men had already been interviewed for the job but were rejected because of the special conditions required. The present MD had been a miner and insisted that knowledge of the industry was crucial because the bulk of Huwood's business was done with the National Coal Board, which was packed with mining engineers. In short, the successful candidate would have links with the mining industry and be acceptable to a strongly partisan Geordie workforce. After persuasion by Archie Thompson, the Babcock top brass decided that I should be interviewed by Fred Bainbridge, the outgoing MD of Huwood. It was acknowledged that he was the best authority on the qualities needed for his successor. I went to see Fred, who was a big burly man with a ruddy complexion owing, no doubt, to his daily ration of whisky. This, I noted, had no discernible effect on his mental alertness and clarity of thinking.

I gave Fred a resumé of my career to date, emphasising the fact that all men in my family for three generations had been miners or steelworkers who worked with a pick and shovel; that is, none of them were white-collar workers. Although I knew I had broken this mould I had started as a boy in the steelworks of Ebbw Vale, and had been both a builder's labourer and had worked on an opencast coalmine before gaining academic qualifications. In other words I had worked my way up to my present position in Winget as MD of the general engineering division.

By the time the interview was over Fred and I were friends, with a mutual respect for each other. Later I was to learn that Fred had told Babcock that in his opinion I could do the job and he had no reservations about my being appointed. I was told by Archie Thompson that Babcock were prepared to offer me the job on condition that Marjorie was completely recovered and there was no reason to believe she was likely to have further medical problems. After discussions with Marjorie and her doctor I was able to assure Babcock she was fit and prepared to move to Newcastle. Although she wasn't sure she would like living there, she followed her usual philosophy of supporting me and agreed to the move.

The children were sorry to leave Rochester, where they had been for most of their lives and where they were happy with their school and friends. However Michael was soon won over by a promise of a season ticket to see Newcastle United, and even Susan finally came around to accepting the move.

The general timetable for my move was agreed with Fred Bainbridge and Babcock. As he was retiring in six months it was felt that for this period I should work as Fred's assistant, on the basis that everybody was aware I would become managing director when Fred retired. We would keep our house in Rochester until it was time for Marjorie and the children to join me in Newcastle, and I would fly home at weekends to see them and dismantle the large model railway in the loft. With this plan agreed, I took leave of my colleagues in Rochester and proceeded to pursue my new career.

After reading the above narrative you may be forgiven for assuming I spent all my time at work and abroad or neglected my family. This was decidedly not the case and I always tried to make up for my absences when I returned home. Owing to Marjorie's past poor health I was acutely aware of the need to pay particular attention to them when possible. Michael started a fishing interest at the age of nine and consequently we would fish together whenever an opportunity presented itself. Susan even came with us on occasion and tried her hand with a rod. We have a picture of her with a 3lb pike she caught, with the help of Marjorie.

When they wanted to go ice-skating I would join them on the ice, although I was a poor skater. Marjorie would enjoy watching us from the safety of the side of the rink. On another occasion the children wanted to camp out in a tent in the back garden, and did; however I was also made to endure this to ensure no harm came to them. So I slept in their minute wigwam, while Marjorie enjoyed perfect rest in bed. The wigwam was sufficient to cover my head and shoulders, but the entire remainder of my body was exposed to the night air and a fine cover of dew blanketed me by morning.

One of my great joys was to tuck Susan into bed at night and tell her a story. My store of tales was endless and completely untrue, but she loved them. Even today she refers to me as a great teller of stories (lies).

At weekends in the summer we often went to the seaside. Broadstairs was a favourite. Each year we would travel to Wales to stay with Marjorie's mother and brother. My parents lived nearby so we often took them to Barry, a popular seaside resort. One of our great joys in South Wales was to go pony-trekking in the Black Mountains near Abergavenny with my father, who truly loved these outings and was always with us.

Michael and I, and sometimes my father, also spent a lot of time in the Brecon Beacons fishing. My father was the world's worst angler but he would sit for hours on the lake's bank and, despite his lack of success, clearly enjoyed himself.

Myself, Marjorie, Michael and Susan (with Bimbo the Chimp) enjoying ice-creams at Broadstairs.

Chapter 14

Huwood

I joined Huwood in the autumn of 1971. As arranged, I started work as an assistant to Fred Bainbridge. This gave me the freedom to pursue areas of interest which would serve me well when I became MD. Fred was happy with this and gave me his full support. My first objective was to acquire an extensive knowledge of the company and its activities, in which I was helped by the middle-managers (managers below those on the main Board).

A tour of the works was most enlightening. The labour force was about 1,750 and largely consisted of shop-floor workers: such as machinists, fabricators, electricians, etc. It seemed that Huwood was the first factory to be built on the Team Valley, which had opened just before the war. When I joined the company it was the biggest factory on the estate. The workforce included 300 white-collar workers who were engineers, clerks and drawing-office staff. All products were for underground use in mines. They included belt and armoured-face conveyors and their drive-machinery, hydraulic roof-supports and a comprehensive range of electrical equipment: all designed to satisfy statutory safety conditions underground.

The company's main customer was the NCB, as I said in the previous chapter, which was split into ten regions (Scotland, Yorkshire, Wales, Staffs and so on). Each region was more or less autonomous with its own regional director who reported to the management HQ in Hobart House, London. To interface successfully with the NCB Huwood had to have regional offices in each of the NCB regions. These offices housed the sales and service personnel, each one being run by a regional sales manager. About 10% of Huwood's sales went overseas, notably to India but also to virtually any country involved in mining. The American market was served by Huwood Irwin, a manufacturing and sales company in Pennsylvania.

One of my first discoveries was that a large proportion of Huwood employees had been with the company for many years: in some cases all their working life. There was also a strong family connection between some of the middle-management and the top brass of the company. This was embarrassing in the situation where a son had a father on the Board and expected to follow in his father's footsteps. I had to keep a close eye on this at all times.

I found that in many ways Huwood was similar to Winget. One thing I soon discovered, which gave me an unpleasant surprise, was that the works director, the engineering director and the company secretary were all planning to retire at the same time as Fred Bainbridge. As if to compound this difficulty there was no effective sales director in the company. Instead this function was partly left to a commercial manager at the factory who co-ordinated operations with the regional sales people. The consequence of this was that when, after six months, I became MD there would be no experienced Board members to support me and, as far as I could determine, no effort had been made to groom any of the middle-managers to take greater responsibilities. It was clear to me that my first duty would be to assess the potential of middle-management with a view to promoting those capable of handling greater responsibility.

Three of the Main Board directors were leaving because they were over 65. The engineering director also left when I arrived: his departure was necessitated by his wife's poor health. My first priority was therefore to address the situation in the engineering department. It was managed by Bob Barber: a quiet, competent and long-serving member of Huwood who proved to be very effective in his job.

In my first six months at Huwood I spent a great deal of my time getting to know the important people in the company and their overall responsibilities. It was a hugely time-consuming task because many of those I had to see were located in the regional offices spread over the whole country. I could, of course, have asked the managers in each office to come and see me but I didn't think this was enough. I was anxious to meet not only the managers but the people who worked for them. Having worked on the shop-floor myself I knew that the men lower down the ladder always appreciated seeing the man at the top make a routine visit to the shop-floor.

I soon realised that the men in Huwood and other mining supply companies had a very close relationship with the men and managers working in the hundreds of pits around the country. This was particularly true of the salesmen and service engineers in the supply companies. Most of them had worked in the mining industry all their lives and often had been underground installing conveyors and other equipment. It was obvious to me that I should make myself known in the collieries as well as in our company.

As planned, I returned home to Rochester every week: a welcome break in my routine. Near the end of 1971 Marjorie and I decided it was time to look for a house in Newcastle so I made arrangements for the whole family to stay there for a few days. We knew exactly what we were looking for: the house had to be comparable in size to our lovely home in Rochester; it had to be near the city centre with a bus stop close by and convenient for schools, hospitals and other essentials; and, of course, it would have to have a big loft for me!

We thought we would have no trouble finding such a property but in fact it was extremely difficult. There were plenty of large semi-detached houses available but detached were few and far between. After we had reached the stage where we thought our quest had failed and were getting ready to go back to Rochester, a house appeared on the market that had everything we wanted. After some friendly negotiations with the owners we agreed on a sale and a possession date. Marjorie and I had been married for nineteen years and this was our tenth house. We hoped we would be in this one long enough for our children to finish their school education!

Early in 1972 we moved to Newcastle and quickly made ourselves at home in our new house. It was in excellent condition and needed no decoration at all. We had arranged for the previous owners to leave all the carpets, curtains and light fittings and all we had to do was install our furniture. We enrolled Michael and Susan at a private school within walking distance and I bought Marjorie a small new car as a special present. She had been using my company car in Rochester while I was away.

The garden was not laid out in a way we liked and we drew up a plan to make it suitable for our needs. This would involve me building a wooden fence and putting in a lot of crazy-paving for the footpaths. I also had to re-lay a lawn. It seemed that every time we took possession of a new house I would spend about two years on the garden alone and then we would usually have to move as soon as I had got it into an acceptable state. The loft of this house was enormous, measuring fifty feet overall. Half of it was nicely boarded out and I did the other half a year or two later. I could now start on my model railway.

Within a couple of months Fred Bainbridge retired along with the other Board members. I was now alone at last with my own company and unlikely to be subjected to much Head Office involvement. Babcock's Head Office was in London and my contact with them would be through Archie Thompson. The plan was for Archie to visit me once a month with his accountant to go over the current state of the company. This pleased me a great deal as I had worked with Archie for some years and got on with him very well. In fact when he came up to Newcastle each month he would call in to see Marjorie and the children, whom he always enjoyed meeting.

My first priority was to form a management team to support me in the day-to-day running of the company. One of the key positions was for someone to run the manufacturing facilities of the works. The bulk of the job was on the Team Valley site but there was also a substantial unit in another factory about three miles away from there. I felt that initially I should find someone from inside the company to do the job. I did not want to start my tenure as MD by bringing strangers in, at least not until I knew more about the potential of the people already available, some of whom had been with Huwood for many years. I finally picked George Steele to be works manager. He had been with the company all his working life and was well-known on the shop-floor. Huwood employed 1,500 men on the factory floor, which was divided into several departments such as fabrication, assembly and so on. Each of these departments was efficiently run by managers who had been in their posts for many years, so George Steele was adequately supported in his new job.

I also chose existing members of the staff to manage the sales and commercial activities of the company. This was mainly the co-ordination of the functions of our area sales managers, who were strategically located in towns near the mining units of the NCB. Finally, Brian Dalglish was confirmed as the new company secretary. Brian had long experience of the job as he had been second-in-command to the newly-retired company secretary.

With this team in place I initiated regular management meetings which eventually gained the status of a management board.

At the start of my new job with Huwood I had realised that three factors were crucial to success:

- Becoming well-known to *all* people in the company;

- Being accepted by the top management of the NCB and the colliery managers and proving that I knew what life was like underground;
- Making regular contact with our regional staff.

To this end whenever I was in Newcastle I made it a practice to call in at our satellite factory on my way in to Team Valley. My visits would include a walk round the different shop-floor departments with ad hoc stops to talk to the men operating machines and assembling equipment. This would happen after I had seen and been briefed by the manager of that particular department. The design and drawing-offices were visited regularly and I took great interest in the progress of various jobs that were being executed.

I usually found the Geordies to be a genuine and friendly people. I had no difficulty in being accepted by them; they were very much like the folk I grew up and worked with. This was hardly surprising as a large proportion of the mining population in South Wales was made up of descendants of miners who came to the area from the North-East, Yorkshire, Lancashire and, in my own case, from Somerset and Dorset.

I got to know a lot of the men on the shop-floor quite well. Some of the employees, who were members of the Felling Male-Voice Choir, often spoke to me and in time I became one of its patrons. There were anglers, war veterans, ex-miners, leek-growers and others who were interesting to talk to. Leek-growing was a great passion with the people in the North-East, and being Welsh myself I was naturally interested. It was not long before I was growing leeks in my garden for entry in the Huwood leek-growing competition, a popular annual event. Various experts were soon visiting my garden with endless advice on growing leeks. They gave me young leeks to plant which, I was assured, were descended from a long line of champion leeks. Sad to say, I never aspired to the dizzy heights expected of me. My leeks usually came in the bottom three in the list of entrants. Nevertheless it was a great day for Huwood personnel and their wives and children, including Marjorie, Michael and Susan. Pigeons and whippets were also Geordie interests and these, too, had figured prominently in my young days in South Wales.

As part of my campaign to make myself well-known to the mandarins of the NCB I enlisted the support of our regional sales managers. One of my first encounters with the NCB resulted in a never-to-be-forgotten episode.

The NCB had its research station at Bretby near Burton-on-Trent and one of our sales managers arranged for me to see its Director. I arrived at the research centre with time to spare and thought I'd go to the cloakroom to freshen up before my important meeting. As part of this process I needed to spend a penny. All went according to plan until I pulled on the zip of my trousers. To my horror the zip had trapped the end of my shirt and stubbornly refused to let go. Since I was due to see the Director in a matter of seconds I did the only practical thing I could. I lifted my briefcase, held it in front of me rather like a Scotsman's sporran and boldly went in to meet the Director. As far as I know he had no idea of the embarrassment hiding behind my briefcase. On the whole I sensed the meeting was a success and that I had made an important friend at the research station. Another such friend was made a little later when I met Dennis Hartley.

Within the first month or so of my tenure as MD of Huwood I visited the NCB's headquarters at Hobart House. I was greatly helped in meeting the top executives by Jack Britton, one of my sales managers, who was well-known in the mining industry. Jack was a particularly great friend of Robert Dunne, the Director General. Dunne was extremely important to suppliers of equipment to the NCB because he was responsible for approving major development schemes. On reflection I can see that my success with various NCB personnel has been because of the excellent relationships between key NCB people and our own regional sales managers.

My visit to Hobart House was followed by those to each of the NCB regional HQs to meet the directors in charge and some of their supporting staff. These visits were repeated and I made some lasting friendships. I became very friendly with Dennis Hartley, one of the Bretby technical experts. Dennis and I spent many happy days fishing together on the River Ure in Yorkshire and on rivers further north. Often we would be accompanied by Allen Richmond, one of our sales managers.

In general I got on well with all the area directors and went to see them regularly. Usually we would find areas of common ground to talk about. Another custom I adopted was that of visiting collieries underground throughout the country. These trips were arranged by our local area sales managers and usually ended with a meal with the colliery staff. While underground I liked to talk to the colliers and discuss the merits and demerits of our equipment. A visit to a coalface is an experience that has to be gained before one can appreciate what it means. Most of my visits were made in the North-East since it was my home territory. The pits in the area, by the time I joined Huwood, were mainly to be seen along the coast. Coal was generally extracted from faces located five or more miles away from dry land and under the sea.

Most people are familiar with the sight of a pithead winding-gear and know that to enter the mine one has to descend the pit-shaft to the working depth where coal can be found. The means of travelling to the coalface can vary from pit to pit, depending on the distance. Sometimes, but not often, it is possible to walk to the coalface but in most cases a mechanical means of conveying the miner to his workplace is required. Methods vary in different parts of the country. Sometimes a narrow-gauge railway system is used but here in the North-East it was common for men to be transported on special conveyors which were designed and produced by Huwood. The conveyors run at a constant speed and stop only in an emergency. Special embarkation and disembarkation platforms are built alongside the conveyor at strategic points. To embark the miner faces the direction of motion, steps on to the conveyor, drops to his knees and then lies flat on his stomach. He remains in this position until he reaches the end of his journey and reverses the embarking procedure to get off. One problem with this system is that the rhythmic motion of the conveyor belt over its rollers has a sleep-inducing effect on some travellers (like me). To wake them, an alarm is triggered and if they sleep through that then the conveyor stops automatically. I have tested this system and can confirm that it really works, although it is embarrassing when the alarm is set off by the managing director of the company who supplied the conveyor. As well as my regular underground visits to the coalmines I also went underground in the salt-mine at Boulby, the gypsum-mine near Penrith and a Cornish tin-mine.

Apart from my responsibilities in the UK I did a lot of travelling overseas to visit commercial partners and to promote our equipment. These trips were always to areas where mining took place, such as Nova Scotia, New South Wales, Pennsylvania and the Transvaal. One thing I noticed when travelling in these countries was their close association with mining areas in the UK. I would come across places which had the same name as British mining towns—Swansea, Ashington and Blyth, to name but three.

I sometimes wondered if any of the miners working in these countries had been in Waunlwyd in the 1930's in the terrible years of depression.

On one of my trips to Nova Scotia I hired a car to see my Aunt Edith, who had married a Canadian soldier during the war and went back to Canada with him. It was wonderful to see her after so many years. She still had an unmistakable South Wales accent. She had produced three cousins and I was godfather to Susan, her second child. All the daughters lived in Halifax and on one occasion I met Aunt Edith and Uncle Bill along with their three children and grandchildren. I always felt sad when I went to Halifax because it brought back memories of wartime convoys leaving on their long voyages across the North Atlantic to the UK. March 1943 was always in my thoughts.

I particularly liked visiting India, where I got to see the mining areas in the north-east of the country. Normally I was based in Calcutta, Delhi or Ranchi and was accompanied on my visits to the mines by managers of the manufacturing company with which we were associated. This company was owned by McNeil and Magor, a large concern whose main interest was in tea-plantations. My early interest in being a tea-planter was known to my Indian colleagues and on one trip which was longer than usual they had a special treat in store for me. It had been arranged that I should spend a weekend on one of their tea-plantations in Assam. I was flown out in the small aircraft owned by the company and stayed in the bungalow belonging to the manager of the tea-plantation. He was the last English manager, all the rest being Indian. It proved to be a wonderful and memorable weekend. I was accompanied by one of the Huwood sales managers and found that we had been allocated a day's fishing on the Brahmaputra River whose source was in the Himalayas, which were visible in the distance. We

Offices in Calcutta at Mangoe Lane.

set off from the plantation in two Landrover vehicles, with a number of Indian servants who looked after our equipment and did the cooking.

We had two boats, which we launched and allowed to drift downstream all day with our Indian friends acting as pilots, leaving us free to fish continuously. In the evening we landed at a point many miles downriver. We found that our attendants had driven ahead in the two vehicles so we arrived to find a big bonfire blazing away and a picnic prepared. Next day we were flown back to Calcutta with a host of marvellous memories and, for me, a sense of relief that I had not pursued my early ambition to be a tea-planter. I could see that I would not have been happy in that role as I was cut out to work in industry.

In 1945 had I made three trips to Bombay in a troopship. This was during the last days of the British Raj. My impression then was of a country teeming with likeable but poor people, many of whom lived and slept in the streets. During my time with Huwood thirty-odd years later I returned to India several times, expecting it to have changed greatly since their independence. I actually found the country very much as it was in 1945, except that the population had more than doubled and the technocrats and managers now behaved in exactly the same way as the British ex-pats.

Traditional dancing by ladies in New Delhi.

An incident that is truly typical of India happened on one of my drives through an intensely crowded city. As I looked through the window of the car it suddenly occurred to me that every bicycle I saw was loaded with three or more people. Motor bikes would carry five or six, suitably distributed around the driver. Cars were also grossly overloaded and people in buses were packed like sardines inside and on the roof, which was really meant to carry baggage. I turned to my Indian friend and said I dreaded to think how many people would be carried by a taxi. My friend was clearly a little upset by my remarks and he said, "No, no, taxis in India are forbidden by law to carry too many passengers." I was impressed and asked how many this was. My friend proudly replied, "In India no more than ten people are allowed in a taxi." I couldn't for the life of me think of an adequate reply to this revelation and decided to keep quiet for the rest of my trip.

A well-laden bus in India.

In 1978 my father died. His death did not come as a surprise for we all knew he had cancer but although he was in pain he kept it to himself. He did not want to cause my mother any anxiety. As a boy he had TB and was sent to live on a farm to improve his health. He had little or no schooling and could barely read or write. He was docile and gentle and was completely devoted to Mum, Pat and me. When he died we found a picture in his wallet of Pat as a schoolgirl and he must have carried it around with him for many years. He never said much when he was alive but this action speaks louder than words.

A suitable epitaph for Dad is provided by Sir Henry Wotton:

This man is freed from servile bands
Of hope to rise, or fear to fall:
Lord of himself, though not of lands,
And, having nothing, yet hath all.

(Sir Henry Wotton)

It occurred to me that many people, like my father, qualify for the above epitaph, meriting as much respect as many well-qualified professional people.

As one would expect, Marjorie and I were often involved in social events centred on the company's activities. There were local events for the mining management in all the regions and we as a matter of course attended many of them. Sometimes they would be held in London but more often in the Newcastle Civic Centre. There were also diverse events at Huwood such as the annual leek show, which I have already mentioned. On these occasions the whole family would get involved.

As time went on I began to realise that Marjorie's health was beginning to cause her trouble again. She did not complain and always stood by my side when her presence was needed. A new problem emerged, however, when it was least expected. She was standing one day in the kitchen near the window when she suddenly said she was having trouble with her fingers (I think it was pins-and-needles) and she thought it was probably the onset of rheumatoid arthritis. She was at one time a trainee nurse but had to give it up because of rheumatism, so I concluded she probably knew what she was talking about. This was the start of a long and painful period for Marjorie. Her condition grew rapidly worse as the arthritis affected all the joints in her toes and fingers. She rapidly arrived at a state where she had to have special boots made but even then she had great difficulty in standing without my help. During this period I kept working at Huwood, but realised I was approaching the stage where travelling, particularly abroad, would be out of the question. Consequently I started to examine ways of carrying on working without the problem of running a big company.

About this time Babcock were having a serious rethink about their involvement with the NCB. The top management wanted to extend their interest in the coal industry to cover the activities of other Babcock subsidiary companies. My feeling was that this could be achieved but that the Babcock companies would need help to break into these new areas of business if the venture were to be really successful. I was then challenged as to how this could be done and, after much thought, proposed that Babcock should form a new company whose sole purpose was to promote the idea of the comprehensive role Babcock could play in servicing the NCB. The idea was accepted and I became the managing director of Babcock Mining Services. My function was to promote Babcock's potential for overall servicing of the NCB by using ten of their subsidiary companies with wide experience of different industries: Huwood; Parsons Chain; Babcock Hydraulic Handling; Babcock Moxey; Babcock Bristol; etc.

My specific usefulness was my widespread knowledge of the NCB people, whom I could contact and introduce to the managing directors of the Babcock subsidiaries. With Marjorie rapidly becoming an invalid this arrangement suited me admirably as I was no longer MD of Huwood on a day-to-day basis and my time spent away from home would be dramatically reduced.

I moved into new offices in Gosforth and for the next three years spent my time assisting various Babcock subsidiary companies to develop their relationship with the NCB. During this time Marjorie got steadily worse and I left my full-time employment with Babcock to become an independent consultant to the company for a further three years.

Chapter 15

Retirement

I retired in 1987 at the grand age of 62. I had started work at 16 in the Ebbw Vale steelworks and, including my seven years in the university, I had been continuously employed for 46 years. I now felt I was ready to spend the rest of my life in more leisurely pursuits. My prime concern at this time was Marjorie and her failing health. She had by now developed problems when she passed water and it patently caused her a lot of pain. To alleviate the problem she started drinking natural spring water, which she felt eased the problem to some extent.

The greatest handicap was her rheumatoid arthritis, which was now so severe that she could only get about in a wheelchair. Unfortunately she could not propel herself because of the state of her fingers, which were badly deformed and incapable of being clenched. Her toes were similarly misshapen which made standing very difficult; in fact, she now relied entirely on specially made surgical boots.

Shortly after I retired, Susan and Mike (her boyfriend) told us they were to be married. We were delighted. They clearly loved each other, were ideally suited and destined for a happy future. The wedding was to be in York, which was Mike's home. I was concerned about Marjorie travelling to York in her state of health, but she was determined to attend the wedding and fully participate in the church service. It must have been extremely difficult for her to stand both in church and for the group photographs, but she did it and I was very proud of her.

Marjorie was now seeing the doctor more often. She also pursued the therapies of alternative medicine, faith healing and acupuncture, but all to no avail. She reached the point where she could not get upstairs but she and I were determined that she would remain at home as long as I could look after her. I was quite capable of doing all the household chores and cooking our meals. Although the latter were rather mundane and uninspiring, we knew we would not starve. I also made some ramps so I could get the wheelchair on to the street, letting us go for daily excursions around the neighbourhood.

The big problem was getting Marjorie upstairs. I solved this by making a special bed for her. It was only about a foot high and I installed it in the lounge. Its low height enabled me to get her to bed at night and to help her if she needed attention. During this period I slept in the lounge on a mattress on the floor, to be near her if required.

It was evident by now that Marjorie was getting progressively worse and in much more pain. Her mind, however, was clear and productive. Each night I would get her to bed in the lounge and spend the last hour or so doing a crossword puzzle with her before going to sleep. One day she told me she had passed blood in her urine. Realising that this was a serious development, I made immediate arrangements for her to visit the Nuffield Hospital to be seen by a specialist. This resulted in a small operation which showed she had untreatable cancer of the bladder. It was a devastating revelation for both of us. Marjorie was understandably tearful and upset but very brave, and she accepted the diagnosis with resignation. The doctor commented on the stoical way she received the news of her terminal illness. Secretly I believe she was relieved to know her suffering would soon be over. After a brief meeting with a counsellor at the hospital she rejoined me and I took her home. By now she was quite calm.

I later saw Dr Mary Bestow, who had attended Marjorie for some years. She lived nearby and was a constant visitor to our house. I asked her for an assessment of Marjorie's condition and she told me she had fewer than six months to live. In a way I was pleased to know the truth, but it was hard to believe I would soon be losing her.

I couldn't help thinking how cruel life can be. Marjorie was kind and gentle but was constantly a victim of poor health. It was a heavy cross to bear and it was so unfair that it should happen to her. I did not tell her the bad prognosis given to me by Dr Bestow as I felt she would not benefit from knowing she was to die within six months. I'm sure she would have accepted it philosophically, and even looked forward to her death as a release from her suffering, but it might have clouded our remaining time together.

Michael and Susan were both adults in their late twenties and regularly visited us at Newcastle. The question now arose about telling them of their mother's cancer. I was surprised to learn Marjorie was opposed to telling them, or anyone else, of her condition. She was adamant and made me promise I would not reveal her secret. I felt this was probably not the right thing to do, but I believed her wishes were paramount. I kept this promise but I know it would have been easier for me if the children and family were aware of the position. When I look back I think she wanted to spare the children the anxiety of learning about the cancer: Susan was recently married and Michael was deeply committed to the research he was doing at Manchester University. She may have been right; who knows?

A few months later I met Mary Bestow, who said that in her opinion Marjorie should go into St Oswald's Hospice for a week or so: for her sake and mine. Both Marjorie and Dr Bestow thought I needed a rest. Although reluctant, I accepted this advice and within just a few days Marjorie was admitted to St Oswald's. I visited her daily and was looking forward to seeing her at home again—an event which I, in my ignorance, thought possible. She had been in the hospice for about a week when I had a telephone call from the doctor there. He advised me to come at once because Marjorie had had a major stroke. I was also advised to send for Michael and Susan.

When I arrived at the hospice Marjorie was conscious but unable to speak. She indicated she knew who I was by closing her eyes when asked to do so if she recognised me. The children arrived in record time. She indicated she recognised them too and understood what they said, but it was clear she was coming to the end of her life.

The hospice made a private room available for Marjorie and gave us permission to stay overnight. She eventually went into a coma and remained this way for several days before she died. We had stayed overnight and were all awake when the nurse examined her and found she was dead.

So ended a relationship that had its roots in the Ebbw Vale infants' school which we had attended from the age of five. Our mutual attraction was apparent from the time we walked hand in hand to the school Christmas party at eleven, followed by our long wait as sweethearts while I took four years to get a university degree. All this culminated in a happy marriage which lasted for thirty-nine years.

On the face of it we were different kinds of people, and one may wonder what factors contributed to our compatibility. Marjorie was a sweet, reserved and very private person, committed absolutely to looking after our children and our home. On the other hand I cannot be described as sweet; I am an extrovert and very determined in pressing objectives, such as an ambition to succeed at work. I suppose in the final analysis we had the same philosophy with regard to marriage. We both agreed that if you really love one another then marriage must be for life and any problems that it brings are faced and solved jointly. Above all we were completely loyal to each other and, although we were often parted by my overseas and UK business trips, we had absolute trust in each other. I owe any success I have had to Marjorie's loyalty, encouragement and support.

Just before we were married Marjorie and I discussed our possible reactions to quarrels we would inevitably have in the future. She came up with a proposal which I thought was both brilliant and practical. She said, "If we quarrel and I realise I am wrong, I shall immediately admit my mistake. If, on the other hand, I know that I am right, I shall not press the matter but simply let it drop." This was sound common sense and we both followed it for thirty-nine years. There were, of course, times when we did quarrel and forget to apply our simple rule, but such events were quickly forgotten.

Now that she has gone I sometimes console myself with these wise words from *The Rubaiyat of Omar Khayyam:*

But see! The rising Moon of Heav'n again
Looks for us, Sweet-heart, through the quivering Plane:
How oft hereafter rising will she look
Among those leaves—for one of us in vain!

One incident which occurred repeatedly during my working career illustrates the above observations. As part of my job as MD I often had to entertain business associates: a number of husbands plus wives who were not known to us particularly well. As the host, acting on behalf of my company, it was my responsibility to ensure that the table-talk kept flowing. Marjorie, of course, knew this and would tell me not to tell anyone her age. She felt this was a very private matter. As usual I would get very absorbed in talking to my guests and would invariably get to a stage where I told them my age. At the same time I would be careful not to let slip Marjorie's age. So far, so good. As the evening progressed and conversation expanded we would often talk about our schooldays. At this point I could always be relied upon to announce proudly that I had known Marjorie since we were in infant school together. I always went home from these parties wishing I'd kept my big mouth shut. It was a trap that I repeatedly fell into and I always got myself in deep trouble with Marjorie as a result… but it was always quickly forgotten.

At work one of my duties was to present a parting gift to retiring employees after a short speech thanking them for their loyal service. Sometimes they would express their concern as to what they were going to do once they had retired and all too often I would learn they had died after only two or three years of retirement. Such people usually had no interests outside their work and had no idea how to fill their time when they retired. Sadly, some of them simply sat at home and did nothing constructive. When I retired I had no problem finding things to do. My top priority was to look after Marjorie but in addition I decided to buy and learn to play an electronic organ and spend more time on my model railway, which was slowly filling my large loft. I also went fishing when I could safely leave Marjorie.

The electronic organ proved to be a great idea, because it involved Marjorie as well as me. She could play the piano, although by now her arthritis prevented her pressing the keys, and still had the ability to listen to a tune and then identify the notes and accompanying chords. This seemed incredible to me, especially as I had had no idea she could do such a thing. So although her arthritis stopped her from playing she could still help me to learn. I once sang *Jealousy* to her and she immediately dictated all the information necessary to write the music down on paper.

Once I no longer had Marjorie, I had to rethink my retirement. I always had a lively imagination and I knew that I would never be lonely. We had been so close to one another in life that her death was not a tragedy to me but simply a change in our material existence. She would always be there in my mind and there was no danger of me indulging in self-pity and mistaking it for grief.

I was now in a position to pursue my love of fishing and to spend more time with my great friend, Gordon Rogers. It was not long after I came to Newcastle that I met Gordon and we soon discovered we were both dedicated anglers. As a result we began going fishing together for trout and salmon—a practice which continued for about thirty years until Gordon died in 2003. He was an ex-army soldier who had fought in North Africa during the war. He was not particularly interested in science and technology, his great passion being history and current affairs, and he was an avid reader of books and newspapers. My fishing trips with Gordon made me realise that our discussions would be improved if I became interested in history. My main source of information came from the books of Jean Plaidy for the post-1066 period and for later years from the excellent history programmes on the television.

On our earlier trips we spent most of our time wading in the river and little time on the bank where we would have our sandwich lunches. As we grew older we spent less time in the river and more time on the bank, where we talked endlessly about history, politics and current affairs. Sometimes, though, we would touch on subjects of a more profound nature and would remind each other of the celebrated Arabic words of wisdom:

"God does not deduct from man's allotted span the time he spends fishing."

We concluded that considering the amount of time we spent fishing we should both live till we were a hundred. Our wish was that when our time came we would die from a heart attack while wading in a river with a twenty-pound salmon on the end of our line. Sadly, Gordon died at the age of eighty from a brain tumour. The end came quickly and was completely unexpected.

Gone fishing: a self-portrait painted by the author.

Gordon was a keen gardener. He had an allotment and spent a great deal of time cultivating all sorts of vegetables which he freely passed on to me. I was never short of marrows, rhubarb, runner beans, etc in the summer.

I miss Gordon and often think of him fishing every day on a celestial salmon-river where the fish are plentiful and not too easy to catch. I'm sure he's keeping a good place nearby for me to join him someday.

After Marjorie died I was able to go to South Wales regularly to see my mother and a number of relatives. Dad had died in 1978 after we had moved to Newcastle. He was 73 and had cancer. During his illness I was able to visit him quite a lot and was with him when he died. After his death Ma left Ebbw Vale to live in Barry and be near my sister. Initially I would use my car to make annual visits to South Wales: about 340 miles each way. Later I went by train as it was easier and cheaper; I also had trouble with an arthritic knee which rendered driving a problem. Ma lived on her own in Barry for many years and was visited daily by Pat. Later in her life she moved to a nursing home, where she was well cared for. Pat, who is a State Registered Nurse, went to see her every day and attended to many of her needs. Ma's mind remained active, although fuzzy sometimes, until she had a fall in 2000 when she was 97. This resulted in pneumonia: the ultimate cause of her death.

Ma's 90th birthday party (1992): with Michael, Mike, Susan, Ma, Pat and Cliff.

Looking back so many years I ask myself what Ma achieved and what Pat and I have to thank her for. An answer immediately comes: she gave us a happy home in which we always felt loved and secure. She had set her heart on Pat and myself getting a good education—something she thought she had been denied. I feel sorry that I let her down at first by opting out of grammar school. It was a great disappointment to her but I know she died with the satisfaction of seeing me finally achieve all she had wished for me.

I still go to Barry every year to stay with Pat and Cliff (her husband) and until recently they came to Newcastle every year for a holiday.

During my working life I spent a sizeable proportion of my time away from home on business and only consorted with my neighbours on rare occasions. After Marjorie's death I saw a lot more of them and became very friendly with Michel and Seryl Spicker, who live next door to me. Michel was an optician and retired about the same time as I did. We get on very well together. He is very interesting to talk to and has a great sense of humour. His father was a Geordie who served in the First World War, subsequently married a French girl and settled near Paris. Because the family was of Jewish descent they had to flee the country in 1940 when the Nazis marched into Paris. They escaped at the last moment and ended up in Newcastle.

Unfortunately Michel has sugar diabetes, which affected his sight in later years and led to his blindness. He is 81 and still going strong with a very active brain. I always like going out for a walk with Michel as he has a good sense of humour and an endless supply of good stories. These are usually about his life in the army during the war and his early days in Newcastle.

Michel's wife, Seryl, has a passion for painting and runs an art class in Gosforth. When I first got to know her we talked about painting and, although I had no experience of the subject, she invited me to join her class to give it a try. She knew I was a professional engineer who had spent some time doing drawings and would have a reasonable knowledge of perspective. So I joined the class and enjoyed myself and soon became addicted to painting although, I must confess, not to a very high standard. The great thing about painting is that it is a creative therapy which allows me to drift through time without being conscious of time itself.

I usually get up about seven in the morning, have a quick bath and eat my breakfast. If I'm in the mood I pile the dishes in the sink and start painting.

This can keep me engrossed until I suddenly realise it's lunchtime or until the smoke-alarm goes off and reminds me I have completely forgotten the meal on the gas-stove and have another burnt saucepan to add to my collection.

There are a dozen or so members in our art class, which has more women than men. With one exception we are all retired and aged about 80. As we grow older we tend to paint less and talk more. Nonetheless, we all look forward to our weekly meeting.

When I was 77 I had to resign my membership of the fishing-club because my arthritic knee was causing me a great deal of trouble. It became difficult to cast a fly without losing my balance and I fell down on a number of occasions. I decided there was nothing for it but to have a complete knee replacement operation and this was done at the Nuffield Hospital in Newcastle. The result was completely satisfactory and I am now walking with no pain and without a stick. Furthermore, I have rejoined the fishing-club and started fishing again.

Each year I have a short holiday with Stan and Doreen in Aberdeenshire. This year I was determined to do some hill walking again after many years of being grounded on account of my knee. Accompanied by Stan, I succeeded in getting to the 1,750 foot summit of Mather Tap, one of the peaks of the Bennachie range north of Aberdeen and a spot of some renown. I found the initial hike to the foot of the peak fairly easy but ran into some trouble tackling the final hundred feet or so to reach the top. With the close supervision and help of Stan I finally made it. The views were fabulous in all directions. There were the remains of an old stone fort around the top of the hill, probably made by Iron Age people between 500 years B.C. and 500 years A.D..

Stan and Doreen Gregory.

My annual visits to Stan and Doreen started the year after Marjorie died. They have been wonderful friends and as a result of their kindness I have been taken all over the Scottish Highlands: from a line south of Ullapool to Inverness. Each year we have a circular tour lasting three or four days, which brings back many happy memories. Glencoe was a happy event as Marjorie and I had toured the area many years before, just after we were married. Glencoe is the ancestral home of Doreen's clan; she is a MacDonald. A visit to Skye was also of great interest as the home of the "Lord of the Isles," the head of the Clan MacDonald. Our visit to Loch Ewe on the north-west coast was more of a pilgrimage than a sightseeing trip for pleasure: it was the starting-point for convoys making the North Atlantic crossing to America in the last war. These memories are now growing dimmer but are still unpleasant.

My trips to Aberdeenshire awakened in me an interest in ancient Britain. The area is covered with Stone Age circles of upstanding stones. Actually, they are found all over Europe. The famous English example is Stonehenge. They all seem to have a religious connection and possibly an astronomical significance.

What a fascinating country Britain is. I was under the impression that it was populated by hunter-gatherers from the Hibernian peninsula at the end of the Ice Age—about 8,000 years B.C.—and that people started farming about 3,000 B.C.. It has now been shown that people settled in Britain as farmers much earlier. For example, in Howick in Northumberland they have discovered evidence that people lived in houses and farmed as long ago as 8,000 B.C., when Britain was still joined to Europe. At that time it was possible to travel to Norway by canoe by following the coast between that country and Britain, as the ice had not melted sufficiently to cover the land and turn Britain into an island. Skara Brae in the Orkneys and Cladh Allen in the Hebrides testify to the fact that our country was settled and farmed much earlier than we previously thought.

With the successful replacement of my arthritic knee in 2003 I am now able to travel more readily, particularly by train. Consequently in the last two years I have visited some of my friends and relations whom I have not seen for many years, notably some of my cousins and Ron and Margaret Lovesey. Ron continued to work for Babcock until he retired; this was, however, with a different subsidiary and location from where I was posted. We were born in the same month and year and came from a similar background. In fact Ron came from a mining/steelworking town further down the valley from Ebbw Vale. He also served in the Merchant Navy.

Margaret came from the same valley and a mining family. They now live in Romsey, near Southampton, and when I go there we can talk endlessly of days gone by. I love walking along the banks of the Test River and watching the big brown trout, and visiting the docks area in Southampton from which I sailed many times on my visits to New York and the Far East.

Both my children, Michael and Susan, continue to prosper. Since I retired Susan has graduated from Newcastle University with an honours science degree. She married Mike Brudenell, whose home was in York. They met at Newcastle University while studying computer-related subjects. As previously mentioned, they married shortly before Marjorie died—an event which Marjorie attended in spite of her rheumatoid arthritis. They now live in York and visit me regularly. That is, they come up to spend a weekend with me at least once a month and each year I visit them for a short holiday during which they ensure I have a pleasant and an interesting time. Over the last ten years or so they have piloted me around all the sights of York and Yorkshire, a region which I love to explore. I have now seen and painted three of their famous abbeys and also Whitby Harbour.

Marjorie, Susan and myself at Susan's graduation (1988).

Mike's mother still lives in York and has become a good friend of mine. She was also instrumental in my adoption of painting as a hobby. Sadly, Mike's father died suddenly before I could get to know him well. I did meet him once and we got on famously. It's a great pity we were not given enough time to become close friends.

Michael is still employed at Manchester University. He is now a senior lecturer and is responsible for the studies of postgraduate students who will

Mike and Susan at Michael's PhD investiture (1990).

eventually become PhDs. He also lectures to undergraduates but his great interest is in research in his specialised field of applied mathematics. He regularly attends research conferences covering his area of interest, many of which are overseas. Michael and I did a lot of fishing together when he was in school, but now our fishing trips are infrequent and limited to an occasional day in my club waters in Northumberland.

It's interesting to note that Michael's field of research is applied maths and he is therefore following in my footsteps. This raises a very interesting question—where did I get the appropriate genes which I have doubtless passed on to Michael? Both my mother and father had very little schooling and certainly had no exposure to mathematics. The same can be said about all my known ancestors, who were essentially ordinary working-class.

The castle on Holy Island (Lindisfarne). Painted by the author.

Epilogue

Afterthoughts

The problem with writing an autobiography is the difficulty of covering the period approaching one's demise. I have always been lucky, so I am assuming my end will come quickly. Bearing in mind that I am eighty I feel it prudent to end my narrative at this stage by simply commenting on some aspects of my life which may be of interest to the reader.

With regard to my general education I feel I have been extremely fortunate with the experiences I had in my early years. All of them proved their usefulness when I left university to pursue a career in industry. I did not consciously set out to gain a general education. It just came naturally to me through remembering and thinking about what I heard and was taught at home and through daily contact with scores of other people.

At home I was taught to honour my mother and father and to obey the Ten Commandments. From my enforced regular attendance at Sunday School and church services I learned to question beliefs and advice handed down to me by well-meaning adults. Some people must have thought I was just being difficult! Actually, it was merely a sign that I was interested in the subject under review. Much later in my life I developed a similar aversion to accepting some scientific theories at face value. In some cases they were subsequently abandoned in favour of new theories.

My long association with the Cubs and Scouts taught me the importance of "Helping other people at all times," and the meaning of such words as honour and pride. My day-to-day contact with the long-term unemployed gave me great respect for such people. Many of them were extremely well-read and intelligent but were trapped by their tragic inability to get work. As a steelworker I learned what it was like to do hard and dangerous manual work on a 24-hour basis. I also learned to work with, and rely on, people from different backgrounds.

My four years at sea during the war resulted in a quantum leap forward in terms of my overall education. I shared living quarters with shipmates of various nationalities and religions, including Africans, Indians and Muslims. They all had their own religious views which I found to be of great interest. Some of my shipmates were only interested in pleasure, particularly when in port. Others were very knowledgeable and intelligent and always worth listening to. I travelled to countries in many parts of the world and witnessed the real meaning of poverty and affluence. The greatest contribution to my education came in my seafaring days when I devoured one book after another which had been recommended to me by well-read and educated shipmates.

My subsequent spell as a builder's labourer and then as a worker on an opencast coalmine gave me a further insight into other aspects of life. My introduction to geology made me rethink some of my views on religion.

As you can see, by the time I gained access to a university technical education I had already received an extensive general education in the University of Life.

After years of hard work studying at home and at university, I finally got a first-class technical education which enabled me to follow a rewarding career with no interruptions caused by unemployment. I chose engineering and applied mathematics as my university subjects in the certain knowledge that degrees in these subjects would lead to a secure and lucrative position in industry. I never entertained the idea of studying anything else because it offered an easier route to a degree. There was no government support for my tuition and I was financed through scholarship awards and vacation work.

I believe that many students these days opt for subjects which offer an easy passage to a degree but which will not be of any great use to them in the outside world. Many would have a more secure future if they studied for a craft apprenticeship, the area where there are definite opportunities for future employment.

The two types of education I have been talking about have given me a unique opportunity to foster my career and ideally provided for my ultimate objective of a top executive post in industry.

The culmination of my industrial career was as Managing Director of a well-known engineering company with a workforce of 1,800 people.

In spite, or perhaps because, of the poor circumstances of my early life, I think that on the whole my pursuit of a good education and a worthwhile career has been a success.